CLINICAL
SOCIAL WORK
TREATMENT

Clinical Social Work Treatment

HOW DOES IT WORK?

By Carolyn Saari, Ph.D.

GARDNER PRESS, INC
New York   London

GARDNER PRESS, INC.
19 UNION SQUARE WEST
NEW YORK, NEW YORK 10003

All foreign orders except Canada and South America to:

AFTERHURST LIMITED
CHANCERY HOUSE
319 CITY ROAD
LONDON, N1, ENGLAND

Library of Congress Cataloging-in-Publication Data

Saari, Carolyn.
    Clinical social work treatment.

    Bibliography: p.
    Includes index.
    1. Social case work. 2. Psychiatric social work.
I. Title. [DNLM: 1. Social Work. W 322 Sllc]
HV43.S12   1985   361.3'2   85-15874
ISBN 0-89876-113-1

Printed in the U.S.A.

Book design by Sidney Solomon

Contents

Contents

Contents

Contents

viii

Preface

In the mid-1960s, I was a young and very dedicated "caseworker" employed at the Family Service Associaton of Philadelphia. Although Florence Hollis' major work, *Casework: A Psychosocial Therapy,* had not yet been published, I had read her earlier work on *Women in Marital Conflict* and several of her articles, including one in which she discussed her classifications of procedures in treatment. I had found her work particularly useful in my understanding of how to conduct treatment. Thus when I heard she was coming to the agency to discuss her work, I was delighted.

Florence Hollis proved to be as charming and delightful in person as her writing had been clarifying to my thoughts. She described to the agency staff her work with her doctoral students at Columbia University. Here she was attempting to learn more about treatment through the transcription of actual client interviews from audiotapes, with the possible categories being: (1) sustainment; (2) direct influence; (3) exploration, description, ventilation; (4) person–situation reflection; (5) pattern–dynamic reflection; and (6) developmental reflection. She reported enthusiastically on her hopes that this approach to the study of the treatment process ultimately would lead to knowledge that could assist in learning more about why treatment seemed to work with some people and not with others, as well as how to learn and teach skill in this endeavor.

Dr. Hollis noted that already some of the research results were surprising. For example, while casework as differentiated from psychotherapy was considered to be fundamentally supportive, very few of the workers' actual verbal interventions on the tapes she had transcribed so far actually could be classified as sustainment. She had expected that this category would account for a large percentage of the worker statements, if not most of them. She indicated that to continue their study, she and her collaborators needed more raw material—that is, more tape-recorded interviews.

I was so impressed by Dr. Hollis and her work that I considered it would be a great honor to be able to contribute in any way to such an important endeavor, and I immediately volunteered to record my work and send her the tapes. Technology was not advanced in those days and it was not commonplace to record interviews—even on audiotape. I had, in fact, never done this, and was quite nervous about what flaws in my treatment might be revealed through objective recording. Nevertheless I proceeded to acquire the use of the necessary equipment and to gain the permission of my very "best" client (in the sense that he was very involved and seemed to be making progress) to tape record our sessions. I had decided that there was no need for me to air the "dirty laundry" of the cases I thought seemed not to be going so well.

When I had recorded the tapes, five successive interviews in all, I decided that although I was ambivalent about what I might hear, I could not bear to send them off to be evaluated by important personages without knowing what was on them. With some anxiety I sat down to listen to them. In some respects I was greatly relieved. I did hear some passages in which I thought I had truly not been with the client, but these were fewer than I had imagined. Furthermore I heard, and could identify, concrete data that confirmed impressions I had had of the client which previously I had thought to be only intuitive suppositions on my part. It was clear that something very constructive was going on between me and this client, which seemed to be helping him greatly with his problems. It was also clear that he, not I, was directing this process.

Since I already knew the framework in which Dr. Hollis and her research team would be listening to the tapes, I tried to listen with the procedural categories in mind to see what I could learn from that point of view. In doing so I was astounded, and very dismayed. Whatever that "something" was that was going on between me and my client, it was not captured in this system of classification. True, my comments could be fitted into those categories, but these seemed of relatively little use to me in further understanding what was helping this man deal with his particular problems. I was so disillusioned that I never sent in the tapes, and for a time I was rather cynical about social work knowledge. After all, if Dr. Hollis did not know how treatment worked, then it was not likely that anyone did. I was not yet ready to recognize fully that Dr. Hollis had given me a present much more valuable than a simple answer—she had given me a question.

In the years since the incident with the tape recordings, I have asked the questions "What is treatment?" and "How does it work?" of every piece of literature I have read and of almost every professional I have encountered. I have pursued the questions with a stubbornness, and perhaps even an obsessiveness, that has provided some amusement, and no doubt some annoyance, to my colleagues, teachers, and students. I have not reached a definitive answer. I doubt that there is a final answer, or that if such were proposed, it would be worth very much. Nevertheless I have learned a good deal in pursuing the questions. This book, therefore, is my attempt to record, in as clear and organized a fashion as possible, the important aspects of what I think I have learned so far.

Currently clinical social workers seem to be in agreement that social work is a process (Ewalt, 1980). Yet defining the features of that process is still a problem, and one about which there is much confusion once the questions are focused at levels that are more than superficial. Evaluating the effectiveness of treatment has now become a very popular theme in both research and clinical circles. Although there is more optimism about the results of effectiveness studies than there was only a short time ago, it is apparent that precise and meaningful data about the outcome of an extremely complex enterprise are likely to be difficult to acquire until we have made more progress in being able to define the significant features of the endeavor itself.

This is not a book about technique. In the past 15 to 20 years there has appeared a myriad of new technologies, methodologies, and modalities—most of which seem to have some effectiveness. I have found it exciting to see such a broad array of possible means of intervention develop. At the same time, I think that perhaps the complexity for professionals of having to learn all of these varieties may have distracted us from asking what they have in common. Furthermore, in a profession such as social work, with its time-honored tradition of "starting where the client is," it has been distressing to see the development of so much specialization that the client is at times expected to fit himself or herself to the worker's techniques rather than the other way around. In professional education the dilemmas created by attempts to teach so much technique have led to a situation in which the student may achieve competence in the sense of a production-line performance, but often does not develop the creativity essential for the comprehension of the complexities of the human condition and of each individual.

I think it quite possible that some of the confusion regarding the understanding of process in treatment would be diminished if there were more consistent recognition that there are actually two processes involved. One is the process of the worker's procedures. The other is the client's growth process. In retrospect I think this is actually what I had intuited in listening to my own tapes, although I could not have verbalized it at the time. To be sure, these two processes occur interactively and simultaneously in practice such that it is difficult, if not impossible, to separate them, except conceptually. Yet to fail to recognize the existence of both, as well as their interaction, is to combine apples and oranges in a fashion that inevitably confuses the end result. In each individual treatment endeavor, the final outcome is determined by an interaction between the worker's individual use of technique and the growth processes of the particular individual involved.

We are, it seems to me, a long way from having a universal model against which to analyze in depth all of the variables that might be involved in treatment transactions. I have not attempted to construct such a model, and do not believe I could do so. What I have tried to do is to attempt what I hope *might* be a beginning in the direction of a general outline for the eventual integration of the two processes of worker procedure and client growth from the point of view of the question, "What makes treatment work?" The general organization of the book owes much to the work of Hans W. Loewald (1980), whose paper "On the Therapeutic Action of Psychoanalysis" has seemed to me an invaluable guide to new insights about the treatment process.

In recent years we have acquired much new knowledge about human functioning as a result of advances in cognitive and developmental psychology, epistomology, and linguistics, as well as in systems and information theory. When this newer knowledge is integrated into basic assumptions about how treatment works, a somewhat new and interesting picture of that endeavor begins to emerge. The book is, therefore, an attempt to show how a reorganization of these basic assumptions affects thinking about the nature of the treatment process as a whole. I do not see the conclusions I have reached as being very radical in terms of technique. Indeed, if anything, the indications would seem to be that traditional social work has more often than not done sensible things, though at times within a misleading or nonexistent framework of explanation.

Acknowledgments

Since this book is the result of an attempt to cull out some of the most important ideas acquired through both personal and professional contacts over a great many years, saying that there are too many people to thank than can be named is not simply pro forma. Were I to attempt to be all inclusive I would have to mention those people who encouraged me to make the professional choice that I did—a choice that I have never regretted. I would have to note my family and all of the friends who have provided support and stimulation. I would, of course, also have to mention all of my teachers, colleagues and students over the years. And certainly I could not neglect those who have taught me the most—the clients with whom I have been priviledged to work. Since I can not name all these people specifically, I hope that they will know how valuable I think they have been to me.

There are, nevertheless, some individuals who have had a more direct relationship to this book in that they participated with me in contemplating ideas and perceptions as I was struggling to organize them. Dr. Florence Lieberman of the Hunter College School of Social Work, who has consistently encouraged me to express my thoughts, commented on papers which represented stages in the work, and

Acknowledgments

ultimately reviewed the entire manuscript is prominent among these people. Dr. Roger R. Miller, Mr. Gerald Schamess, and Mr. Thomas Givler, all of the Smith College School for Social Work, have also consistently been generous with their thoughts. Dr. Thomas Kenemore was the person who first suggested to me that I needed the new concept which I ultimately decided to call "concordance." My colleagues and students at the School of Social Work at Loyola University of Chicago have been extremely encouraging and helpful. In particular Dr. Randolph Lucente read the entire manuscript and provided a dialogue about it was always stimulating.

I would, however, literally never have been able to complete the book at all were it not for the assistance and support of Dr. Helen J. Lane and Ms. Louise Fassler.

CLINICAL
SOCIAL WORK
TREATMENT

1 Introduction: The Nature of Clinical Social Work

One of social work's major strengths as a profession is that it has never been wedded to any single explanatory theory. Thus it has been able to make use of new developments from a variety of knowledge bases as these have become available. To be sure, this has also produced a strain in that there has been a tendency for the development of schools of thought that have competed for dominance at particular times in the history of the profession. History, however, also shows that each school of thought has had contributions to make, and that these valuable ideas ultimately became integrated into the mainstream of the knowledge base. For example, the battles that once were waged between the psychodynamic and the functional schools now seem irrelevant, if not a little silly. Both points of view had strengths and limitations, and both have now been transcended by new developments.

One side effect of the fact that the profession had no single theory has been that for a very long time a debate raged among its practitioners as to whether it really was a full profession since it had no exclusive knowledge area, but utilized and adapted content from many disciplines. This was seen as a weakness because defining the profession became a problem. Fortunately today there seems to be more comfort with this state of affairs. New knowledge is growing so rapidly that all professional groups must integrate discoveries from other fields in order to remain relevant. Furthermore it has become increasingly apparent that social work is, and has always been, more defined by its goals, values, and ethics than by the specific content of the theories it may utilize to achieve its ends.

In its more recent history, clinical social work in particular has been through a period of considerable stress during which some colleagues have criticized it for merely helping people to adapt to a sick society and thereby perpetuating social ills that needed to be more directly addressed. Such voices have become muted in the 1980s through the recognition that many of the social programs of the 1960s and 1970s not only did not warrant the optimism that accompanied their inception, but also that at least some of these programs themselves created new and unforeseen social problems. Today clinical social work seems to be somewhat more "in vogue," but the clinicians themselves appear to be more aware of the continuing devastating effects that inequities in social justice and resource distribution can have on society as a whole as well as on its individual members.

Perhaps the most important lesson to be learned from the events of the past two decades is that social work as a profession is itself a part of its environment and is very much influenced by the tenor of the times in which it is operating. In this regard Bertha Reynolds' words (Reynolds, 1942, pp. 3–4) would appear to have been quite wise.

There is a temptation to think of social work as something "good" which those who believe in it should defend while it is making its way in a world which is to some extent hostile to it, or to think of social work as "bad," a palliative in place of justice to the poor, a confused, sentimental, time-and-money-wasting activity which we somehow have to tolerate. Both conceptions are static, failing to take into account that social work is dynamically one with the society of today. It is neither good nor bad; it is fact, to be studied like any other fact in a changing scene.

In the 1980s the major challenge to clinical social work appears to be to prove its effectiveness. This is, of course, a very practical concern in a time when financial and programmatic resources are rapidly diminishing. It is important in such times to recall that humanitarian values and the importance of the quality of life for all are variables that cannot be measured in terms of dollars and cents. Effectiveness has become an issue, however, not only because of monetary problems. Outcomes studies, indicating that results may not always have been what was desired, have raised many questions that need to be answered. These questions are partly in the area of the research methodologies utilized in particular studies, but also transcend that dimension into the arena of the manner in which the treatment itself is conceptualized. Specialists in research methodology cannot, after all, be expected to construct designs that measure variables that have not been called to their attention by experts in clinical methodology.

Research into effectiveness, therefore, is fundamentally dependent upon the adequacy of the model of treatment upon which it rests. Actually there exists no lack of treatment models from which to choose. In fact there are so many competing treatment models that the clinician has a difficult time in mastering them all and most practitioners are tending to become specialists in one or a small number of them. There are, however, other difficulties with this state of affairs. One of these difficulties is that the clinician seems to be becoming a technician, expected to have mastered a series of intervention strategies that guide activity within the therapeutic encounter. In this situation the clinical educator is pulled toward the endorsement of one particular model and the clinical student or practitioner is left with relatively little help in knowing how to judge the strengths and weaknesses of the variously available models. Clinicians thus become subject to a certain faddism whereby the newest techniques may be adopted without consideration of how these may fit into a holistic picture. Worst of all, the client may be expected to fit himself or herself to the expertise of the particular clinician he or she happens to encounter. In this manner the old, time-honored, and very valuable social work tradition of "starting where the client is" becomes threatened.

Given this state of affairs, it may quite legitimately be asked why anyone would bother with the construction of yet another new model of treatment. Are there not enough already? There is, however, a difference between most of the existing models and that which is outlined in this book. Most of the current models are conceptualized at a level quite close to the immediate concerns of the practitioner so that they can be useful in leading to particular techniques. The model presented here is not directly concerned with technique or modality issues, although it does have some implications for these. Instead in asking the question, "How does treatment work?" this model assumes that treatment may come in a variety of different forms that may be appropriate at different times, but that have certain goals, processes, and assumptions in common. This model concerns itself

3

with those common elements and a knowledge base that may underlie them all. It is, therefore, conceptualized at a slightly more abstract level in hope that it can provide a framework useful for the integration of many of the already existing models.

As has already been pointed out, knowledge about human behavior from a variety of disciplines has been growing so rapidly that it has been exceedingly difficult to keep pace with it. This has created a gap between the knowledge available from the behavioral sciences and the practice theories that direct the clinician more immediately. Furthermore where there has been an attempt at integration, this has often been done, for understandable reasons, in a manner that has, in the end, been more additive than it has been integrative. Thus many of the practice theories contained some unexamined assumptions that leave them either with internal inconsistencies or with apparent conflicts with other practice theories, which are in fact unnecessary. It has only been within the past ten to 15 years that the implications of the newer knowledge have become sufficiently clear as to make an attempt at a more complete integration even conceivable.

There is a major danger inherent in the proposition of any new model. This danger is that the model, if it achieves some degree of acceptance, will be interpreted so concretely and rigidly that its very existence may retard further examination and modification. Any model will necessarily have both strengths and weaknesses and no claim is being made for this as an exception. It is, in fact, perhaps only a beginning of a more integrative approach to treatment theory in clinical social work, and should be considered as such. In another sense it can be argued quite sensibly that the elements of this model are not new. Indeed that is the case. The only real claim for novelty that can be made here is the manner in which the elements are put together.

Social Work Traditions

*I*f it is necessary periodically, as knowledge expands, to reevaluate the totality of what is known and to attempt to integrate the new, one must also take cognizance of the traditions into which the new is to be integrated. This is particularly true in relation to clinical social work. From its inception social work has been an extremely ambitious profession. Social work has positioned itself at the interface of the most debated issues throughout the history of humankind—the nature of human beings, of their relationship to the environment, and of the relationship between environment and heredity, as well as of that between the mind and the body, between thinking and action, and between people and their systems of government. Viewed from this perspective, it is hardly surprising that there have been myriad disagreements within the profession that have not been resolved in its short history. Rather it seems surprising that social work has survived at all.

It can be argued that one of the major reasons for the survival of clinical social work is that it has always been an activity-oriented and goal-directed profession. In this regard it has often been better known for its practical wisdom than for the quality of its more intellectual productions. This may have been a weakness, but it can also be seen as a very real strength since its observations, although at times accused of being intuitive rather than scientific, have also been rooted in direct encounters with client populations. Mary Richmond (1917) attempted to make the profession scientific by utilizing the best theoretical knowledge available to her, but she began with the data she and other practitioners of her time had gathered in their work. Social work, therefore, has always had a solid empirical base underneath its practice wisdom. The result is that much of that practice wisdom is well worth preserving. Indeed its wisdom is proving more and more "wise" as we learn more and more about human beings from presumably more scientific research studies and carefully conceptualized theoretical attempts.

As has already been mentioned, one of social work's traditions, and perhaps its most valuable one, has been that of beginning where the client is. This has been determined, of course, by the values and ethics of a profession that has insisted on respect for the inherent dignity of every individual as well as on the person's right to self-determination in a social system that also preserves the rights of others. There is little doubt that it was in an attempt to learn more in depth about the characteristics of the human being that the social workers of the 1920s turned in great numbers to the new discipline of psychoanalysis. While a major segment of clinical social work has remained closely aligned with psychoanalytic thinking since the 1920s, the two professions have not had identical goals, and so have not had identical perspectives. Social work has benefited tremendously from this relationship, but there have been some disadvantages as well.

Much of this book deals with the theoretical assumptions underlying a psychoanalytic point of view, with the evolution of thinking within that discipline from a very orthodox view point that concerned itself with the vicissitudes of the intrapsychic life of the individual, through ego psychology, to what is called the psychology of the self. In this review an attempt is made to cull out those aspects of the theory that can provide guidance to the clinical social worker today. In this process no attempt has been made to survey in any depth the social work literature or the various schools of thought within social work itself. Specifically because this is the case, it is necessary first to outline some of the traditions that have been present in social work from its beginning in order to make clear the many ways in which current theory from outside the social work profession is now confirming the wisdom of those traditions.

THE PERSON AND THE ENVIRONMENT

*L*ong before systems theory became popular with other helping professions, social work was maintaining that there was an inherent relationship between a person and the environment that had to be understood in order to be helpful to that person. In fact Richmond utilized the sociology of her day to conceptualize the types of data the worker needed to collect from sources other than the client in order to understand that particular individual. It has always been presumed that human beings are fundamentally social animals and that interpersonal relationships with significant others are of critical importance for self-definition, self-esteem, and behavior. Much attention has been paid to the importance of gathering the history of the interactions between the person and the environment, both animate and inanimate, in order to assess the forces that have influenced the client in the past and the present. Home visits, even though thought time consuming, have been advocated as one invaluable way of gaining an understanding about the client and about the things the client might not think to explain. In fact social work has traditionally seen itself as having expertise in problem solving within the client–situation configuration.

Introduction: The Nature of Clinical Social Work

THE SOCIAL MOTIVATION AND
MEANING OF BEHAVIOR

Social work has always assumed that the human being is fundamentally a social animal. From this point of view, it has been generally taken for granted that the motivation and meaning of behavior, whether of the individual or of the group, have a direct relationship to the form of social organization of the environment. Interpersonal relationships have been considered of prime importance in the lives of all people, and the family has been recognized as the primary social institution from which one derives understanding of the world and one's relationship to it.

While social workers have continued to espouse this point of view, in large part because it simply makes more "common sense" in relation to the observations made in the course of clinical work, this orientation has led to some difficulties in regard to the profession's relationship with the popular intellectual and academic disciplines that have surrounded the profession. It was clear as early as the 1920s that a purely sociological approach, in the sense of epidemiology or of an understanding of the "facts" of an external social order, had serious limitations when utilized to comprehend individual behavior. Data from this approach could indicate group trends, which certainly do have an impact on individuals, and which, to some extent, could be predictive of normative behavior in a statistical sense, but were of little use in understanding how the individual came to define himself or herself within that overall system.

Clinical social work, therefore, needed a psychology as well as a sociology. However, although orthodox psychoanalysis provided some propositions that made considerations at an individual level possible from its concerns with the inner life of the person, this discipline fundamentally assumed that much of that inner life was biologically inherited and developed according to almost genetically determined timetable. Thus this approach neglected the interpersonal and social aspects of the human being in its basic foundation. Orthodox learning theory appeared, at least superficially, to be more in tune with the notion of social influences upon behavior, but since it could not account very well for the existence of any inner life in the individual, this approach also had its limitations in an attempt to understand the total person.

Ways of understanding the relationship between the person and the environment, the very field in which social work had positioned itself, thus were limited within the theoretical structures that were available outside the profession itself. Social work has always been in need of a theoretical framework that could define more clearly the interactions and interrelationships between the inner and external worlds. It is fortunate that it is in precisely this area that considerable progress has been made in recent years.

ACTIVITY AND GROWTH

Social work has always been an activity-oriented profession. This has been particularly evident in its programs for advocating social change, but has been apparent as well in its clinical approaches. Social workers as intervenors have not, for example, had the same tradition of seeing themselves as "blank screens" that has been a part of a model common in psychoanalysis or psychology. Indeed social workers have often found themselves working more in the "field" than in a consulting room, and in general have found ways to be comfortable with this role. Even when operating in an office, social workers have been attracted to more active forms of intervention; for example, the popularity of "activity group therapy" for children. In addition, social work traditionally has seen itself as focusing on the healthy aspects of human beings in order to foster inherent growth potential rather than as eliminating or curing pathological states.

While social workers have known "intuitively" that the approach they have taken has led to ameliorative results for many people, this activity orientation also has led to many problems for the profession. It has left social workers open to charges that they are simply do-gooders who are out to mold the rest of the world into their own images, or that they do not take the inner experience of the individual into sufficient consideration, and so could not effect changes that would have any lasting value for the person's long-range behavior. Psychoanalysis, as a discipline, greatly neglected the role of action in human behavior other than in rather negative conceptualizations of "acting out" and "repetition-compulsion." Thus social workers have had few ways to articulate a rationale for their successes, which has left them open to self-doubt and has allowed other helping professions to dismiss much too quickly any data supporting such successes.

Introduction: The Nature of Clinical Social Work

SUPPORTIVE TREATMENT VERSUS INSIGHT

*U*ntil about the mid-1960s, social "casework" was generally considered a legitimate form of treatment, but one that differed from psychotherapy in that it was "supportive" rather than "insight oriented." Two things appear to have occurred simultaneously that led to a recognition that this division was a false one. The first, from within the profession of social work, was the influence of studies from the perspective of Hollis' (1965) typology of casework interventions. Hollis, operating according to a definition of casework as a supportive therapy, assumed when she began her work that a large percentage of the verbal interventions of skilled social workers would be classified in the category she had labeled "sustainment procedures." This proved not to be the case. In fact the studies indicated that only a very small percentage of the interventions could be so rated, and there appeared to be a general trend in the direction of fewer such interventions as the worker gained in experience and skill. Clearly, then, if social casework was to be considered a "supportive" therapy as distinguished from other forms of treatment, then "support" would have to be defined in a more sophisticated or differentiated manner.

At the same time, psychoanalysts were finding that traditional psychoanalytic techniques involving the utilization of "the couch" and conceptualizations of the therapist as a "blank screen" for the reception of the projections from the client were having less treatment success than they had supposed. Furthermore psychoanalysts became much more interested in working with the more psychologically disabled (the borderlines) as it became clear that only a very small percentage of the general population was truly "neurotic" in the sense of having purely "oedipal" rather than "preoedipal" problems. Psychoanalysts, therefore, began to consider ways of adapting their techniques and their theories to a population they had previously seen as being appropriate only for the less sophisticated interventions of the social worker through supportive treatment.

As a result of these two changes, it has become increasingly difficult to define "casework" as essentially different from "psychotherapy" in a broader sense. In some ways, this has had benefits for the profession of social work. But it also has had its negative aspects. Since psychoanalysis and psychotherapy were considered the "status" professions in the eyes of society, social workers have tended to assume that the practice of psychotherapy could best be learned from practitioners trained primarily in those disciplines. There thus has been a tendency to adopt the traditions of those disciplines even in areas in which the old "practice wisdom" of social casework might have been more applicable.

In the long run, however, interdisciplinary competition is not the central issue. The critical issue has become that of understanding the nature of support as this relates to treatment, and concomitantly also the nature and function of "interpretation," both of which have been in need of a modified understanding as knowledge about the nature of treatment has expanded and become more sophisticated. Involved in a redefinition of supportive versus insight therapy, two additional concepts must be reexamined. The first has to do with the unconscious and its nature. Traditionally social casework was conceptualized as working only with the conscious content of the mind, whereas psychoanalysis dealt with the unconscious. In retrospect it becomes rather clear that, in dealing with real people in real interactions, such a division was false since one could hardly make a division between the conscious and unconscious influences on behavior in other than an intellectual manner.

The second of the concepts that needs reexamination here has been the assumption that social casework dealt with the provision of "concrete" services whereas psychoanalysis did not concern itself with such mundane aspects of life. Traditional social caseworkers knew very well that concrete services were not "concrete" merely in the sense of being external and unrelated to the inner life and its inner meaning for the individual. However, since no adequate theory of symbolization related to social organization seemed available, this connection could not very well be explicated at an academic forum. Thus there has been a tendency (and not a very useful one) on the part of those clinical social workers interested in doing psychotherapy to attempt to dissociate themselves from the provision of concrete services. Germain's (1976) whole ecological school has, at least in part, been an attempt to demonstrate the importance of the external world for the inner life of the individual. Unfortunately this approach has not been sufficiently well related to interventions within the interpersonal framework of the therapeutic situation so that its impact has been more limited than might have been useful.

THE TREATMENT RELATIONSHIP AND ITS EFFECT

*T*raditionally social work has assumed that the client–worker relationship is central to the achievement of any therapeutic effect.

Caseworkers were presumed to utilize themselves as instruments of stabilization or change. This was, of course, consonant with a view of the human being as a social creature. Furthermore clinical results have indicated that this relationship is indeed critical. Yet there have remained difficulties in being able to conceptualize in precise detail just what this has meant in practical terms.

Although it has been clear that positive regard from others makes a major difference in relation to phenomena such as self-esteem, it has also been apparent that Bettelheim (1950) had a point when he noted that *Love is not enough*. Empathy became popular in psychology as a concept, but just how this differentiated itself from simple positive regard has not always been clear. Psychoanalysis offered a number of concepts, such as introjection, internalization, and identification, which were presumed to have some relationship to the treatment relationship within that discipline. However, until at least the expansion of object relations theory, these seemed poorly integrated into a total theory of how such things could effect change. This was especially true if psychoanalytic theory considered that the relationship was merely a context for the interpretation that was the ultimate tool for effective change.

Social workers seem to have known intuitively that the relationship was of more importance than simply being a tool that could allow for the reduction of "resistance" such that an interpretation could be heard as valid. However, they may not have known how best to define its therapeutic value. The question remains: If the client is to have self-determination and is not simply expected to mold himself or herself after the worker in some sort of imitative fashion, and if the simple prescription of love is not a sufficient explanation for the therapeutic effect of worker interventions, then how does one conceptualize what makes treatment work?

Definition of Clinical Social Work

*C*linical social work has been defined in a variety of ways. Most of these definitions would be compatible with the manner in which it is conceptualized for the present work. However, for purposes of clarity in understanding the point of view to be offered in this book, a definition from its vantage point is necessary.

The goal of clinical social work is the improvement of social functioning through the enhancement of the meaningfulness of life experiences and an expansion of the range of choices for individual behavior in an environment capable of supporting a variety of adaptive patterns. This goal rests upon the foundation of a belief in the dignity of all human beings and of the necessity for a communal responsibility for all members of society. Services provided may be geared toward the prevention of future difficulties, toward more effective coping with current situations, toward the stabilization of achieved coping capacities, and/or toward remediation for the effects of stresses from the past. While the individual as a biopsychosocial system remains a basic unit of concern, persons may be served alone, in families, or in small groups.

The practice of clinical social work involves a process in which assessment, goal setting, planned intervention, and evaluation are prominent features. The effectiveness of the interventions is presumed to rely upon the strengthening and reordering of the organizational structures in the client's life, including those structures that have traditionally been seen as intrapsychic, interpersonal, institutional, and/or societal. Practice invariably takes place in the context of a purposeful relationship within which the tools selected for intervention may involve available and appropriate social resources as well as the professional self of the social worker. The practice of clinical social work is neither an art nor a science, since such a division is artificial—it is both.

2 Reality and the Person–Situation Configuration

Much of the theorizing in both psychoanalysis and social work has had roots in a scientific view of the world that was inherited from the Victorians. Within this world view, "reality" has been considered to be external, objective, concrete, and to some extent stable. It is an assumption that until recently had not been directly challenged and had simply been taken for granted. It has, however, created many problems. There is an implicit understanding here that those persons who do not share the dominant view of reality must be mistaken, if not actually demented. All too often, in the treatment situation, there has been a hidden assumption that it has the prerogative of the therapist to define reality for the patient through the use of interpretations. Should the patient object to that view of reality, this could be dismissed as a part of the patient's pathology and "resistance."

Although the situation in which the therapist serves as the definer of reality has frequently arisen, almost no theorist would endorse a notion that this was what should be happening in the treatment situation—with the possible exception of work with the psychotic individual whose illness has often been viewed as meaning that the patient is "out of touch with reality." Freud, who still indicated even in his late works that he did not think he fully understood schizophrenia and did not believe that it could be treated through psychoanalysis, nevertheless did view that illness as evidence that the patient had "withdrawn libidinal cathexis from the external world" and had retreated to the world of primitive thinking or of the primary process.

According to this explanation of schizophrenia, then, the individual who suffers from that ailment should show no interest in the phenomena of the external world. However, this explanation contradicts much clinical experience in work with schizophrenics (e.g., Hill, 1955), which has been that such individuals are often more observant of the concrete details of the external environment than are persons who presumably are normal. Today the dominant view of schizophrenia in psychoanalytic circles is that such persons have insufficiently formed self–other boundaries so that they cannot distinguish between that which is internal and that which is external (Blatt and Wild, 1976).

In a classic, but relatively unknown, paper entitled "Ego and Reality," Loewald (1951) pointed out that because the child at birth does not know the difference between inner and outer, internal and external, self and other, a loss of reality is always a loss of self. According to Loewald it is through the interaction with an organizing structure in an external world, at first the primary caretaker, that the internal organization develops into a sense of self. This process, which although assuredly much affected by physiological need states and affective interchanges, can also be seen as a type of learning or socialization. It is, then, through interacting with the environment that the child learns to tell the difference between the inner and outer, the hallmark of reality testing in the strict sense of psychoanalytic theory. The importance of this ability and its centrality to human functioning has certainly been proved by sophisticated brain-washing techniques, which have demonstrated that people are more easily broken by sensory deprivation or by a conflicted or elusive reality than by mere physical pain, as horrible as that may be.

What is fascinating about the traditional approach of psychoanalysis to the subject of reality, however, is that even today there is an underlying tendency to assume that, once the self–other boundaries are relatively well established, the individual can comprehend the outside world perfectly well. Much of the writing about the treatment of borderlines, for example, will almost dismiss the subject of the patient's comprehension of the external world following the statement that reality testing in such individuals is intact. This is, of course, technically correct since the psychoanalytic definition of reality testing has been that of an ability to tell the difference between that which is internal and that which is external. But an in-depth understanding of the world calls not only for this basic reality-testing ability, but also for the ability to select and abstract organizing principles within which to place, order, and assign meaning to observed data. Robbins and Sadow (1974) noted that psycho-analysis did not even have a term for any ability beyond limited reality testing and suggested that the term "reality processing" be utilized.

To understand how it happened that a theory as sophisticated as psychoanalysis should not have included a term for reality processing, it is necessary to examine the assumptions underlying Freud's original thinking. Freud's approach to cognition and reality was based partially on the representational approach taken by the philosopher John Locke. Locke saw mental content as a series of internal representations or pictures of the external world. Perceptions, therefore, were rather like photographic images of an objective external reality. As Schimek (1975) and others have pointed out, this approach involved a view of the mind as passive and as initially a blank tablet upon which images are engraved and preserved. In this sense, then, perception was assumed to be pure, and its knowledge accurate and free from affect. Freud never totally changed his early model in which he considered that these accurate perceptions were distorted by the effects of the instinctual drives and the need states associated with them. Freud also believed that, under circumstances such as those provided by psychoanalysis, the distorting effects of the drives and need states could be eliminated, and that the original perceptions and memories would then emerge. This is the reason it was considered unessential for the analyst to know much about the patient's "real life" circumstances or to be concerned with the environment. Once the distortions had been eliminated through the curative effects of working through the transference neurosis, the nonpsychotic patient would be able to recover what reality was and act in accordance with it. However much clinical social workers may have been influenced by psychoanalysis, they have normally had a more dynamic view of reality than this.

Since Freud's day numerous studies, not only by the object relations theorists such as Spitz (1965) and Mahler (Mahler et al., 1975), but also by more cognitively oriented psychologists such as Hebb (1949) and Piaget (1973), have demonstrated that perception is not a simple matter in which the mind is the passive receptor of copies of external reality. Instead perception is a complex, active process in which some stimuli will be recorded while others are ignored, and in which there is an internal organization of that which is perceived into a system of comprehension that is influenced by previous experiences and perceptions. Memory is not the result of a recall of events that have been recorded as if on a tape recorder, but of the processing of past impressions through the structures existent in the organization of experience at the time these are revived (Piaget & Inhelder, 1973). In treatment this means that the fact that a client may give different accounts of his or her history at different times is neither simply the result of repression not that of varying levels of comfort in the relationship. The way in which the person organizes and understands his or her past will have changed by virtue of intervening experiences, of which treatment presumably is one (Loewald, 1976).

The recall of past subjective realities is not the only constant change, since external reality is also changing. The empirical science of Freud's time did tend to assume a static reality whereas today's physics teaches that change is constant. The existence of an average expectable environment cannot be assumed with the ease with which Hartmann (1958) posited this concept. It has become commonplace to recognize the unsettling effects of constant change in the world. While there is no question but that the rapid pace of environmental, particularly technological, change does place a significant strain on the human ability to maintain a sense of stability in the organization of a comprehension of the world, it may be a little reassuring at least to note that it was the Greek philosopher Heraclitus who first pointed out that the essence of reality is change.

While there is currently little debate about the importance of empirical observations in understanding the environment, there is also little question that it is an error to believe that such observations can ever be truly objective. As Lacan (1981) has pointed out, a human being simply cannot achieve a "God's-eye view" of the whole. To divide reality into the subjective and the objective is to create a false dichotomy of the same type as that of a division between the mind and the body. Although we may not fully understand the nature of the interconnections between these entities, such connections and interactions do exist. To assume that the human being can know about an "objective" reality is also to ignore the fact that much of reality is defined by social agreement.

In the helping professions, an underlying assumption that an understanding of an objective reality was possible has led to many problems. For example, intelligence measured solely by the ability to memorize fails to capture the phenomena of creativity, reasoning ability, and the effect of cultural differences on thinking. Treatment evaluated on the basis of variables that poorly reflect the influences of the treatment relationship so central to that process, or on variables that give little credence to the world of personal meaning, fails to demonstrate effectiveness. It is inevitable that the assumption that the organization of the intrapsychic world has little to do with the organization of the external world will lead to conflict between clinicians and advocates of changes in social policy.

Reality and the Transitional Process

Piaget's work has been critical in the demonstration of human knowledge of reality as being "constructed" within the structures of the mind over the course of experience. It has helped considerably in providing a base for the amendment of orthodox psychoanalysis so as to correct for some of the faulty assumptions that Freud made. Translating Piaget's theories directly into practice theories has also been difficult, however, primarily because Piaget did not take into consideration the central variable of the human relationship and its quality as this affects the development of cognition. What is necessary for the practitioner is a point of view that can integrate and encompass the points of view of both Piaget and Freud in a manner that can also be consistent with other knowledge gained about human developmental patterns.

Freud's model of cognition has been severely criticized even by such friendly critics as David Rapaport (1951). This model was a dualistic one involving the primary and secondary processes. The primary process, characterized by the irrational instinctual impulses of the id and the pursuit of the pleasure principle, has proved to have some usefulness in describing the content of intrapsychic conflicts and the early primitive levels of organization of the mind. The secondary process was seen to be dominated by the reality principle, which was established by the child's encountering the demands of an external reality that Freud tended to see as harsh but thoroughly logical and objective, like the strict and sometimes punitive father of the Oedipus complex. The concept of the secondary process has similarly had its usefulness. Most current thinkers, at least in the tradition of the Western world, do assume the existence of an objective external world even though human beings never *experience* this world as such. Hard data and survey research related to the measurement of facts from a secondary process world do have their value. And it certainly should not be necessary to remind social workers that external, factual reality can be harsh and punitive.

Freud's ideas about primary and secondary processes may have utility, but the model within which they are located is a dualistic one. Such dualistic thinking, as has already been noted, similarly can be found underlying most conceptions of the person and the situation, of the mind and the body, of subjective reality and objective reality, of reality testing, and of a division between affect and cognition as well. It is further worth noting that dualistic thinking is not unrelated to the type of splitting that Kernberg (1975) has made so central to his theories of the functioning of the borderline adult. It would appear that if theorizing in social work is to make real progress, precisely this type of model construction must be eliminated.

In spite of Freud's tendency to rely upon concepts that localized conflicts as between two polar opposites, he transcended this in at least two areas: the tripartite structure of the personality, that is, the id, the ego, and the superego; and the three-person conflict of the oedipal situation. It has been the model of the id, ego, and superego that the subsequent thinking of the ego psychologist has found to be such fertile ground for the further development of the understanding of the individual human being. Whatever legitimate discontent there may now be with Freud's interpretations of the meaning of the Oedipus myth, the universality of the affective appeal of this story and its three main characters would seem to have been fairly well substantiated if only by the enormous number of varying human situations it has been used, or misused, to explain. It is at least possible that the value of the oedipal theory has not been its specific content, but rather its implication that, at least at the higher levels of intrapsychic development, the person's conflicts are indeed triadic and not dyadic.

It is probably true that ultimately the number of explanatory variables necessary for a full accounting of human thought and behavior is so large that only advanced computer technology could analyze them. On the other hand, there appears to be a significant qualitative advance in utilizing a triadic model of categorization as opposed to a dyadic or polarized one. Recently several psycho-analysts who are interested in understanding creativity (Arieti, 1976; Pruyser, 1979; Rose, 1980) have suggested the possibility of a third or tertiary process in cognition. This process involves an interaction between elements of the primary and secondary processes and is seen to be related to the development of the functions of the transitional object and of transitional phenomena, concepts that were first developed by Winnicott (1975).

In his simple observation of the young child's first favorite toy, usually a soft blanket or stuffed animal, Winnicott pointed out that, while this object did not yet seem to be a fully developed symbol for the mother, it could substitute for her under conditions of stress or separation. Tolpin (1971) has suggested that the affective functions of the transitional object are internalized such that the child learns to be able to console himself or herself with processes of the mind such as fantasy, an idea that has received almost universal acceptance in psychoanalytic circles. However, linking the transitional object to the development of the capacity to symbolize suggests that the transitional object has cognitive as well as affective functions.

The ability to symbolize,—that is, the ability to utilize something, normally a word, but often an object, to represent another thing,—appears to be a uniquely human characteristic, the capacity for which seems to be inborn. Just what this inherited capability involves remains a mystery (Chomsky, 1968). The importance of symbolization in human life is, however, not a mystery and perhaps can be best illustrated through the now famous event in the life of Helen Keller, when she suddenly comprehended that what her teacher was spelling into her hand at the well was the word *water*. Keller (1903) later discussed this realization as giving her not only sight, but life itself. It was the gift of meaning. The meaningfulness of life is difficult, if not impossible, to capture in the statistics of the factual segment of objective reality and the secondary process. It belongs instead to the realm of the transitional process. It can be said to occupy the space between the subject and the object.

Personal meaning also can be described as a knowledge of one's own relationship to the external world as it is constructed in the mind over time through the development of the representational world. It involves content, which comes from both the world of the primary process and that of the secondary process; that is, from both the inner and the outer realities. Those personal meanings that are common enough to be shared with others become institutionalized as art, culture, religion, and theory. Thus all of these social phenomena grow out of the transitional process, which also may be considered to be the space between the subject and the object, between the person and the situation. In fact the transitional process, having as it does the three basic elements of the infant, the primary caretaker, and the external world, is social from its very definition as well as triadic in its conceptual structure.

In traditional sociological theory, the family is seen as the primary unit for socialization, with language as the primary tool utilized for this educative function. Language is, of course, a series of shared verbal symbols through which people communicate to others the personal meanings that the world around them holds. A developmental psychologist by the name of Heinz Werner (Werner & Kaplan, 1963), who was aware of Winnicott's concept of the transitional object, formulated a conceptualization of how the child learns to utilize verbal symbols, through which, it should be noted, adults also think. For Werner the capacity to symbolize developed out of the child's sharing of perceptions, initially of a primarily affective nature, of the significance of concrete external objects with a primary caretaker. Werner's theory is a highly sophisticated one that remains relatively little known, but is beginning to receive more attention in psychoanalytic circles. In one sense it can be seen as an attempt to delineate the development of a transitional process.

Werner believed that the capacity to symbolize developed along the lines of increasing separation and individuation in a psychological sense. Thus both perception and the ability to convey meaning developed from the more global to the more discrete and from the concrete to the more abstract. He indicated that this development could be found to have certain generalized stages, which can be quite easily examined in relation to the stages of development of object constancy from ego psychology. Werner's work seems to provide not only a basic framework within which to consider the transactions among the components of the transitional situation, that is, the person, the other, and the external world, but also a framework within which to consider the development of individual abilities in these transactions. It would thus appear that utilizing the notion of a transitional process, as further elaborated by Werner, not only could provide a manner of relating the person and the situation to each other, but could do so within a developmental framework that is potentially compatible with knowledge acquired about human functioning from other sources.

Significantly, Freud began his discoveries and his theories with ideas about the meaning of symbols in the unconscious, dreams, and parapraxes—concepts this approach would place in the realm of the transitional process. Freud did not, however, pursue this aspect of his work very much in subsequent years. This was partially because he assumed that language was learned in an essentially memorized fashion and that the symbols utilized in dreams and id processes were universal, had fixed meanings, and were a part of an inherited language. That even unconscious symbols do not have fixed, constant, and inherited meanings has been recognized by many psychoanalysts for some years (Rycroft, 1956). There may have been a more basic reason, however, why Freud did not pursue this line of thinking. Although his discovery of human irrationality shocked the world, Freud himself had a marked preference for empirical science and a *relative* disinterest in elements of the transitional world such as art, music, and religion. It may be that had he continued to investigate the place of symbols in human life, Freud might have been forced to deal more directly with the impact of his own discoveries than he wished to.

Currently it appears that, while human beings are not rational, the need for a sense of organization and meaning in experience is absolutely basic. For example, Loewald (1980) has pointed out that psychoanalytic theory has moved from seeing organization as serving defensive purposes to seeing defense as serving organizational purposes. Thus there may be a need for an illusion of rationality and of certainty even if it is only an illusion. Winnicott noted that the mother's task is ultimately to disillusion the child, but that she cannot do this if sufficient illusion is not first allowed. Forty years after Freud's death, social workers are relatively comfortable with his ideas about the existence of childhood sensuality. These have had their very real value. Perhaps now social work is ready totally to discard outmoded notions of a purely empirical science, to accept that rationality is illusionary, and to give full credence to the concept of a transitional world that it has so badly needed. If this can be accomplished, perhaps psychoanalytic theory might finally fulfill more of the early promise that attracted the social workers of the 1920s.

Relevance to Treatment

*B*lanche (a pseudonym that seems appropriate because of certain similarities to Blanche DuBois in *A Streetcar Named Desire*) had grown up in a small town in the southern United States. The family, part of the local aristocracy, resided in a large old mansion that had been inherited by her mother along with extensive land holdings farmed by tenants. It was, in fact, the income from the tenants that provided the family living—a quite meager one for the life-style to which they both aspired and pretended. Blanche's father had grown up in a tenant shack (in another town) but had worked his way through college prior to his marriage. At one time he had been the principal of the local high school, but left that position, ostensibly because of a disagreement with the local school board in which he felt his values were being violated and he could not compromise. Blanche, however, always suspected that the real truth was that her father was incompetent.

During most of Blanche's life, her father did not work, but played the role of the local intellectual, spending much time in his study—though Blanche claimed he had not read most of his impressive looking books. In his walks through the town, her father carried candy in his pockets to disperse to the children who would crowd around him, but Blanche noted that she never got any of it. Meanwhile she claimed to have had to make do with clothes that were made over to look like new—a skill at which her mother became quite adept. Thus Blanche's image of her father was of a man who was a total sham in almost all aspects of his life. At least she could convey a picture of what her father was like, however. Her descriptions of her mother were much more vague. Mother seemed to have remained the long suffering, but quiet, aristocrat who really managed the family affairs competently, but did so from the background and in a manner that was emotionally distant from her two daughters, of whom Blanche was the junior by about two years.

In high school Blanche began to see her role in life as being to expose the hypocrisy, not only of her own family life, but also of the entire conservative and religious culture of the small southern town. This choice of role evoked much disapproval from her father, but Blanche seemed to enjoy their angry confrontations, which were also somewhat sexualized and which gave her a sense of her own boundaries. Her mother apparently remained silent and apart from the frays. Blanche began drinking, and flirting openly with any male in the proximity. She noted that no one in that town would have believed that she was actually a virgin on her wedding night, and that furthermore she did not want them to believe such a thing. When she left home for college, she wrote detailed letters about often fictitious escapades to supposed friends whom she knew would repeat these tales. In actuality she was a good student, majoring in literature since she loved fiction. Following graduation she returned home and taught for two years, but found life dull as there was little left for her to do to shock the community. Thus, though she was frightened about the prospect, she convinced her older and more conventional sister that they should both move to the sin capital of the country—New York City.

Once in the city, both sisters obtained employment and began a life in which they met a variety of young men, attended many parties, and consumed a good deal of alcohol. Blanche often wrote home embellished letters about their wild existence. However, before long her sister became seriously involved with a young man and decided to marry. This threatened to leave Blanche alone until she received a proposal of marriage from the best friend of her sister's fiance. She did not especially care much about him, but he had the advantages of being reasonably reliable, wealthy, and Jewish, which would surely make a good tale back home. Although she claimed that she never really thought the marriage would last very long, and indeed there were problems from the beginning, Blanche soon decided that she would like to have the experience of being a mother. Her husband did not want children so she pretended to use birth control, while not actually doing so. The result was a son, Robb.

Blanche thought motherhood a wonderful experience and became extremely invested in her son, a situation that made the marriage worse since her husband complained loudly of her relative lack of attention to him. In spite of the fact that the marriage was very unsatisfactory, Blanche decided that Robb should not go through life as an only child so she manipulated a second pregnancy, which resulted in a daughter. Shortly after this pregnancy, Blanche asked her husband to leave, which he did, though continuing to meet all her financial demands and to retain contact with both her and the children. Now basically alone in a city of which she was still very frightened, Blanche considered returning to her home town, but did not want her children to grow up with the kind of hypocrisy she thought herself to have experienced as a child and did not want them to have to cope with the negative reputation she had purposely built for herself there. She therefore remained in New York.

Other than her activities with her children, life became relatively bleak and isolated. Blanche retained a small circle of friends, and had at least one opportunity to remarry, but had no desire to do so. She described herself as the type of person who could get along beautifully with the doorman and the grocer, but simply could not manage anything more intimate. She spent much time alone and became increasingly depressed, a condition for which she ultimately sought psychoanalytic treatment. Treatment lasted several years and Blanche thought of it as being quite helpful in some ways. However, she concealed from her analyst the fact that she had become an alcoholic, invariably being quite inebriated in the late evening hours. When she eventually did reveal this, along with her inability and reluctance to change it, there came an agreement to end the therapy with the idea that all that could be achieved had been accomplished.

Blanche continued to be quite invested in her children, especially Robb, who was very responsive to her reading stories to him at night. Separations such as the beginning of school were difficult but managed with the help of her analyst. Thus the children grew to be intellectual achievers and were seemingly well adjusted. Blanche attempted to protect them from her periodic irrational rage attacks and her alcoholism by having her ex-husband buy for her the apartment next to hers. She had a door made in the wall between the two kitchens and declared that the children lived in one while she lived in the other. The children were forbidden to enter her quarters, except at certain times, and she similarly gave them relative privacy. However, in the late evenings following considerable alcohol consumption, Blanche would have difficulty retaining her resolve and her boundaries. Thus she established a pattern of going to her son's bedroom in an inebriated condition. She would sit on his bed and the two would engage in long intellectual discussions. This continued throughout his adolescence in spite of her recognition that it was not good for him.

Robb experienced very serious psychological difficulties in college. At the request of the agency treating him, Blanche presented herself for treatment, even though she noted that she was terrified of venturing out alone in the sinful city. She quickly pointed out that she was herself beyond reclamation, and furthermore had no desire to change even though she had become a virtual prisoner in her own apartment. However, she would do whatever was required to help Robb. With the rationale that treatment needed to begin where the client was, a contract for weekly attendance at individual sessions and at a parents' group meetings, along with occasional meetings with Robb, was made. Blanche admitted that she fortified herself against the terrors of the trips, but she kept appointments regularly in a relatively sober condition.

With the support of her worker, Blanche withstood Robb's angry attacks against her and maintained a position that, while she knew she had been far from a perfect mother, she had done the best she could. When Robb would aver that he could not get better unless she changed, she would inform him that her life was basically over, that he had his life yet to live, and that he would have to live it for himself independently of whatever she did. She used her individual sessions productively to deal with her own guilt over her failings and with her sadness in seeing the seriousness of Robb's problems and the pain he was having to endure.

Initially Blanche protested that the parents' group meetings were not for her. She noted that at the time she terminated analysis, group therapy had been considered, but that her analyst had told her she was not a good candidate for it since it would only give her an opportunity to act out her not inconsiderable tendency to be exhibitionistic. Indeed this tendency was quite apparent from the outset. Blanche would, for example, arrive for her individual appointments flamboyantly dressed and would greet her worker with a dramatic hug and kiss in the waiting room while quickly glancing around to see what effect this would have on the worker and on whomever might be around to see the behavior. When alone with the worker, this seductive behavior was replaced with a very serious demeanor. Therefore, a decision was made not to challenge the defensive public behavior but to leave it alone.

Blanche joined the parents' group with some reluctance, and did cause quite a stir at the initial session. Fairly quickly, however, she became impressed that she had achieved acceptance in the group in spite of her provocative behavior, became an active participant in discussions, and began expressing in individual sessions her feelings of sympathy for the other parents and their problems with their children. She proudly referred to them as "my family group" and began to talk of long neglected memories of a variety of distant relatives and family friends who had often been in and out of her childhood home. She recalled that while the southern culture had indeed been a sham in many respects, there had also been a certain quality of warmth and sharing in the small town. At Christmas time Blanche spent several days making brandied fruit according to a recipe she recalled from her childhood, and proudly presented each parent and her worker with a jar as a gift. She noted that this was the first time in years she had felt as if she had some truly meaningful work to do.

During this time Blanche's drinking did not decrease significantly. She did manage, however, to avoid going to her son's room at night on the relatively few occasions when he was at home. These visits were apt to be stormy and Blanche, who had managed to acquire her worker's home telephone number from the public directory, developed a habit of calling the worker in the middle of the night instead of going to her son's room. While the ensuing discussions were rarely useful in terms of pure content, they did assist her in maintaining her intent not to invade her son's privacy.

On one weekend evening, Blanche called the worker when the latter happened to be having a party. Hearing the background noise over the phone, Blanche inquired if there was indeed a party going on, to which the worker answered honestly. Blanche, clearly surprised, then asked, "Have you been drinking?" Not sure how to handle this, but concerned that the truth might be evident, the worker again honestly answered "yes." Blanche indicated that under the circumstances she would prefer not to keep the worker on the telephone and hung up. At her subsequent appointment, Blanche indicated that she had been surprised as she had not pictured the worker as the "life of the party type," but said little more about the incident. However, at her session two weeks later, she proudly announced that she had joined AA, had been attending meetings almost nightly, and had decided to try to stop drinking—at least as much as she had been. This, she announced, was for herself, not her son. She then also pointed out that she had been impressed with the worker's honesty on the night of the party, saying she assumed that the incident must have been a little embarassing to the worker since presumably such behavior was not supposed to be part of a therapeutic and professional image. She indicated it must have taken courage to admit the truth, but she thought that if the worker could deal with being truthful and face the consequences, then she guessed she could learn to do it too.

Subsequently Blanche continued to attend AA meetings regularly and to cut down on her drinking. She began talking more and more about her need for others in her life now that her children both were grown up. She made a trip to her hometown and returned saying that she had found she still had some friends there, had enjoyed attending church services, which she had not done in years, and had made contact with the AA organization there. Thus within a few months she had made arrangements to return home to an environment in which she thought her life could have some meaning. For a time after her move, she kept in touch with her worker, indicating that she still went occasionally on "binges" but that for most of the time she was sober, was occupying herself with keeping up her house, and with church and AA activities, and had found life in general to be far more satisfying than it had been for her in many years.

Today Blanche would probably be diagnosed as having a narcissistic personality disorder. Yet there are also similarities to the type of immigrant problems with which the early social workers were concerned, with the obvious exception that she was not poor. Blanche clearly had many strengths, including her genuine concern for her children as well as some self boundaries, though these became shaky at times of stress and when she was under the influence of alcohol. Her interest in fiction and her desire to share this with her children was clearly partly related to a curiosity about the real inner lives of others, a knowledge of which she felt that her family had not provided her. She had some inner life of her own, but this was limited and partly experienced by her as hypocritical and fictitious. No doubt, as she thought, her earlier treatment had been useful to her in helping to strengthen her internal resources. Nevertheless she had lived for years with a relative vacuum of meaning in her life.

Adaptive capacities require a mixture of internal and external resources. It would appear reasonable to say that the capacity to call upon these resources is related to the development of the transitional process. Blanche certainly had some skills in this area, but her development was incomplete. Thus it was not possible for her to maintain meaningfulness in her life in a new context. Meaning always is dependent to some extent upon context, or one might say upon culture or environment, in both written exposition and personal experience. For Blanche, then, one might say that her transitional process had not progressed to the point where she could abstract meaning and transfer it from one context to another. She had always defined her self in relation to its meaning for the significant others in her hometown. In this regard her meaning system retained some concrete qualities. For her to regain a sense of meaning in her life, therefore, she needed to make a decision to return to the context within which her meaning system had developed.

Even before she could make that decision, however, Blanche needed to review the content of the meaning system itself, and to reorganize it in relation to its relative good and bad aspects in relation to her own self-esteem. She accomplished this through her relationships with the other parents in the group and her individual worker. It should be pointed out here that it was a coincidence, but one of which Blanche was aware, that her worker also had been raised in the South, so that some of the process in the treatment could be considered to have been a sharing of observations, from different perspectives, of what that culture meant. It is, of course, from this kind of sharing with a significant other that the child's first construction of the meaning of reality develops. It can be supposed that the perceptions of the significant other are not taken in unchanged, but rather are integrated into the existent data about the relative meaning of both the primary process (the existing internal world) and the secondary process (the external world) in regard to the safety of the self. It may be said, then, that the importance of the treatment relationship may lie in its provision of both a holding environment in which perceptions can be called forth and of a sharing process in which new dimensions of experience can be differentiated and integrated into the meaning system itself.

It should be pointed out that the realities of Blanche's past did not change during treatment, not was there any emergence of significant new unconscious material. Rather what occurred was the reinterpretation, by Blanche herself, of the meaning of her past experience. This is suggestive of the possibility that the effectiveness of treatment may lie, not so much in the recovery of deeply repressed material, but in the reordering of structures that underlie personal meaning and the symbolic capacities of the individual so that new meanings can be differentiated, constructed, or abstracted. It is just possible that, if research into treatment effectiveness were to focus on inquiring into the variables associated with a transitional process and reality processing more deeply, the effectiveness of that process might be more convincingly demonstrated than it has been to date. After all, social functioning is in part dependent upon the individual's capacity to identify a range of choices for behavior. Yet without an adequate internalized meaning system, options for behavior are likely to go unrecognized or unrealized by the individual.

3

The
Nature
of the
Unconscious

A RE-EXAMINATION

Freud is quite commonly credited with the discovery of the unconscious. Technically speaking, however, this is incorrect. The existence of an unconscious had been recognized for some time prior to Freud's work. What Freud actually did was to demonstrate that unconscious mental activity had a direct significance in relationship to human behavior, as well as to formulate a theory within which it became possible to study the influence of such processes in the individual, especially in situations in which an existent pathology was interfering with adaptive functioning. Thus Freud made the unconscious a legitimate arena for study—indeed a monumental achievement in the history of human thought. On the other hand, the study of the unconscious was only beginning, and Freud's assumptions were based on the knowledge then available to him. Some of these were faulty as viewed from the perspective of advances in developmental and psychological theory today.

Freud's assumptions, nevertheless, have continued to influence clinical thinking in ways that have not always led to constructive therapeutic results. A brief, but common, clinical example will help to illustrate some of the points involved.

Mrs. Cook was the mother of a hospitalized and tragically ill adolescent boy who had been diagnosed as schizophrenic. It was Mrs. Cook's practice to visit her son frequently at dinner time. She would bring her own food, which she insisted on feeding her son herself. She proved highly resistant, in fact impervious, to suggestions from the hospital staff that she stop this. When asked by her social worker about this behavior, Mrs. Cook responded with angry charges that the hospital food was inedible and not good for her son. Since Mrs. Cook did have an occupational background in food service, she was able to present her arguments in quite specific ways, detailing the nutritional insufficiencies of the hospital fare. Mrs. Cook also voiced these criticisms quite loudly to other staff and to other parents she met on the ward. Naturally none of this behavior won Mrs. Cook many friends on the staff, most of whom considered her to be the epitome of the "intrusive schizophrenogenic mother" who was deliberately undermining her son's treatment in order to keep him infantilized and symbiotically dependent upon her. Several staff members attempted to interpret this meaning of her behavior to Mrs. Cook, which, of course, only enraged her further.

For a time there was an impasse in which neither Mrs. Cook nor the hospital staff could see the validity of the other's point of view. Mrs. Cook did not acknowledge that her son needed to feed himself, while the staff overlooked the fact that the food was indeed poor, a situation the hospital administration had tried unsuccessfully to change for some years. Several highly sophisticated professionals considered the situation to be simply untreatable and wanted to deal with Mrs. Cook by forbidding her to visit if she wanted her son to be treated.

Here one can see that the conflict between Mrs. Cook and the hospital staff is partially based on differing constructions of reality in which both points of view have some validity. It is, therefore, possible to say that the problem was that of a failure to "begin where the client is"—that is, to begin with Mrs. Cook's construction of the reality. While this may be the case, it is not of much assistance in knowing how to proceed with the situation therapeutically since clearly Mrs. Cook's construction of the reality in this instance was interfering with the staff's being able to carry out its proper function—the treatment of her son, who needed to become more independent and to grow up. In this situation one needed to begin the work with Mrs. Cook, but precious time would be lost in the work with her son, who might be far less amenable to treatment if he were not reached during the critical time of his adolescence. Therein lies the dilemma.

When examined closely, however, it is apparent that the staff was making another assumption, which remained unexamined and which has caused considerable difficulty for treatment in this and similar cases. That assumption is that Mrs. Cook unconsciously wished her son to remain ill, and that this was the primary motivation behind her behavior. Many parents have been quite vocal about their feelings that a psychoanalytic point of view has scapegoated them in this manner. Increasingly it has been recognized that such parents have a point, and treatment programming has tried to avoid this problem. Frequently, however, insufficient attention has been given to an examination of the theoretical problems that led to this impasse. Theory, unexamined here, essentially is used in a way that becomes socially repressive. To understand what has gone awry, one must examine in more detail the original theory that supported the later unexamined assumption.

Freud theorized that the drives were motivational in their nature, that is, that their influence was attributable to their expression as unconscious wishes or fantasies existent in the mind of the human being from birth. Utilized in a reductionistic fashion, then, it is possible to say that if the behavior of a person leads to a certain result, then that person *unconsciously* must have wished for that result. Loewald (1980, p. 108) has called attention to this situation in the following manner.

Not enough attention has been paid to the intriguing fact that in psychoanalysis unconscious processes and phenomena are interpreted in terms of personal motivation, while conscious processes and especially volitional acts—whether of thought or deed—tend to be viewed as less personally motivated than superficially appears to be the case but as determined by instinctual-unconscious forces. It is as though what counts in mental life takes place on a kind of middle ground between two poles, and the two poles are being interpreted in terms of each other.

Leaving aside the fact that what Loewald is pointing out is awkward, and to some extent circulatory theorizing, it can be seen that Freud's original formulation led to the confusion of thought and causation. Modell (1968) has done a masterful job of pointing out the fact that one of the aspects of primitive thinking (or primary process) is that it believes in action at a distance. Modell describes this as part of magical thinking. In this mode of thinking, the wish causes the deed. Thus persons with schizophrenic or borderline thinking may believe that their anger will be directly injurious to those at whom they are angry. Within the realm of pathological magical thinking, there is no concept of the fact that the anger as a feeling state must be acted upon in some manner to cause actual injury. The existence of internal feelings does not lead human beings into trouble, though action based on those feelings may.

The Nature of the Unconscious

In an attempt to understand what led Freud to confuse motivation and causation in his theory, it may be useful to refer to the general paradigm that was common in psychology at the time Freud was writing. Essentially it was of the nature of a simple formula:

$$Stimulus > Response$$

Freud amended this formula to include the intervention of the mental apparatus:

$$Stimulus > Mind > Response$$

In making this change, Freud greatly increased the explanatory value of the theory such that individual variations could be considered. Even this change in the paradigm, however, is not enough to account for the complexity of behavior. Today, with the influence of systems and information theory, such a paradigm would have to be seen in the form:

$$Stimulus > Mind > Response > Feedback > Mind > Stimulus$$

Now several things can be noted in relation to the altered paradigm. One is that it is circular, so that the possibility of change is automatically built into the system. In addition, however, this paradigm makes it possible to assume that perhaps Mrs. Cook's problem is not so much based on problematic motivations or intentions as on her inability to process adequately the data she receives from feedback about the results of her behavior. It should also be noted that this formulation means that the therapist may intervene in influencing the client's mind at one of two possible points, that is, either in relation to the original intention of the behavior, or in the evaluation of the results that behavior has brought about. It is the thesis of this model that, while there is an interaction between intention and result so that feedback about the results of a person's behavior *may* then also change the motivation, social work treatment has, by and large, been designed so as to effect the evaluation of the results, leaving the intentional aspects to the individual. Thus the client has been left with self-determination, or the choice of what to do with his or her own life.

A book that explores like never before the questions...
"What is treatment?" and "How does it work?"

CLINICAL
SOCIAL
WORK
TREATMENT
How Does it Work?

"An outstanding contribution."
—FLORENCE LIEBERMAN, D.S.W.,
Hunter College School of Social Work

BRIDGING THE GAP BETWEEN THEORY AND PRACTICE

CLINICAL SOCIAL WORK TREATMENT
How Does it Work?

By Carolyn Saari, Ph.D.
School of Social Work,
Loyola University, Chicago

Current clinical social workers seem to be in agreement that social work is a process. Yet defining the features of that process is still a problem, and one about which there is much confusion…especially once the questions are focused at levels that are more than superficial.

In this illuminating book, Dr. Saari relentlessly pursues the questions, "What is treatment?" and "How does it work?" The result is an extraordinary model for understanding the treatment process within which a variety of techniques can be used. It also provides an encompassing framework for consideration of potential intervention effectiveness.

Through her years both as an educator and in direct practice, Dr. Saari has been clearly able in this book to bridge the gap between theory and practice. Social work practitioners or anyone involved in the helping professions will find that Dr. Saari is able to logically develop theoretical aterial so that it can be readily utilized from a functional point of view treatment.

Within the framework of psychoanalytic theory, she evaluates the ertinence of such constructs as the self, the unconscious, and transference to clinical social work and sets forth a coherent theoretical framework that adheres to traditional social work values and practices such as a orientation to action and client support. In addition, she focuses attention on specific issues, such as meaning and context, in the hope that ese will receive further consideration in the future.

CLINICAL SOCIAL WORK TREATMENT: HOW DOES IT WORK? is mandatory reading for anyone involved in areas of interventions with individuals, families, and small groups.

A Review By

FLORENCE LIEBERMAN, D.S.W.,
Hunter College
School of Social Work

Though the title of this book focuses on social work treatment, it covers more than that...the book is a contribution to the theory and practice of psychotherapy, integrating a variety of theoretical formulations in an original manner. Many fields of knowledge are utilized to illuminate the theory underlying professional practice.

The various chapters examine the meaning of reality, the unconscious, affects, values, sexuality and identity. Exquisite attention is paid to the relationship between theoretical concepts and the treatment process. Clinical vignettes are used to illuminate the integration.

Alternate Selection
Published 1986
(38559)
Publisher's Price $26.95
Member's Price $20.95
Earns **two** bonus credits toward the four
required for your next Bonus Certificate

Behavioral Science Book Service®   July 1986

The Origin of Content

*T*raditionally social caseworkers claimed that one of the primary features distinguishing their techniques from those of psychoanalysis was that these were geared to working only with conscious material whereas psychoanalysis dealt with the unconscious. This distinction is clearly in line with a formulation that locates the point of intervention at the point of the evaluation of the results of behavior rather than with the initial motivation. Furthermore social workers were always very careful to note that the client must retain the right of self-determination; that is, the right to make independent choices regarding his or her own life. Once again this approach can be seen as underscoring the importance of dealing with the conscious. While unconscious forces may indeed affect behavior, only conscious material can have any influence on the choices over which the client has any control. Taking this point of view from a superficial perspective, it can be, and sometimes has been, argued that the social worker need have no knowledge of the operation of the unconscious. Yet most social workers also seem intuitively to have known that the conscious and the unconscious were so intimately interrelated that to understand one of these it was necessary to comprehend the functioning of the other as well.

Classical psychoanalytic theory provided an insufficient basis for a full understanding of the relationship between the unconscious and the conscious, thus preventing social workers from being able to articulate convincingly the nature of the interrelationship they nevertheless suspected existed. To understand the difficulty here, it is necessary to examine in some depth the fundamental assumptions behind Freud's work. In the process of this examination, it is important to remember that Freud was originally trained as a neurologist and so began his work with a hope of being able to make direct connections between the physical structures of the brain and the motivation of behavior. He was, of course, unable to do this, since brain functioning was not yet sufficiently well understood then (nor is it now). His theory thus became increasingly less physically oriented and more psychological as his work progressed. But, since he never provided a finally comprehensive and integrated picture of the totality of his thinking, there remain many ambiguities and contradictions within his theory. [See Nemiah (1965) for a concise but useful overview of the development of Freud's thinking.]

For a period of time, relatively early in his work Freud put forth what has been referred to as the topographic theory of the mind. This was the tripartite model of the unconscious, the preconscious, and the conscious. It is apparent that at least initially he thought these would correspond directly to anatomical layers of the brain. As it became clearer to him that such a correspondence did not exist and, furthermore, that an explanatory theory based only on these concepts was not adequate for his purposes, he abandoned the topographic model as his primary mode of explanation, but did not fully explicate how constructs related to the unconscious should be integrated with his later tripartite theory of the id, the ego, and the superego. There was, nevertheless, a tendency to equate the id with the unconscious and the ego with the conscious. It is clear, however, that Freud did not intend that this equation should hold entirely, since, for example, he considered that the defenses that were part of the ego were unconscious.

Because many early psychoanalysts had defined their discipline as having concerns with "depth psychology," or the exploration of the contents of the id and the unconscious, the advent of the school of ego psychology was initially quite controversial. It seemed to direct attention away from the fundamental drives, instincts, and wishes that were posited as the primary motivators of human behavior. This controversy was so strong that, for example, Anna Freud (1946) found it necessary to begin her classic work, *The Ego and the Mechanisms of Defense,* with a justification of the legitimacy of a study of the ego within psychoanalysis. Anna Freud's point of view, however, essentially highlighted the defenses as primary in understanding the coping and adaptational efforts of the individual, certainly a critical area for social workers to understand.

It is, therefore, not at all difficult to comprehend why social workers were very much attracted to the school of ego psychology within psychoanalysis. This theoretical approach allowed them to say that they were concerned with coping, with adaptation, and with the conscious in a way that, at least originally, seemed to provide an intellectual structure within which to house the clinical interventions common in social work. The ego psychologists emphasized that the existence of defenses was a normal state of affairs and that these could not be directly challenged in a wanton manner without threatening the stability of individual functioning. This also appealed to social workers who preferred to see themselves as working with the normal and healthy aspects of the personality rather than with pathology. Moreover, social workers had discovered in clinical work that too much confrontation with a client regarding issues of fundamental motivation usually led to the loss of the client from treatment.

But if this early ego psychological framework had its appeal and usefulness for social workers, it also had serious drawbacks. Defenses were, technically speaking, formulated as being structures the operational purposes of which were to protect the individual from a knowledge of the frightening and overwhelming aspects of id contents. While it was relatively easy for social workers to say that what they did was to work within the structure of the defenses, the question "A defense against what?" presumably was not to be asked. When it was asked, social workers often responded with descriptions of social or external life circumstances, which, although perhaps quite real and quite relevant to the client's situation, did not fit into the theoretical concept of the defenses in the manner in which they had been defined, that is, as being against unconscious content. In this manner defenses, for social workers, were often utilized as a way of classifying adaptive behaviors that had little explanatory power or value other than the perhaps psychologically consoling effect of a labeling system.

The essential point here is that to utilize the concept of defenses in its traditional sense, but then to cut it off from the possibility of an explanation for the reason for the defenses themselves, fundamentally limits the practitioner from being able to comprehend the reason for or the ultimate meaning of the defense. Within this construction of theory, unless social workers were willing to say that they were indeed working with id content and the unconscious, there was no way to explain very easily the meaning of client behavior in any depth. Furthermore this approach was of little use in a connection between the client's life history and current behavior (again, unless one were to say that one was dealing with unconscious material). Social workers continued to gather history quite extensively in the belief that this mattered, but the actual connections between current client behavior and the past remained only vaguely defined.

Under the circumstances described, it is not hard to understand why a substantial number of social workers turned to conditioning theory or behavioral theory as an explanatory framework for treatment interventions. Behavioral theory was simpler to learn as it did not involve such complicated conceptualizations, yet, based on the notion of learning as a type of associational process through which certain habits were induced, it allowed for a connection to social phenomena and the effects of life experience. Moreover, it appeared to allow for client self-determination without the danger of repressive use of interpretations regarding motivation of the type illustrated in the case of Mrs. Cook. Best of all the use of behavioral theory promised both a simple way of understanding the connections between a therapeutic intervention and its effectiveness and a "scientific" means of measuring outcome. Behavioral theory seemed to have at least as much explanatory power as psychoanalysis. The movement of social work clinicians toward behavioral theory probably would have been even more pronounced than it has been were it not for the fact that it had little way of dealing with the importance of the therapeutic relationship, always a critical part of traditional social work formulations of treatment.

For a period of time, arguments between social workers attracted to a behavioral theory and those who remained within a more traditionally psychodynamic framework seemed to be both powerful and insoluble, since the two groups simply did not speak the same language and both could point to legitimate inadequacies within the other's framework. When such conditions exist, it is usual that the theoretical solution derives from a point of view essentially outside either of the two poles. Indeed this is precisely what appears to have occurred in this instance. The foundation for a solution seems to derive from neither of the two schools of thought as narrowly defined, but rather from the influence of the work of Jean Piaget.

Freud, it must be recalled, began as a neurologist at a time when the discoveries of Darwin about the evolution of the species were still relatively new and fascinating. Darwin's work had much influence over the scientific thought of the time. The notion was, of course, that human beings had inherited much from their biological predecessors and were in the process of further evolution. People were envisioned as highly developed animals, but as animals nonetheless. It was recognized that certain cognitive capacities, especially of the ability to symbolize through the use of language, made human beings significantly different from other forms of animal life, but it was assumed that they also still retained characteristics of the more primitive forms of inner life. It is not so surprising that, within this context, someone who was concerned with understanding the content of the unconscious might have supposed that this content, which appeared to be irrational and primitive, might have been biologically inherited. This is precisely what Freud supposed through his theory of the instincts.

Just as Freud initially supposed that the unconscious might have been housed in a physical layer of brain anatomy, so he initially thought of instincts as biologically based. These instincts, which were the stuff of the primary process, were then mediated through the acquisition of higher forms of thinking (the secondary process) over the course of the child's development in the first few years of life. The infant was conceptualized as being, fundamentally, a little animal with primitive impulses that would have to be socialized in order for the child to become a well-adapted and functioning member of society, but the primitive impulses would remain. There are, however, some indications in Freud's work that he also believed that evolution toward even higher forms of life was on the side of increasing secondary process and rationality as well as that the science of psychoanalysis ultimately might have some effect on the speeding up of such an evolutionary process.

As Freud's work progressed, it became more psychologically than biologically based, and the precise definition of the instincts became more and more obviously unclear. By the end of his life, Freud (1940) was stating:

The theory of instincts is so to say our mythology. Instincts are mythical entities, magnificent in their indefiniteness. In our work we cannot for a moment disregard them, yet we are never sure that we are seeing them clearly.

It is quite conceivable, if not likely, that had Freud lived, he would have amended his theory of the instincts.

As was noted earlier, in Freud's theory these instincts became the primary motivators of behavior through their expression in wishes and unconscious fantasies. What is important about this conceptualization is that those fantasies had specific universal content and it was this content that formed the core of the id and the unconscious. It was, therefore, through a presumed knowledge about the contents of the id that the psychoanalyst was able to make interpretations about the primary and fundamental motivational system of the individual. This was a part of the theoretical structure that allowed at least some professionals to believe that they could interpret Mrs. Cook's behavior as being based on an unconscious desire to keep her son in a pathological state. It is, in a sense, a supposition that she had a biological need for the continuance of a relationship based in early instincts toward mothering.

The idea that women, including Mrs. Cook, have tendencies, based in biological structures of some sort, related to the function of motherhood is hardly absurd. Nor is it absurd to think that these tendencies might be in some way involved in Mrs. Cook's relationship with her son. On the other hand, to assume that this is her primary motivator does not explain why all mothers do not behave as she does. In other words, it can be said that to make this assumption is to reduce all of Mrs. Cook's personality to this one factor—to utilize a type of single causation that Freud himself warned against. It is too simplistic an explanation.

Even if it were to be assumed that biology had some bearing on Mrs. Cook's behavior, it would be necessary to know in what form that biological patterning was inherited—an issue which, from a physiological point of view, modern science has still not resolved. It is no wonder then that Freud considered his instincts to be vaguely defined. Loewald (1980) has attempted to solve this problem by pointing out that, since the problem of the precise nature of the relationship between the mind and the body has not been solved, and since psychoanalysis deals with psychological rather than physical data, any concept of instinct in a psychological theory must be considered to be of a psychological nature. Loewald then goes on to say that instincts, in the sense of their psychological content, are not inherited as Freud had supposed, but are shaped by the influence of the environment, particularly the early care-taking environment. In this formulation a concept of instincts becomes potentially more useful for a social work theory simply because a relationship between life experience with the external social world and inner life is posited.

Freud did not only assume, however, that the instincts were inherited. He also assumed that they were inherited in a specific form. Because of his assumption that the brain works in a camera-like fashion, he assumed that primitive thought was in the form of visual images. Primary process, for example, could be understood from the visual images of dreams. He then assumed that these could be interpreted as symbols and their language translated into verbal language that would move their meaning from the world of the unconscious to that of the conscious. This is the reason why dreams were considered so important in the practice of psychoanalysis, why they were the "royal road to the unconscious."

Although Piaget's work focused on the purely "cognitive" issues of how the child learned and thus had quite different aims and intentions than those of a psychoanalytic theory, it also had to deal with an understanding of the unconscious. Piaget was quite familiar with Freud's theories in this regard and was not fundamentally disposed to challenge them. However, Piaget studied in some depth the actual behavior of infants and children, something Freud had never done. Piaget's methods were creative, but carefully based on empirical observation. He came to the conclusion that there was no reason to assume that thought, in its initial and most primary stages, consisted of visual images. This is a possibility Freud appears never to have considered. Instead Piaget assumed that the earliest stage of thought was one in which action was primary; he termed this the sensorimotor stage of thinking. For Piaget the utilization of visual images in thought is a later stage of development in the child.

Piaget's observations are not fundamentally in conflict with observations made of children by psychoanalytically trained observers. For example, Despert (1949) reported a study of dreams in young children in which she noted that dream content was not generally reported by children younger than 2 years old. Even in older children, considerable variability in the ability to report dream content was observed. Here, however, it was assumed that the variation was attributable to the capacity to report, not to the possibility that dreams with visual content did not occur prior to about age 2. Piaget's theory that thought developed out of action was, however, so fundamentally different from some of the fundamentals of psychoanalysis that it has taken some time for its implications to become integrated into psychoanalytic thought, but is now occurring. Dowling (1982), for example, has utilized Piaget's theories in pointing out that in young children's "night terror"—in which the child's visual image is much more global and less differentiated and in which there may be a single, vaguely perceived, image—precedes the more elaborate experience of the nightmare in which there are normally a series of visual images that are more or less related in the form of some sort of drama.

Defense, Motivation, and the Organization of the Self

An understanding that the unconscious does not originate in the form of specific content indicates that the human being, in order to maintain a sense of identity or of an intact self, must work at the construction of a sense of organization in which to provide a meaning for the world. This world consists, or course, of both the individual, including internal experiences, and the surrounding environment—in social work terms, the person–situation configuration. At this point it would be legitimate to consider whether such a possibility might be observed in clinical experience.

David was a severely ill young man who had been diagnosed as paranoid schizophrenic and was being treated on a long-term basis in a private hospital at some distance from his family's home. David's father was a successful, self-made businessman who believed in the work ethic and in the possibility of overcoming problems through the utilization of determined effort. The father, therefore, had considerable difficulty in comprehending David's limitations, a situation that caused considerable strain between the two. In spite of this strain, however, David did have some sense of the fact that his father genuinely cared about him and wanted him to be well and functioning.

On one occasion David's father wrote a letter to his son while also sending a check to the hospital to pay the monthly bill. Presumably by error the father included the check for the bill in the letter to David rather than in a separate envelope addressed to the hospital. Thus David received a check for $2,356.39 in a letter that made no mention of the check or the reason for its inclusion. Since hospital rules included a limitation on the amount of money any patient could keep on the ward, David was used to receiving his allowance checks made out to the hospital to be placed in an account upon which he could draw as he needed money. Therefore, the real explanation for the check did not seem immediately apparent to David.

Pleased that his father should have given him such a generous gift but uncertain as to what he wished him to do with it, David decided to do what appeared to be obvious in order to clarify the situation. He telephoned his father. The father was not home at the time, and his mother answered the telephone. When David inquired about the check, his mother indicated that she had no knowledge of it and asked what he was talking about. Unfortunately communication in this family left a great deal to be desired, and so David's conclusion was that his father had not wanted his mother to know about the check. He quickly brushed over his mention of the check, pretending it did not really exist. There had been no mention of the check in the letter and David now concluded that the message was that he was not to talk about it.

David still was left with no satisfying explanation for the existence of the check or its purpose. He was very puzzled by this, as well as by the question of how it was that his father had arrived at the precise amount shown. He doggedly pursued various ways of trying to figure how his father might have come up with a payment to him of exactly $2,356.39. None of his original ideas seemed to work. It was not related, for example, to any combination of figures from his regular allowance or from any previous savings of his. But David did not give up, and after a number of days spent on the problem, he ultimately found an explanation that satisfied him as being the only possible and correct one.

David knew that his father valued work and that he had been pleased when David had been able to work at a relatively menial job for a brief time just prior to his hospitalization. He calculated how much he had earned on that job. He then calculated how long he had been in the hospital. Through some manipulation of the figures, he was able to come up with the notion that his father had paid him the exact amount he would have earned had he remained on the job and not become so ill as to need institutionalization.

Once this solution had been reached, it became, for David, something like ultimate truth. Such is the nature of delusional thinking; although it may not be in concert with reality as perceived by others and is extremely rigidly held, it nevertheless has an internal logic to the individual and provides that person with at least some explanation of reality. At levels of primitive thinking, the possibility of no explanation at all is absolutely intolerable. No explanation leaves the person with no sense of self and open to the experiencing of a terrifying vacuum of nonexistence.

In terms of the psychological paradigm discussed earlier, it is now possible to point out that feedback following behavior must be integrated into the sense of the self. Thus that paradigm might be further amended to read:

Stimulus > Mind > Response > Feedback > Self > Stimulus

Here the purpose of the defense is not the prevention of conscious awareness of an unacceptable unconscious idea, but the construction and preservation of a sense of an intact self. This is very much in concert with Loewald's idea that originally psychic organization was seen as being in the interest of defensive purposes, that is, that the psychic apparatus was constructed so as to maintain repression of unconscious motivations. Current theory, however, has reversed this relationship such that defense now is seen as operating in the interest of organizational purposes.

Although not technically correct in terms of the original theory, it has become commonplace to utilize the notion of a defense in interpersonal terms. If, for example, a person is confronted in a manner he or she perceives to be angry or critical and reacts to this, that individual is said to have become defensive. Here the defense is not against an internal threat in the nature of allowing an unconscious meaning to become known, but rather against an external or interpersonal threat. It is, however, still against an assault on the integrity of the self, out of fear either of actual physical attack or of a change in the organization of the meaning of the self if the criticism should prove to be factual. Thus it can be seen that the term defense has come to be used quite normally in ways that are not well explained by the original theory. However, this usage of the term does make sense if the assumption is that the primary motivation of the individual is an attempt to preserve an intact sense of self or identity.

4 The Role of Action

Social work has always been considerably more comfortable with action than have the other disciplines within the psychologically oriented helping professions. In fact this orientation may have been even more of a distinguishing feature of the profession than the more frequently noted concern with the environment. This has, of course, been particularly true in social work programs for the advocacy of improved social conditions, but also has been true within the conduct of clinical interventions. An examination of the resolution of the work with Mrs. Cook (Chapter 3) will illustrate this point.

Although there did exist for a time an impasse between Mrs. Cook and the hospital staff in relation to the feeding issue, Mrs. Cook did not remove her son from the hospital. Instead she continued to try to negotiate, albeit somewhat angrily, with the hospital about what she saw as in her son's best interest. Eventually Mrs. Cook's social worker suggested to her (and to the administration) that perhaps her expertise in food service might be of some value to all the patients. Mrs. Cook immediately became interested in this idea. With some assistance from her social worker, Mrs. Cook organized a committee of parents to study the problem. In time a new food service, which was not run by Mrs. Cook herself but which was much improved over the old, was instituted. Mrs. Cook was extremely proud of her ability to contribute to the welfare of her son and the other patients. As she became more involved in feeding her son from a distance, she had less need to feed him in person, and she became much more willing and able to reflect on her own needs (and her son's) in her continuing treatment sessions with her social worker. Her son began to show some improvement.

What can be seen here is that Mrs. Cook's sense of herself required her to be able to define herself as a good mother. This would appear to have been her primary motivation. The difficulty was that she had a very limited picture of what a good mother is and of how she could meaningfully perform that role. What the social worker's intervention did was to offer her an opportunity for a redefinition of that role and of herself, through the use of actions that could be compatible with other aspects of Mrs. Cook's self. It is important to note that, because of a rather low level of personality organization, Mrs. Cook's ability to think through the situation, in the absence of action, had been limited. Once, however, she was engaged in actions she could define as constructive from the point of view of her own understanding of reality, she could also become more engaged in a process of thinking through other aspects of her relationship with her son.

This example is only one of numerous implications for understanding clinical social work practice that can be derived from an understanding that action precedes content in the evolution of thought. Another example of a mother who was slightly more developmentally advanced than Mrs. Cook will demonstrate another point.

Mrs. Allen, a borderline woman with considerable, previously successful treatment, sought help again during her son's adolescence. Aware from her earlier therapy that she had a strong tendency to have difficulty in allowing this youngster to separate from her, Mrs. Allen had made a conscious effort to allow his independence. She knew that she had been ambivalent about his acquiring a girlfriend, but also knew that this was a normal step for him, could see nothing to be concerned about in the girl he had chosen, and even managed to like this girl at times. When, however, her son and his girlfriend exchanged friendship rings, she became filled with rage. It was the experienced violence of that rage, along with the fear that she might act on this feeling, that made her once again seek treatment. She could not explain to herself why this particular event should elicit such a strong reaction in her, nor could she describe her feeling except to say that she was simply outraged and furious at both her son and his girlfriend. She had considered a connection between friendship and wedding rings, but knew her son to be nowhere near marriage and did not think this explained her reaction, nor did knowing this diminish her fury.

After a number of sessions during which time Mrs. Allen did not act on her rage, but experienced no relief from it, the social worker noticed that Mrs. Allen fingered a small object on a chain around her neck during the sessions and casually asked about this. Amazed that she could have totally forgotten that she had worn this object day and night ever since her son had passed babyhood, Mrs. Allen removed the chain and showed the worker a baby ring that had been a present from her own mother at the time of her son's birth. Mrs. Allen now knew the significance of the friendship rings. In several subsequent sessions, she reviewed the significance of the first ring with its connection to both her son and her mother, as well as to marital problems at the time of her son's birth. She terminated the treatment feeling secure that, although her feelings might seem strong, she understood and could deal with them.

In this brief vignette, it is clear that Mrs. Allen sought treatment because of her own awareness that there was some unconscious meaning for her connected to the friendship rings, and that this meaning, in its unconscious state, might lead her to taking actions she would regret. In other words Mrs. Allen already knew that making the meaning conscious would give her the ability to control her behavior—that is, to make a conscious choice over what actions she wished to take. Here is a concrete example of the relationship between an intrapsychic process and social functioning, a relationship that too often has been left at a very vague level. The expansion of the conscious allows for choice in behavior. This may not ensure that choice will always be in the direction the social worker, or society, might wish. It does, however, mean that the individual can have more self-determination and society can more reasonably hold the person responsible for his or her own actions and the resulting effects of these actions.

Access to the previously unconscious meaning here is not, however, through a process of free association or through the route of dream interpretation. Instead it is through the examination of an action. The point is not that free association and dream examination are not routes to the discovery of unconscious meaning, but that the examination of actions may also be such a route. This is particularly true in dealing with people, like Mrs. Allen, who are organized at levels of psychological development that are more primitive than that now considered neurotic. This would be the case specifically because, if actions precede the ability to utilize visual images or verbal forms of expression developmentally, then much of the most primitive meaning in human beings may still be embedded in actions. From this point of view, it becomes clear that traditional social work processes, which have always dealt with helping people examine their behavior, also always have dealt with the unconscious in the sense of transforming it into the conscious.

Mrs. Allen did have some sense that some meaning was attached to the rings of which she was unaware. However, this does not necessarily indicate that the meaning existed in a preconstructed and preexistent form that was ready for her simply to rediscover through a visionary experience. There has been too much emphasis on the notion of "unconscious thought" rather than on the idea that there may be additional ways of thinking of which the person is not conscious. Once Mrs. Allen had an idea of the possibility of connections between the baby ring and the friendship rings, she did not immediately leave her treatment—nor did her worker suggest that she do so. In the remaining, and very critical, hours, Mrs. Allen worked to review the various meanings of the baby ring in order to understand the nature of the connections to the friendship rings. She was not recovering "repressed" thoughts. Instead she was actively involved in a process of reorganizing old meanings into a newly constructed consciousness.

The Theoretical Background

*O*n a theoretical level at least, orthodox psychoanalysis paid almost no attention to action. This derives from the fact that Freud defined pleasure in the human being as equated with a lack of tension or a state of rest, an assumption that pervaded much of his meta-psychology. Developmental studies, going at least as far back as Hebb (1949), have indicated that this is a false assumption. A state of rest is experienced as pleasure only when the organism has already expended energy and is in need of replenishment. There are, therefore, times when a state of rest will be experienced as pleasurable, but there are also times when action will be experienced as pleasurable. Hartmann (1958) pointed this out in his notion of "pleasure in functioning," a type of pleasure that is quite readily observable in, for example, the toddler who has just learned to walk.

Hartmann et al. (1950) discussed the fact that action could aid in the differentiation of the self, but only very recently has there been much real attention paid to the growth-producing aspects of action. Orthodox analytic theory also had a tendency to see the infant as a passive dependent being who was nurtured by an all-giving breast. Josselyn (1976) has pointed out that this is fantasy, not fact, since it overlooks the reality that in the feeding situation it is the breast which, relatively speaking, is passive while the infant must engage in the vigorous activity of sucking. Such a widely held fantasy about dependent passivity in human beings is undoubtedly related to the fact that there is a long period of time during which the human child must be cared for by others in order to survive. It also seems related to a biological need for contact with others of the species, as well as to a fundamental conflict about fusion between the self and the human other. That it is a fantasy, however, needs to be recognized. Furthermore this fantasy, like many others, would be more unpleasant than not if actually lived out. The real human infant is, and needs to be, a creature who seeks stimulation through action.

Treatment formulations that have been drawn from an assumption of fundamental passivity have sometimes erred in the direction of assuming too readily that pathology has resulted from a failure to have dependency needs met in early childhood and that treatment thus must consist of an environment that provides total acceptance and caring in order to meet these needs. On the other hand, the belief that the individual is pleasure seeking and that pleasure is equated with a state of rest has also led some clinicians to assume that an adult individual with severe pathology may have such severe unmet dependency needs that these can never be met. This type of thinking has often led to fear of making very much of a relationship with a client on the basis that it will only stir up a dependency that never can be satisfied. In this instance appropriate treatment sometimes has been avoided or not provided.

This assumption that pleasure equaled a lack of tension also, perhaps unwittingly, emphasized a treatment relationship in which the therapist was seen as the authority who also was the owner of nurturant supplies that could be doled out in some manner to the dependent client. Thus the client was seen as dependent upon the authority figure of the therapist. To be sure, the human being, especially early in life, does need to have an environment within which there is a sense of security, safety, and a connection with other human beings. However, this may imply an environment quite different from one in which the person is viewed simply as having a need for a type of passive dependency. A truly empathic relationship, such as should exist in treatment, should be based on far more than a simple notion of positive regard and total caring for the individual.

Certainly some theorists have attempted to take into account the need for action in the human being. Freud himself actually struggled with this issue in some of his works and talked at times of the possibility of ego energies. White (1963) utilized this idea in building a theory around the notion that the child gained both pleasure and self-esteem through being able to see that he or she could have an active effect on the environment. Others, such as Maslow (1971), have posited an instinct toward mastery. These have been important considerations in the gradual building of theory. Too often, however, these theories have tended to be too simplistic. Additionally, some individuals unfortunately have tended to think that if one of these two extremes, basic passivity or basic activity, were the case, then the other point of view was automatically invalid.

Human needs and pleasures, it would appear, are best viewed as being variable rather than static. What at one moment may be experienced as quite pleasurable, may be infuriating at another and fear inducing at a third. It is not possible to know what these needs and pleasures may be without considering the environment of the moment—from the point of view of both its external and internal, or inner life, aspects. This is one of the reasons why the social work clinician must learn to be constantly alert to how the client is interpreting and experiencing his or her own reality. It points to a requirement that there be good and constant communication and helps to explain why treatment relationships can be such hard work.

Klein (1976) made a list of what he considered to be the vital pleasures of the human being. These were (1) a reduction of unpleasant tension; (2) sensual pleasure; (3) pleasure in functioning; (4) effectance pleasure in experiencing the self as an agent of change; (5) pleasure in pleasing others; and (6) pleasure in synthesis or the achievement of a sense of organization as in artistic or creative pursuits. Klein considered that this list might not be complete and that there might be others. Certainly all of these need to be taken into consideration in any theory regarding human behavior and human motivation. However, there is now some reason to believe, as has been indicated previously, that there may be a need for a sense of organization regarding the self and its relationship to the environment that is quite fundamental and to which all of these various pleasures may contribute.

Activity can be seen to play a part in the achievement of all of Klein's pleasures. An understanding of the importance of action has led Klein, and others as well, to a reconsideration of such notions as acting out, repetition–compulsion, and even repression. Loevinger

(1966) may have been the first to point out a tendency in the human being toward the "active reversal of the passively endured experience." Such a notion can easily be seen to relate to situations in which the concepts of acting out and repetition–compulsion had previously been evoked. It also has a bearing, however, on behavior that has also been labled undoing and identification with the aggressor. The difference is that Loevinger's manner of stating the concept puts more weight on the notion that the action itself, even when it fails to achieve goals that appear to be in the direction of constructive change, is an attempt at active mastery rather than evidence of an existing pathological condition. For social workers this is an important difference since the conceptualization helps in the search for ways of aligning with the healthy aspects of the client—a search social work clinicians have always considered critical to their efforts.

Piaget's theory (Piaget, 1962; Wolff, 1976) makes the assumption that the infant has certain inborn reflex patterns, such as sucking, which become activated by contact with the external world. In the sense of the exercise of these action patterns, the infant has a need to function. Although there may be some similarity between the assumption of this need to function and the need for affirmation of one's existence as discussed by Lichtenstein (1977), the need to function is not a differentiated motivation of the same sort as has usually been discussed in orthodox psychoanalytic terms since motives in that theory have generally been considered as related to experienced internal affective need states. As has already been pointed out, current data suggests that in the past psychoanalytic theory tended to posit need states on the basis of adult projections. While some affective orientations do exist in early infancy, these are extremely general and undifferentiated at that time in life. According to Piaget the action patterns involved in the early reflexes serve as sufficient stimuli for their continuing repetition. Gradually, through these actions, the infant also encounters novelties that serve as attractions the infant wishes to repeat. In this manner schemata of action become formed and increasingly refined. The important difference between this and orthodox psychoanalysis is that the action itself causes the internal need for its repetition.

The action pattern, according to Piaget, is modified in each encounter with the environment, and then is integrated into all past encounters through a process termed assimilation. In each encounter, as a result of the modification through assimilation, the function of the action pattern itself changes slightly. This change is called accommodation. It is important to note here that the environment plays a significant role in the determination of directionality of development of the schema, but this is not in a reflexlike pattern since the infant will not be able to assimilate stimuli that do not fit well with an internal structure or schema that already exists. There is thus a type of selective perception and response. At the same time, the internal structures that do exist impose an order on the environment as it is perceived. For Piaget motives (goals and aims) thus are determined, not by the organism or by the environment, but rather through the interactions between the two.

As the action patterns become more complex, the need arises to put together a type of action chain in order to be able to repeat a previously discovered novelty. To be able to do this, the child also must be able to avoid the distraction of becoming more involved in the intervening action. The child must, in this sense, remember what the goal of the action is. Such action chains and the ability to maintain a goal independent of the immediate action at hand are the basis of intentional or purposive behavior, and are what Piaget sees as the basis for all intelligent action. It is important to note here that the popular notion that action and thought are mutually exclusive is misleading. In Piaget's theory action precedes thought but contributes to its development. Piaget's research (1976), for example, shows that children can perform active tasks such as throwing a ball correctly before they can describe accurately how they accomplished these tasks.

While Piaget's theory has proved to be fundamental in helping to clarify some of the misconceptions related to treatment that were based in early psychoanalytic formulations, it also has its limitations in relation to a direct translation into a theory for use by clinical social workers. These limitations derive from the fact that Piaget did not consider the role of affects or feelings in development, avoided study of the development of individual children or of pathological development, and did not consider the nature of the child's interactions with caretaking adults as contributors to that development. His ideas, therefore, need to be integrated with others to explain fully how learning and development occur.

Although orthodox psychoanalysis may have placed too much emphasis on the pathology of action in repetition–compulsion and acting out, there is no question but that the constant repetition of similar ways of dealing with problems, even when these do not lead to change or apparently constructive results for the individual, is commonly observed in clinical work. Active involvement may be necessary for problem solving, but it is not sufficient. It must be asked, therefore, what other conditions must exist in order for constructive change to take place. The work of two developmental psychologists, Heinz Werner and Bernard Kaplan (1963), is of considerable assistance here.

Werner and Kaplan use the term physiognomic to characterize the perceptual world of early infancy. By this they mean that at that time in life, the world is understood primarily in globally experienced affective terms in relation to its capacity to provide pleasure. This is not in contradiction to Piaget's idea that actions precedes thought. It simply means that the actions themselves and their results were themselves valued in terms that related to states of primarily physiological functioning. They do, however, consider that a critical part of that early biological programming includes an orientation toward other human beings, an orientation that is evident particularly in the infant's attraction for human faces. The infant's attraction to human faces has been noted by many child developmentalists (e.g., Brazelton, 1974; Kagan, 1978; Lewis & Brooks-Gunn, 1979; Mahler et al., 1975).

Werner and Kaplan point out that in the early world of the child, the environment consists of what they call "things-of-action." The idea is that the world has meaning for the child purely in terms of what actions the child can perform upon or with these things in order to achieve pleasure. However, in the course of development during the first eight months or so, the child's attitude toward the world changes. Although Werner and Kaplan do not note this directly, it is likely that this transformation comes about at least in part through the awareness that the external world sometimes seems to respond to the child's globally experienced desires but at other times does not. The change of attitude consists of a shift to seeing the elements of the environment as "objects-of-contemplation." For Werner and Kaplan, it is out of this perspective on the world as an object-of-contemplation that thought, the capacity to symbolize, and the use of language develops. It is, therefore, a very critical shift.

The shift toward objects-of-contemplation can be seen in a gradual increase in staring behavior and eventually in the development of pointing. Pointing behavior is a particularly significant development because it indicates a desire to share with the human other the internal perceptions of the external world. Werner and Kaplan consider pointing behavior to be the first real step in the process of the development of the capacity to think and to symbolize. At the time that pointing behavior occurs, they posit what they call the "primordial sharing situation," which consists of the child, the mother, and the concrete external object. They note that their concept of the primordial sharing situation has many similarities to Winnicott's (1975) concept of the transitional object.

In Werner and Kaplan's theory, which is well grounded in observations, the ability to think in mature terms (usually accomplished through the utilization of language) develops out of the increase of psychological distancing and differentiation in the primordial sharing situation, which ultimately includes a fourth element—the symbol used to characterized the concrete environmental object the child has noticed. Thus mature thought and communication through language must have four distinct elements: the addressor, the addressee, the object of reference, and the symbol utilized to capture the elements of the object of reference that are being noted. It should be pointed out here that in this theory the development of both thought and language is social from its very onset.

By utilizing a combination of the theories of Piaget and of Werner and Kaplan, it can be posited that the growth that occurs in clinical social work may derive from the sharing of perceptions of the environment, including its internal and external aspects, as well as of the action chains that make up the behavior of the self and the human others in the community with the social worker. It is through such a process that new constructions of reality, including the building of an expanded conscious internal life, occur.

Clinical Application

M r. and Mrs. Flynn were a couple in their early 40s whose 10-year-old son Patrick had been diagnosed as probably having childhood schizophrenia. Although a very bright youngster, Patrick had severe learning difficulties due to an apparent inability to concentrate in classes. He could not manage peer relationships and was often a behavior problem in class, where he would distract other children, sometimes by passing strange drawings or notes, and at other times by severe teasing as well as hitting or stabbing with sharpened pencils. Patrick had an active fantasy life, but one that was disorganized, chaotic, and frequently violent in content. Outside of school Patrick was a loner and an avid reader, usually of science fiction comic books and *Mad Magazine.*

The parents considered Patrick a behavior problem at home as he frequently would not mind, although he was not usually actively destructive. However, he had a habit of reading his magazines at the dinner table, even though this was expressly forbidden. Patrick seemed to know that this was bothersome to his parents. To them it seemed to be (1) a representation of a distorted picture of the world; (2) a statement of his mental problems, about which they felt quite guilty; (3) an accusation that they were also crazy; and (4) a statement about anger and hostility, affects with which they could not deal very well. Although Patrick's problems were fairly severe, a detailed developmental history and testing indicated that he did have neurological impairments that probably accounted for much of his pathology. Therefore, while there were problems within the family, these were not necessarily the fundamental basis of the pathology.

Upon referral from school authorities, Mr. and Mrs. Flynn sought treatment through a child guidance clinic. They indicated from the outset that they were quite upset by their son's difficulty, which also made them feel quite ashamed of him. Mr. and Mrs. Flynn were outwardly willing to cooperate with treatment, which, for two years, consisted of weekly appointments for Patrick and weekly appointments with a separate worker for both parents. During this time Patrick's progress was discernible but very slow. His teachers did report improvement, but the parents thought there had been none at all at home. The parents' worker also thought there had been no progress at all in the work with the parents.

During this initial two-year period, Mr. and Mrs. Flynn kept appointments quite regularly and never showed any unwillingness to do so as long as the clinic thought this necessary for their son. The worker considered the parents to be quite dependent people, but who handled any suggestions about how to deal with their son in a highly passive–aggressive manner. Each week Mr. and Mrs. Flynn would dutifully report on their son's behavior and request help with handling it. However, they would then return to point out, without any overt show of anger, that the suggestions had not worked. Over the course of these two years, it also became quite apparent that Patrick was scapegoated within the family. His younger brother and only sibling, Sean, was openly recognized as being more responsible and competent than Patrick. Sean was allowed, and at times even actively encouraged, to tease Patrick for mistakes or shortcomings. At other times it appeared that Mr. and Mrs. Flynn themselves joined in making fun of Patrick's behavior. Meanwhile Patrick continued in his defiance, primarily through his magazines at the dinner table, which infuriated his parents and often led to very angry scenes about which the parents complained bitterly but could not seem to stop. Mr. and Mrs. Flynn's worker, whose philosophy regarding treatment of parents consisted primarily of a simple belief in educational guidance through helping parents understand their child better, was extremely frustrated by them and believed that no significant process was possible.

Following two years of treatment, Mrs. and Mr. Flynn were transferred to a new worker. This worker also quickly discovered the Flynns' pattern of presenting problems, openly requesting help and then demonstrating how this help had been ineffective. However, the Flynns' genuine guilt over what they saw as their own parental failure was also apparent. The new worker, therefore, quickly attempted to divert discussions from just reports on Patrick's behavior to an attempt to learn more about the parents as a part of getting to know them as individuals. Mr. and Mrs. Flynn were cooperative about offering general information about themselves as they had been about other aspects of what they saw as being demanded of them.

Mr. and Mrs. Flynn had grown up in the same lower-middle-class, ethnic neighborhood in which they now lived. They had known each other from childhood. In fact they had lived across the street from each other but, as he was a few years her elder, had not especially played together as children. Both reported their childhoods as being reasonably pleasant and uneventful. Both had graduated from high school with unremarkable records. There was no expectation of further education for either. Following high school Mr. Flynn had served several years in the service prior to returning home to live with his mother and support himself by working as a skilled laborer. His father had died while he was in the service and he expected to live with his mother until he married. Meanwhile Mrs. Flynn had graduated from high school and secured a clerical job for a time while also continuing to live at home. The two families had always considered each other to be good neighbors and Mrs. Flynn would occasionally visit with her future mother-in-law, whom she liked, especially after the death of Mr. Flynn's father.

Thus when Mr. Flynn returned from the service, his mother began to invite the future Mrs. Flynn over for dinner, especially on Sundays. Mr. and Mrs. Flynn considered it quite natural that they should have eventually begun dating and become married. When the house next door to Mrs. Flynn's parents was put up for sale, the Flynns had bought it, so that they continued to live on the same block with parents from both sides of the family. This was not an unusual pattern in the neighborhood and, in fact, Mr. Flynn also had a brother who lived down the street and Mrs. Flynn had a sister only a few blocks away. It was evident that, while some might read intrapsychic pathology into this failure to separate geographically, it was actually culturally quite normal.

Both parents reported the marriage to be satisfactory. Indeed in treatment sessions they presented a somewhat united front in which there appeared to be a genuine affection for each other and a mutually supportive relationship. While Mr. Flynn appeared to get along well with his fellow workers on the job and Mrs. Flynn maintained some contact with girlfriends from high school and her former place of employment, their primary social contacts were with members of the extended family, again a pattern that neither parent had ever questioned as a natural part of an expectable lifestyle.

Mr. and Mrs. Flynn shared an interest in the maintenance of their modest home, which occupied a large part of their time. They also shared a kind of passion for the sport of hockey. During the hockey season, their evenings were nearly always devoted to watching the televised games. Mr. Flynn would drink a can of beer or two, and Mrs. Flynn would sometimes share in the beer, though there was no evidence that either ever over-indulged. The two would become very involved in the activity of the game, often yelling invectives over frustrating situations or cheers when their team was doing well. Although both parents considered this enjoyment quite normal and their major form of recreation, Patrick found it to be somewhat frightening because of the hostility that was expressed and because he seemed to fear that his parents were, or might become, out of control. Although Mr. and Mrs. Flynn recognized that this behavior on their part troubled Patrick, they considered his reaction quite out of proportion since they did little more than yell or occasionally pound a pillow out of frustration. Indeed it did seem that this recreation was the only time when the Flynns ever allowed themselves to experience or express any anger, with the exception of their battles with Patrick. While the Flynns were not proud of their own anger at Patrick, which they knew was expressed in the dinner table confrontations, they simply could not understand why he did not behave as a normal child and abide by their directive not to read during dinner, which was considered to be a time for family sharing and discussion.

As the Flynn's new worker encouraged an informal atmosphere in the sessions and evidenced a noncritical interest in the details of their lives, they began to appear more relaxed in the interviews. On one occasion Mr. Flynn asked if the worker liked hockey, to which the reply was a truthful and matter-of-fact statement that she did not. Mr. Flynn then said that he bet she did not know anything about the game and she acknowledged this to be the case. After a long protestation that the public impression that people watched hockey only for the violence of the physical fights that were typical of the game was inaccurate, Mr. Flynn announced that he thought it was a fine game and that the worker would enjoy it if only she understood what was going on. He then directed the worker to watch a game, saying that he would teach her about it.

The following week Mr. Flynn asked if the worker had watched a hockey game. She replied that she had, but that she had not understood the rules. She began asking questions while Mr. and Mrs. Flynn tried to explain the intricacies of the rules, the playing skills, and performance records of the various local players. This pattern continued throughout the remainder of the treatment so that parts of sessions would often have sounded to an outside observer as a social discussion of the sport in which the Flynns were the experts and the worker the learner.

Before very long, just before a major national holiday, Mrs. Flynn mentioned the fact that they had always gone to one of their parents' homes for dinner on these occasions, and had never invited their parents to their house for a holiday meal. She thought it was time they did this, but acknowledged that she was very nervous about putting on the dinner. Mr. Flynn indicated he thought it was a fine idea, and volunteered to help in the preparations. The worker encouraged the activity and subsequently shared in listening to the plans for the event as well as the details of how it had gone. It had worked well, with a few minor hitches that provided for some later mild amusement, and Mr. and Mrs. Flynn were very proud of their accomplishment. Later on in the treatment, Mrs. Flynn, who had been encouraged by this initial success, decided to give a fairly large bridal shower for a member of the extended family. Once again she was actively supported by both her husband and the worker. The event proved to be a total success, which had considerable meaning to both parents.

Apparently encouraged by his wife's new successes, Mr. Flynn decided to undertake some major remodeling jobs inside the house. Thus the sessions also included discussions of his work, his plans, and her participation with him, especially in projects involving sewing new curtains or new slipcovers. Problems encountered in the work were discussed, with both parents offering suggestions to each other about different ways of trying to solve these. The worker on occasion also shared an observation or two about possibilities, but primarily served as an interested and encouraging person. Over the course of time, this discussion took place about most of the rooms in the house.

The last room to be remodeled was the master bedroom. During this project Mr. and Mrs. Flynn came to one session with a markedly different demeanor than was typical for them. They were clearly angry with each other and they reported that they had been engaging in a major argument—the first serious disagreement they could remember. Mrs. Flynn wanted to buy a new queen-sized bed and Mr. Flynn was opposed to the idea. Both were very angry and hurt and neither could understand the other's position. The difficulty was that neither had been able to discuss openly the reasons behind their positions. Mr. Flynn finally was able to admit that he was hurt because he assumed this meant his wife wanted to get more distance from him during the night. He said he liked sleeping with her, enjoyed feeling her body next to his, did not want this to change, and did not like to think that she wanted such a change. Mrs. Flynn was clearly shocked that this had been his assumption. She shyly, and with some embarassment, indicated that she liked having sex with her husband and had been thoroughly enjoying some fantasies about what fun they could have together in a larger bed. Both parents indicated that they never before had really been able openly to discuss their feelings about their sexual relationship with each other.

The events in the treatment with the new worker occurred over a two-year period. During this time there were also discussions about Patrick's behavior and progress. However, increasingly the nature of these discussions changed from the parents reporting problems and expecting the worker to pronounce solutions, which were doomed to eventual failure, to a process in which Mr. and Mrs. Flynn would engage in problem solving in relation to Patrick in the same manner as the discussions about planning family events and remodeling the home. In these discussions about planning family events responsibility for their own handling of their son and seemed not to be as concerned about not doing the "right" thing. They became much more relaxed about Patrick's reading at the table, though they did not like it, and finally reported that they had directly told Patrick that he could do this if he wanted, but that they wished he would not since it excluded him from the family discussions. For a time Patrick did continue his reading, but the parents tolerated it and eventually he stopped. Gradually Mr. and Mrs. Flynn's relationship with Patrick changed and they no longer allowed Sean to tease him in their presence.

Patrick continued to have serious difficulties, but his improvement was marked. He continued to need special help at school, but was doing well within this structure. Mr. and Mrs. Flynn seemed much more comfortable with the idea that their son had limitations and would probably always have trouble of some sort. They no longer, however, saw this as evidence that they had been bad parents and were more freely engaged in cooperating with the school. At this point active treatment was terminated with the understanding that in all probability Patrick would need further help in the future, but that at least he was making as much progress as could be expected. In the process of terminating, Mr. Flynn pointed out that he thought the main thing he had learned was that as a parent one had choices over how to handle situations and that one had to think about how best to deal with them. The worker had never verbalized this principle to them.

Mr. and Mrs. Flynn did not have severe intrapsychic difficulties or conflicts. Had they not had an impaired son, in all likelihood they never would have come to the attention of any mental health program. They did, however, have a type of developmental arrest, which was apparent even within the context of their own culture. It was clear, for example, that others in their generation had been able to take a more active role in entertaining within the family. Their environment had encouraged them to be passive, pleasant, and somewhat dependent individuals. While it would be quite accurate to say that there was behavioral evidence of anger against the authority figures in their lives, neither parent seemed to be consciously aware of this. Thus, instead, they acted out their anger by scapegoating Patrick. They appeared also not to be aware that this was what they were doing. Therefore, simply pointing this out to them would not have been of any use since it would have confirmed their own sense of inadequacy as parents and their own roles as perpetual children.

The Flynns' scapegoating of Patrick can readily be seen as an "active reversal of the passively endured experience." They felt humiliated by him because of his failure to appear normal to their family and to the school authorities. In turn, of course, Patrick engaged in a similar active reversal in his behavior with peers at school. No doubt the parents also felt humiliated by having to deal with authorities at the child guidance clinic. This desire for active reversal can also be seen in Mr. Flynn's wish to teach the worker about hockey. The worker's ability to allow him to do so, while both accepting this and willingly participating as a learner, provided him with an opportunity to have this reversal have constructive rather than destructive results—the worker made it clear she did not feel humiliated by his having more expertise than she did in this area. Additionally, of course, placing Mr. and Mrs. Flynn in the role of teachers was treating them as adults with something to offer rather than as children. Furthermore, since the teaching had to do with the one area in which parents could accept their anger, this provided a message that this aspect of themselves was acceptable.

From one point of view, it can be said that these parents had never really noticed that there were other possible ways of dealing with Patrick's behavior because they had not built up the internal structures into which such things could be assimilated. To them in parent–child relationships the parents laid down directives and the children simply obeyed. When Patrick did not follow the expected pattern (Sean did), they did not know what else to do. This was to a large extent a deficit from a lack of experience, and they needed to acquire some experience of a different sort that would give them clues as to how else to conceive of parental roles.

From another point of view, it can be said that Mr. and Mrs. Flynn's world was to some extent still at a level of things-of-action. They did not engage in a contemplation of Patrick's behavior, but simply reacted to it. Similarly they could not respond to suggestions from their first worker as ideas to be contemplated and used selectively. They heard these as actions to be carried out, and no doubt did so in fashions that were rigid, stereotyped, and not well integrated into their own lives, and so doomed to failure. These parents were, however, always involved in pointing behavior in the sense that they would actively come in with identified problems. The treatment need was to help them become more actively involved in the sharing of perceptions regarding those things to which they could point.

The treatment process with the Flynns could, in a sense, still be considered to be one involving parent education, but it is not so in the simple sense of providing suggestions or ideas. People who are not able to engage fully in a sharing process involving a contemplation of objects, either because, like the Flynns, they may have had little exposure to such processes in life, or because there is a developmental arrest as a result of a more active pathology, often need to be helped to learn how to make use of the treatment relationship. It is an error to think that all people automatically know what this relationship is about and how to use it. This is the case with all clients and not just with parents.

For new behaviors to acquire some stability, it is undoubtedly necessary for the individual involved to achieve some pleasure from them. In relation to the work with the Flynns, it can be seen that the treatment helped them in the achievement of more pleasure in the sense of all of Klein's pleasures. There was reduction of unpleasant tension in the relief of conflict over the shame over Patrick's problems, as well as the reduction of some of their fears about their own ability to handle him in the future. There was a pleasure in functioning seen in their ability to become more adequate adults— even to be able to give themselves permission to be less self-conscious about being fully functioning and sexual beings, in which there is, of course, sensual pleasure. There was effectance pleasure in being able to see themselves as agents of change since they ultimately could recognize that Patrick did respond positively to some of their own changed behavior. There was pleasure in pleasing others, which was clear in the treatment relationship as well as in their relationships with each other and with other members of their extended family. Finally, there was pleasure in the achievement of a sense of synthesis, both in the sense of a reorganized sense of themselves, and in the creation of a nicer environment for themselves in their home.

It can be said that the Flynns seem to have been greatly aided by an ability to share perceptions of their own actions and those of their son, while engaging in these actions and interactions. In a similar sense, it can be said that Piaget's child, who has the ability to throw a ball but cannot describe accurately how it is done, will also be helped to learn how to describe his or her actions through sharing perceptions of such actions with others.

5 Affect and Aggression

The case of Mr. and Mrs. Flynn (Chapter 4) also raises issues related to questions of the nature of aggression and of hostility as an affect. In this case it seems fairly clear that the Flynns had considerable difficulty in dealing with their anger. In fact it can be hypothesized that had the worker not given them permission to express and feel anger through her engaging with them regarding their interest in hockey, no further progress would have been made. How best to understand and deal with anger and aggression has been a troubling issue, not just for the Flynns, but throughout human history. It is still a highly controversial subject in treatment theory. There does, nevertheless, seem to be a developing consensus about some of the issues involved.

One of the major difficulties in dealing with an understanding of anger from an orthodox psychoanalytic point of view comes from the fact that Freud considered the affects as derivatives of the instincts, although the precise nature of the relationship between the two was never totally clarified and seemed to changed as his theory developed. Anger, however, was seen as being related to the aggressive instinct, the existence of which was controversial even among his followers from the time he proposed it. Part of the controversy had to do with the fact that, whereas Freud seemed to think that aggression was inherent in the human animal, many psychoanalysts preferred to believe that it was not necessarily inherent, but was the result of frustration encountered in interactions with the environment. In addition Freud posited the ultimate aim of the aggressive instinct as being death, another idea that many found hard to accept.

There are many reasons why the arguments in psychoanalytic circles over the existence and nature of the aggressive instinct have been so difficult to resolve. However, a major reason was simply the fact that activity of any sort was considered to be related to the aggressive instinct. Within this formulation, then, any sort of assertiveness could be assumed to have a hostile impulse at its base. To a not inconsiderable extent, this idea has been generally accepted in Western culture and can be seen to have created difficulties for many people. The Flynns, for example, seemed to be so frightened of their angry impulses that they could not be appropriately active in areas of their life where it would have been beneficial for them to be so, such as in their relationship with their parents. In clinical circles in recent years, there has been considerable effort to change this notion through the vehicle of assertiveness training. The underlying theoretical problem has been the equation of action and anger or hostility, which seem to be better understood if dealt with separately than as both related to an aggressive instinct. This position is being taken by an increasing number of psychoanalysts (e.g., Blanck & Blanck, 1977).

Once it has been posited that action is fundamentally neutral in relation to affect and that anger and hostility, although these may be expressed through action, are in fact affects that are fundamentally separate from any specific actions, this seems to make good sense to most people. It is, therefore, worth taking the time to wonder why such a simple principle should have been so difficult for people to formulate and espouse for a long time. Although there may be many ways of attempting to understand this, one of the most productive seems to be through the concept of magical thinking [see Modell (1968) for a more complete explanation of magical thinking and its nature].

In the most primitive form of magical thinking, the extremes of which can be found in schizophrenic states, there is a psychological fusion between the self and the external world such that the thought seems to cause the deed. Persons in an acute schizophrenic episode may believe that they have become gods and that their wishes automatically will be fulfilled. This may not be troublesome so long as the wishes and thoughts are pleasant. However, such persons may have to resort to extremes to prevent themselves from thinking angry or hostile thoughts, or they may become responsible for the destruction of the world, usually including themselves. In actuality, of course, thoughts do not cause events in the external world unless they are acted upon in some manner. What can be said then is that in a primary undifferentiated state, there is a failure to make a sufficient distinction between internal thought and external action. Since the primary undifferentiated state presumably has been the psychological past of all human beings, more magical thinking may survive into adulthood, even in presumably normal persons, than has been supposed.

The Flynns do not seem to have been unusually troubled by the idea that thoughts can cause harm. They were not, for example, fearful of acknowledging to their worker that they were angry at Patrick over his behavior. They were, however, not quite so certain that assertive actions might not harm him. They knew that he was upset by their behavior when watching hockey games and, while they refused to stop this, they seemed to have some expectation that an expert would tell them to do so.

There is a second form of magical thinking that is very common when people do not really understand the nature of cause–effect relationships. In this element of magical thinking, there is a belief in action at a distance. In primitive cultures, for example, a magical ritual may be performed to bring rain. If rain does not result from the prescribed dance and ritual, it is assumed that the actions were not done properly enough to please the gods. In this manner the human beings involved have invented an organization or explanation of the reality of the world around them that can provide a sense of understanding and control even when it is a false one. Thus while the ceremony actually may have little to do with the weather, it has a very important positive meaning for the participants. Such thinking may seem primitive to some in the "scientific" world, but upon closer examination it proves to be not so very far from the daily lives of people in today's culture.

Most people do not know enough about the products of modern technology to be able to explain them. A television set is turned on and, as if by magic, it works. Certainly there is an awareness that a chain of events is set in motion by turning the knob. When the set breaks down, a repairperson is called. On the other hand, as people do not have the technician's knowledge of television and do not know what it is that has been done to fix it, they normally think of a casual chain in which turning on the knob causes the picture and sound to appear.

Human relationships are much more difficult to understand since the elements of the casual chain regarding responses to our actions are far more intangible and abstract. Even presumed experts have much more to learn about the elements in the action chains involved in human behavior and thus may become involved in magical thinking far more than they may wish to acknowledge. This is a type of magical thinking that is based on a lack of experience and understanding. Mr. and Mrs. Flynn did not understand what about their behavior might be contributing to Patrick's problems. They did sense that they were angry at him in a global sense and that he was angry at them. Anger, or perhaps more accurately frustration, was also involved in their behavior in watching the hockey games. Therefore, it is not unreasonable that they should hypothesize (or that Patrick himself should) that these might have some connection. It can be seen, however, to be a belief in action at a distance—a belief in magical action. In a similar sense, one can say that the Flynns wanted a magical ritual, that of treatment or of the prescriptions they requested, to "fix" the situation.

Fundamentally, of course, there remains the failure to separate action itself from the emotion of frustration, anger, or hostility. Viewed from this vantage point, it is also perhaps understandable why early psychological theory, not yet fully comprehending the intricacies of the action chains between human beings, might also have proposed some formulations that involved a belief in the effects of action at a distance. Indeed there are probably many such naive assumptions underlying clinical work. Eventually other professionals will discover these and provide better explanations. For the time being, however, an explanation is necessary to help clinicians do as much as possible to provide adequate treatment and to be able to feel that they are not helpless in dealing with human suffering. Explanations also make it possible for clinicians to gain some effectance pleasure from their often frustrating work.

Affects and Objects

*I*n the initial formulations of psychoanalytic theory, it was thought that affects, as derivatives of instincts, were present from birth. Thus these were presumed to be well formed even in early childhood, and to be experienced in much the same manner by all people at a primitive level. Changes, therefore, in the experiencing of affect over the course of life were presumed to be due to the intervention of repression or some other form of defense. As object relations theory within psychoanalysis has progressed, there has been increasing questioning of this formulation. Many theorists now believe, on the basis of observational data from studies of children, that affects have a developmental course that closely parallels that of the development of object relations (e.g., Mahler et al., 1975; Blanck & Blanck, 1979; Jacobson, 1971; Schimek, 1975).

Affect, in the form of sensations of pleasure or unpleasure related to physiological relations, is indeed innate in the human infant, but affects in the sense of organized perceptions of the intricacies of an inner experience are abstractions, the capacity for which must evolve during the course of development. For example, Bruch (1969) and Coddington and Bruch (1970) convincingly demonstrated that even the perception of a sensation as basic as hunger must be learned. A precise course for the development of affects has not yet been delineated in detail, although there is currently much interest in this topic and there have been some initial attempts (e.g., Blatt, 1974). In fact there is still considerable disagreement about the nature of early affective experience and there are those who would argue that the affects are more differentiated at birth than others suppose (Gaensbauer, 1982).

It is becoming increasingly clear, however, that although present in all individuals, feeling content and the capacity to experience this in very differentiated ways vary considerably from one person to another. The differences are presumed to be related to the individual's life experiences in general, but in particular to the experiences with other human beings who have been of significance in the person's life. Certainly there is a physiologic base upon which affects are based. Some infants are clearly born with dispositions that make them more prone to activity than others, and some infants seem to be much more irritable than others from birth. However, these basic moods become much more elaborated and can be changed to some degree. The person with a frustrating early-life experience is more likely to be prone to angry reactions in later life. This is what Loewald (1980) apparently means by the idea that the psychological instincts are formed in the course of the interactions with caretaking adults.

In the undifferentiated psychological matrix of the newborn (Hartmann, 1958), affects, activity, and the external world are all fused and are poorly differentiated from each other. Parens (1979), who has studied the development of aggression in much the same manner that Mahler studied the development of object relations, has indicated that at least four different types of "aggression" can regularly be seen in young children. These are (1) activity that is not destructive; (2) aggressive action that may or may not result in destructiveness but does not appear to have a direct connection with affect; (3) rage reactions that appear to result from excessive frustration or unpleasure; and (4) destructiveness from which the child appears to gain pleasure. Parens' observations lend further support to the idea of the necessity to separate action and anger to understand both.

There is another sense in which the early theory's failure to deal adequately with the notion of anger would appear to have created misleading notions for the clinician. Freud tended to think of his instincts of libido and aggression as polar opposites. Mature functioning, as in sublimation, then depended on the adequate mixture of these two drives. The problem here is that such a formulation leads too easily to an assumption that love and hate are mutually exclusive opposites rather than that both are normally felt toward any person who becomes important in an individual's life—the notion of the ubiquity of ambivalence.

Currently Kernberg's (1975) formulation regarding the pathology of the borderline individual, which has been much in vogue, relies heavily on the notion of splitting as the primary defense in these disorders. Thus the borderline personality seems either to love or to hate important people in the environment. Certainly this readily can be discerned in such individuals. Furthermore it has often been noted that most of the population treated by clinicians today can be considered borderline, so much so in fact that as a nosological category the term "borderline" has often been considered a meaningless "wastebasket." Since much of early psychoanalytic thinking has now been absorbed into the culture of the Western world, it is an intriguing, though unanswerable, question as to the extent to which the early theoretical assumptions might have contributed to the general population's believing that the two were mutually exclusive, and then to behaving as if this were the case. On the other hand, of course, Freud was himself very much a part of his own culture and may simply have translated into his theory a preexistent assumption he found there. Psychological theory is, after all, highly intermeshed with the culture in which it is found, and the interrelationships between the two are so complex as to be impossible to separate through any thought system currently available.

The idea that affects are connected with objects, as well as that love and hate are experienced in relation to all important people in one's life, is not difficult to demonstrate. Figures on the prevalence of family violence and child abuse, as well as murder, clearly attest to the fact that the person by whom one is most likely to be injured is not a stranger, but a person to whom one has become important. These statistics also, somewhat frighteningly, attest to the widespread symptomatology of having difficulty in separating anger as an affect from action. Clients with these difficulties need to understand, in a fully integrated sense, that the inner experiencing of anger, even of the with to injure or kill, is not abnormal or pathological in any sense. Acting on such feelings, however, is.

Winnicott, in an article of some importance, has noted that anger, even to the point of hate, is normally felt by all mothers toward their infants. He pointed out that, no matter how much a mother may love and want her child, that child will also at times be experienced as an inconvenient intrusion into her life. To demonstrate his point, Winnicott (1975, p. 202) noted how frequently mothers sweetly sing:

Rockabye baby, on the treetops,
When the wind blows, the cradle will rock,
When the bough breaks, the cradle will fall,
Down will come baby, cradle and all

And they apparently have no realization at all of the actual meaning of their words.

Winnicott further noted in this same article that hate plays a role in assisting the child to learn his or her own boundaries and to gain a sense of self. He believed that to experience himself or herself as separate, the child needed to be centered upon as such, an experience that hate can provide whereas love cannot. Understanding the function of anger and hate in this manner is quite important in the conduct of treatment. It, therefore, makes a considerable difference as to how the clinical social worker thinks of anger and of how comfortable that person is with its expression.

Fromm-Reichman (1959), certainly a superb and admirable clinician in many regards, believed that aggression derived purely from frustration and deprivation in the environment, and did not believe, as Winnicott did, that this frustration played a constructive part in the development of the individual. She reported a case in which she was working with a severely regressed schizophrenic woman who had the habit of smearing feces. Fromm-Reichman reported this as a technical problem because when she was with the patient in the treatment hours, the patient would smear feces all over her. Since Fromm-Reichman found herself objecting to this behavior, she saw it as interfering with her ability to accept the patient as she was. Fromm-Reichman ultimately solved the problem by wearing washable housedresses to her hours with this patient so that the feces smearing would not be a problem for her.

Although Fromm-Reichman reported therapeutic progress to have taken place following her solution to the feces problem, such a solution seems a bit extreme. It not only runs the risk of allowing the patient to think that feces smearing is acceptable social behavior, but it also raises the issue of whether or not there might have been a message in the feces smearing to the effect that the patient wanted the depth of her anger to be recognized as real. The normal social reaction to anger is, after all, to become angry in return. To ignore a client's anger, when directly expressed toward the clinician, can be a message that the clinician simply does not take the client very seriously; in effect it can be a put-down that robs the person of the experience of having a significant impact upon the environment (effectance pleasure).

While having to cope with feces smearing during an interview with a client may be a relatively rare experience for clinical social workers, dealing with expressions of anger and the need for setting limits is not. The principles rest upon the same theoretical foundations. For clients to learn that their anger is acceptable and will not destroy either the clinician as an object or the relationship with that object, the clients often need to have actual experiences in which this occurs. Inexperienced clinicians, genuinely wanting to convey to a client that anger is acceptable in the treatment hour, will often attempt to accomplish this through words by saying something to the effect that is is alright for the client to express anger. Particularly when this statement is made prior to any demonstration of anger by the client, the real message that is conveyed is that the social worker will not take the client's anger very seriously and so does not take the client very seriously. It is, in effect, a social put-down that maintains the worker in a safe authoritarian position, but does not advance the therapeutic work.

Taking the client's anger seriously and helping the client to learn that this anger will not destroy a relationship often requires actions as well as words, as in the following example,

Gary was a 17-year-old borderline youngster being seen in a residential treatment center. Within this environment it was necessary for Gary to keep regular appointments with his social worker in order to maintain his privileges to go out into the community to movies and other entertainment events. Normally Gary not only kept such appointments quite regularly, but had been very invested in working actively on his problems. In his background was a mother who had attempted suicide on several occasions, events during which Gary had been responsible for taking measures to save her life. One of the dynamics, therefore, was that of experiencing important women in his life as very vulnerable and of fearing that perhaps his own anger might be a part of the cause of the suicide attempts.

In the middle phase of the treatment, Gary began showing much anger toward his social worker, first by talking to others of disliking her. Then he began one session by telling his social worker that he thought her to be totally incompetent. She had, he indicated, been of no help to him, and he did not wish to talk with her anymore. Gary said he had come to the appointment only because he would lose his privileges if he did not. Initially the worker attempted to get Gary to explain to her the basis of his anger at her, inquiring what she had done that had made him feel this way. Gary sat glaring at the worker in silence, but it was a silence with an air of triumph and mockery.

After a few moments of enduring the silence to see if Gary would decide to break it, the worker told Gary that she was sorry that he felt the way that he did, but she saw no point in wasting her time if he did not wish to talk. The appointments, she indicated, were his time to help himself, and if he wished to waste it, that was his choice. She said that she, however, took how she spent her time seriously, and so if he was not going to talk, she would do some paperwork. At that point she moved to the chair behind her desk and proceeded to begin working. She told Gary that if he wished to talk, all he had to do was say so, and she would stop doing the paperwork. Appearing furious, Gary got out of his chair and moved toward the door, announcing that if she was going to treat him in this manner, then he was going to leave. The worker told him that if he left, she would see to it that he lost his privileges by not attending his sessions. Gary returned to his seat, where he remained in silence for a time, during which the worker proceeded with the paperwork, but kept an eye on Gary as well. In a little while, Gary began to speak in a much calmer manner about his grievances toward the worker and she moved back to her chair to engage with him around these.

In this example Gary had an experience of learning directly that the worker was neither vulnerable to nor afraid of his anger. He also had an experience through which he could learn that his anger had not destroyed the worker or his relationship with her. Because of his relationship with his mother, this was a particularly important event in his treatment. Simply discussing his anger in an abstract sense would not have had the same impact or importance for him. The worker's behavior may not have made her appear to an outsider to be a heroic, all-loving therapist, but then the goal of therapy is not to make the clinician look like a superhuman; it is to help the client. It should be pointed out here that the context of the worker's behavior is that of an ongoing and previously workable positive relationship. Had the worker behaved in this manner in, for example, an intake interview, the meaning and its effects would have been entirely different, and would have been contraindicated.

Affects as Communicative Regulators

Social work has always stressed the importance of a positive working relationship with the client in the treatment. Merely having the relationship, however, is not sufficient. One must do something with it. Similarly, social workers have traditionally considered that paying attention to the client's affective state is of critical importance. But the precise connections between these things and the growth of the client have not always been very clearly spelled out. Understanding that the affects help to build the sense of a separate self, as in the case of Gary, can begin to make the connections between a treatment relationship, affects, and client growth much more evident.

Empathy is often considered a critical element in the conduct of any therapeutic enterprise. However, too often empathy has been interpreted to mean a type of all-giving, all-accepting positive regard. This conception ignores the fact that at times the individual may need something other than this type of positive regard. Lichtenburg (1978) has noted that the infant's first experiences with empathy come from the consensual validation of the caretaker's perception of the infant's true state of physiologic need. If one assumes, then that the human being's need states are variable, rather than static, this means that empathy must always be related to an assessment of the particular needs of the moment. A mother who feeds her child every time the child cries will not be experienced as truly empathic since the child may not be hungry, but cold, wet, in need of more freedom to move about, or a variety of other possibilities. In similar fashion a social worker who assumes that a client has only dependency needs or needs for positive regard will not be experienced as truly empathic either.

Psychological needs vary as much as, and quite probably more than, physiologic needs. Furthermore, as there are connections between psychological needs conceived of in a narrow sense and both physiologic and environmental needs, the social worker must take all of these into account in any response to a client situation. One of the advantages of utilizing the concept of the self, and of the human being's overarching need for an intact sense of self as a primary motivator, is that this can enable a definition of psychological need in a much broader sense such that the physiologic and environmental needs can be seen to be important parts of that more generalized psychological need. This is very much in concert with Hartmann's (1958) concept of the primary undifferentiated psychological matrix within which the self, the other, and the external world are not yet delineated.

Accurate empathy, at least as conceived here, must also take into account an understanding that the human being also has something akin to a built-in timetable for growth and maturation, and therefore a need to function in concert with the demands and limitations of a particular life stage. Kohut's (1977) point that human beings are pulled by their wishes for self-fulfillment at least as much as they are driven by their desires is relevant here. A static conception of the self is not functional for the individual, not just because environmental and social demands change over the course of an individual's lifetime, but also because the person's internal needs change. Empathy is, therefore, not a quality that an individual either possesses or does not possess. It is an achievement that must be actively worked at constantly in order to establish and maintain it. Issues relating to the appropriate timing of interventions in social work treatment must be based on accurate empathy, that is, on the needs of the individual at the moment.

One of the major variables to be assessed in the treatment relationship is that of the degree of interpersonal closeness/distance the client needs at any given time. Kestenberg (Kestenberg & Weinstein, 1978) has noted that breathing causes a regular back-and-forth movement in the bodies of both the mother and the child. She postulates that this may be influential in the foundation of inter-personal relationships from very early infancy, and perhaps even prior to birth. Whether Kestenberg's speculation is accurate or not, it is now becoming quite evident that human beings need to regulate the degree of psychological distance between themselves and others. A constant state of intimacy with another human being (psychological symbiosis) is neither desirable for functioning nor experienced as pleasant.

Burnham and Gibson (1969) have characterized schizophrenia as a need–fear dilemma in that the individual both wants psychological merger with another human being because of the comfort it promises, and also fears that merger because it involves a kind of death of the self through the loss of individuality. While for the schizophrenic this need–fear dilemma is fundamental and often experienced as a life or death issue, this same desire for intimacy at times and for separation at other times can be observed to be an important issue for all humans at all levels of development. This can be observed in the practice of marital counseling, where it is seen that too much contact with the partner may create as much conflict as too little. A flexible balance must be achieved.

Lichtenstein (1977) has taken the notion of psychological distance one step further than other theorists by positing that the real dilemma of human identity is that the human being has a fundamental conflicting need for both existence and nonexistence. Whether or not Lichtenstein's proposition is accurate, it can be seen that positive affect and its expression tend to create closeness whereas negative affect creates a sense of distance. Viewed from the sense of the manner in which the affects regulate the psychological space between human beings, love and hate perhaps can be seen as opposites since they have, in general, opposing effects. It may have been this fundamental distinction that led Freud to consider libido and aggression as polar opposites in his formulation of the drives. It is, however, understandable only when one considers them in their functioning in relationship to human objects. Anger, for example, is often an expression of the fact that too much closeness has been experienced with another human being and is an attempt to gain some distance.

Affects then, have communicative properties that serve to regulate the interpsychic space between people. In infancy, prior to the formation of a relatively stable sense of self, this interpsychic space is relatively small and, furthermore, must be regulated in a rather rigid manner. It is through the process of growth and the development of the self that this space becomes both potentially greater and more easily traversed such that it can be regulated with some flexibility. At the same time, however, it is through the activity of these same regular back-and-forth movements, regulated by affect, that the individual can build a sense of the self as a reliable and stable organization.

Mr. and Mrs. Hernstein began outpatient treatment for marital problems after she had assaulted him, threatening his life. The marriage had been a poor one for many years, and for many years Mr. Hernstein had indicated that he was trying to make up his mind as to whether he wanted the marriage or not. A woman from a very emotionally impoverished background, Mrs. Hernstein had believed her husband's accusations that she was psychologically quite disturbed and had seen herself as being fundamentally helpless in relation to any decision regarding the marriage. She had, therefore, periodically sought individual treatment upon her husband's insistence that she do so in order to try to save the marriage, but rarely remained in this very long as she would discover she did not fundamentally wish to change herself, but only to satisfy her husband. Following the assault Mr. Hernstein became quite frightened, and finally agreed to his wife's demand that both be involved in the therapy in order to deal with the question of whether or not the marriage should continue.

Initially joint sessions were held with both marital partners. In these sessions it became clear that Mrs. Hernstein fully expected that the worker would side with her husband since her difficulties in performing the roles of wife and mother had been quite apparent and she did not attempt to hide these. Mr. Hernstein, however, also had his own issues, which led him to be chronically unable to make a final decision to terminate a marriage that he would, nevertheless, acknowledge he no longer really wanted. In the joint sessions, Mrs. Hernstein gradually began to recognize that the marital failure had not been entirely her own problem and to gain some confidence in herself. As this occurred she decided that if the impasse were going to come to an end, it was she who would have to take the steps toward setting up separate households.

Following the separation Mr. and Mrs. Hernstein were seen jointly for a brief time during which they negotiated their mutual anger at each other and the plans for care of their two adolescent children. Then, as both partners had individual issues that required continuing assistance, both were seen on an individual basis by the same worker. Mrs. Hernstein also entered a therapy group run by another worker in order to gain additional support and assistance as she tried to establish herself in a totally new life-style. The year that followed was a very rocky one for Mrs. Hernstein. She did manage to set up her own household for herself and the one child who remained living with her, as well as to obtain employment even though she had not worked in 20 years. Although she utilized both her individual and group treatment very well to assist her in negotiating these changes, she also experienced considerable anger and depression in the process. These affects were particularly aroused for her in relation to her attempts to parent the one child alone, which created a necessity to deal with how inadequate she felt, as well as how inadequate what she had received from her own parents had been. In spite of these feelings, however, Mrs. Hernstein was quite determined that she was going to prove that she could accomplish these life tasks.

At one point during the course of the year, Mrs. Hernstein became so depressed that she contacted a psychiatrist to request medicine and eventually hospitalization since she feared that she would commit suicide. She was hospitalized for a brief time, following which both the psychiatrist and the social worker agreed to Mrs. Hernstein's plan that she continue with her clinic treatment, but also maintain periodic contact with the psychiatrist, who would again intervene in the event of an emergency. As her daily routine became more established, Mrs. Hernstein seemed to be able to achieve more equilibrium in her life, so that her periods of depression seemed to be less severe and less frightening to her.

Although a very troubled woman, Mrs. Hernstein was also highly intelligent and very articulate. In the initial phases of her treatment, she had been quite able and willing to communicate not only the details of her life situation and her plans to deal with these, but also of her background and her current affects. A woman with a highly developed inner life, she experienced this as often chaotic. Mrs. Hernstein also had difficulties in maintaining a sense of herself as a separate person, and so on occasion believed that she had special powers that enabled her to understand others, especially her daughter. Similarly, she at times had difficulty realizing that the worker did not know things she had thought about communicating, but actually had not. Thus a diagnosis of borderline seemed indicated.

As Mrs. Hernstein became better able to manage the details of her daily life more adequately and with more confidence, her demeanor in her appointments with her individual social worker changed markedly. She kept appointments regularly and on time, but communicated very little of what was really going on in her life. Instead she would begin her sessions with a vigorous challenge to the worker that life was miserable and that the worker had no right to tell her she could not commit suicide. The worker would respond, just as vigorously, that life certainly was miserable, but that this did not give Mrs. Hernstein the right to commit suicide, and that she would simply have to put up with it. A repetitive argument would then ensue, taking up the bulk of the time in the session. Following these sessions Mrs. Hernstein would attend group therapy, where she was more open about her life circumstances. When other group members would inquire about Mrs. Hernstein's state of mind, she would convincingly announce that she was fine and had left all her depression in her worker's office.

On one occasion Mrs. Hernstein's demeanor in her appointment was entirely different. She slumped into her chair and mumbled that life was miserable and that the worker had no right to tell her she could not commit suicide. The vigor was gone. The worker, knowing little about what might have occurred, became quite concerned and began asking Mrs. Hernstein what had been going on in her life. Though she answered the questions, Mrs. Hernstein did so with little detail and seemed reluctant to talk openly, mildly protesting that she was doing all right and that the worker had no faith in her. Since the group session followed immediately, the worker did not confront Mrs. Hernstein further, but alerted the group therapist that some action might have to be taken jointly before the night was over.

Mrs. Hernstein did not wait for the group therapist to say anything, but began the meeting with the announcement that she was terrified. She claimed she had been feeling tired but alright until she got to her social worker's office. She said she knew that her worker was concerned that she might commit suicide. She said she had not even thought about it recently, but feared that if her worker thought she was going to do this, then perhaps the worker was right. Through the intervention in the group, Mrs. Hernstein was encouraged to talk again with her worker, as well as to contact her psychiatrist in order to reassure herself. The crisis was negotiated without a second hospitalization.

It was, however, necessary for the worker to confront Mrs. Hernstein with the fact that she could not always know how Mrs. Hernstein really was if she was not told. Mrs. Hernstein indicated that she would respect that, but did not want to spend her hours on what she considered to be the minor details of her life. A compromise was finally reached in that Mrs. Hernstein agreed to write out what was going on in her life for the worker prior to the sessions, and then would be free to use the time with the worker as she wished. The arguments resumed, with the previous vigor, but with Mrs. Hernstein bringing her letters with her. Eventually, as treatment progressed into a different phase, Mrs. Hernstein's letters became shorter, with more of the material entering into the sessions themselves. Ultimately both the worker and Mrs. Hernstein agreed the letters no longer were necessary.

Mrs. Hernstein's self–other boundaries were not well established. Thus she had for some years allowed Mr. Hernstein to serve as the definer of her own qualities and saw herself as unable to separate from him. In part the assault that occurred during a fit of anger was caused by frustration because of Mr. Hernstein's chronic refusal to promise continued security within that relationship, but it was also partly the result of Mrs. Hernstein's own need–fear dilemma in relation to intimacy with him or with anyone else. It is quite likely that, had Mr. Hernstein decided that he wished to continue the marriage and to try to achieve a true sense of intimacy from it, Mrs. Hernstein would have been unable to tolerate this either and the marital situation would have been difficult from that perspective. Thus for many years the marriage continued for both, with Mrs. Hernstein periodically utilizing treatment contacts to vent her spite at her husband. As Seton (1981) has pointed out, spite expresses a somewhat different relationship to the object than does anger in that it achieves a psychological distance from the object and yet maintains a connection with that person. Many seemingly destructive marital relationships are maintained through the utilization of mutual spite due to both partners' inability to negotiate issues of closeness/distance with flexibility.

Although it hardly can be considered a directly adaptive or constructive means, the assault can be seen as an attempt to achieve a more satisfactory resolution of the problem on Mrs. Hernstein's part. It, as well as her subsequent insistence that Mr. Hernstein engage in treatment with her, can be seen as evidence of a desire to grow. It is the utilization of action toward the further differentiation of the self, as, of course, was the later action taken in attempting to formalize an end to the marriage.

Once Mrs. Hernstein had lost her husband as the self object who defined her own qualities, she needed a substitute for him and it can be hypothesized that for a time her social worker performed this role to a significant extent. In part the utilization of the therapy group was intended, however, to provide Mrs. Hernstein with a variety of other self objects, such that this function would not have to be located in one person, thus making that relationship into a potentially very threatening one. Even so, however, Mrs. Hernstein eventually needed to be able to achieve and consolidate a more adequate sense of boundaries and of herself through an increase in the interpsychic space between herself and her worker. At lower levels of functioning, such attempts are at a global level, such as is the case here. In fact such maneuvers probably often account for client termination of treatment as a middle stage of treatment in entered.

Mrs. Hernstein, however, achieved some sense of interpsychic space in a rather creative manner. She managed to turn the relationship into a chronic argument in which a psychic fusion was not possible, thereby gaining a sense of distance and a more stable sense of an independent self while she practiced her new life-style and new definition of herself. At the same time, she managed to obtain from her worker constant reassurances of the worker's concern about her through the worker's assertions that she did not want Mrs. Hernstein to kill herself. That this was a balance of interpsychic space that was, for the time being, a comfortable one for Mrs. Hernstein is attested to by her indications in the group that she had left her depression in her worker's office.

The continuing fragility, however, of Mrs. Hernstein's sense of a separate self is indicated in her fear that the worker knew more about her probable behavior than she herself did (perhaps through a reading of her mind rather than her actions) on the occasion when she was "tired." This, then, meant that the worker needed to clarify the need for more direct communications about the state of Mrs. Hernstein's self, in itself a message that there existed, in fact, no state of psychic fusion between the two. Only as Mrs. Hernstein gradually developed more firm self boundaries and more confidence in these could she allow the interpsychic space to be held with less rigidity and, therefore, to begin sharing once again the details of her life and her inner state in person during the sessions rather than through the treatment, thus ending the therapeutic endeavor prematurely.

6 Affects as Knowledge

Basch (1976) has defined emotions as "subjectively experienced states and always related to a concept of self vis-á-vis some particular situation." If this definition of emotions is utilized in examining Mrs. Hernstein's (Chapter 5) experiences, it becomes possible to say that her depression during the time following her separation from her husband and her attempts to make a new life for herself were related to her own evaluation that perhaps she could not manage these tasks. In other words, she did not experience the organization of her self to be strong enough to accomplish the goals she very much desired. From this point of view, emotions not only serve regulative and communicative functions in relation to interpsychic space, but also provide an evaluation of the subjectively experienced well-being of the self.

Basch's definition of affects, now receiving considerable acceptance in psychoanalytic circles, provides a somewhat different perspective on depression than an earlier formulation that relied on seeing depression as a "turning of anger against the self." At the same time, the two are not necessarily mutually exclusive since it might be assumed that the individual who senses himself or herself to be inadequate to reach a desired goal might also experience anger at himself or herself because of the perceived lack. Basch's definition also builds on Bibring's (1953) now classic contribution to the theory of affects. Bibring, a psychoanalyst who became quite depressed when he was diagnosed as having terminal cancer, began to wonder how, theoretically, he could explain his feeling state. He knew that he was going to die, and that he was helpless to prevent this. He, therefore, translated this into the theoretic notion that depression was the result of the ego's being in a state of helplessness.

Bibring utilized his own state of depression to make a significant contribution to knowledge about human experience. However, in doing so, he also presumably decreased his own sense of depression. He creatively switched his attention away from a reality he could not change, and one in which he was helpless, to an attempt to utilize the knowledge that the affect gave him in another way, thereby assuming a task in relation to which he was not helpless. Bibring did not become as overwhelmed by his feeling state as did Mrs. Hernstein. What is the difference between the two individuals? Both were struggling with difficult real-life problems, but from a purely external vantage point, one would have to say that Dr. Bibring's problem seems the more severe of the two.

It might be hypothesized that the amount and intensity of affect that Dr. Bibring and Mrs. Hernstein experienced were different. Since affect is qualitative rather than quantitative in form, there is really no way to measure this. Furthermore, because each is a separate person, from each other and from any outside observer, and since emotions are subjective and individual, the hypothesis is fundamentally not answerable. There are, however, other ways of approaching the differences between the two people. Mrs. Hernstein deals with her depression to a large extent as a thing-of-action, and thus fears that she will commit suicide. Dr. Bibring responds to his feeling state instead as an object-of-contemplation, and thus tries to comprehend its meaning both for himself as an individual and for humanity in general. Emotions, when still embedded in an action framework and when insufficiently differentiated from action, can be experienced as dangerous. When utilized for their meaning in relation to an understanding of the well-being of the self, emotions can be extremely useful in adaptation. The difference may not lie in the intensity or quality of the affect itself, but rather in the way in which the person deals with that emotion. This would be in consonance with Erikson's observation that in diagnosis the issue is not how much conflict a person has, but how much the conflict has the person.

Learning to hear the communicative, regulatory, and evaluative messages related to affects in treatment situations and to respond therapeutically to these messages is a substantial part of the achievement of empathy on the part of the clinical social worker. A brief example will illustrate this point. A client arrives for a regular appointment and begins the session with the statement, "Stay away from me today, I have a cold." Presumably this means, "I have a viral infection that has been making me ill and I do not wish to pass it on to you." On one level this communication can be heard purely as a thing-of-action. A response to this message then would be to keep some physical distance from the client who is trying, out of a positive regard for the worker, to protect that person from a physical illness. It may be that this is all the statement is meant to convey.

Viewed as an object-of-contemplation, however, this statement may have a number of other meanings. The client may really be saying, "I am angry with you as a specific individual and would like to give you my cold, but am going to try to restrain myself from doing so. I would like you to cooperate in helping me achieve that goal." On another level the client may really be saying, "I am today feeling very global and generalized anger that makes me experience myself as potentially dangerous. Under these circumstances I am frightened about what harm I might bring to you without being able to control that." Yet another possibility might be "I am finding myself very attracted to becoming close to you as a person, but I am frightened about what such closeness might do to my sense of myself as a separate person. Therefore, I want you to give me a little distance until I can feel more secure about what such psychological closeness would be like for me." Nonverbal affective communication, through tone of voice, physical movements, and facial expressions accompanying the words, may give the social worker clues as to which of these meanings is the predominant one. They do not, of course, have to be mutually exclusive.

In considering the statement from an evaluative point of view, the client may be saying, "I am experiencing my boundaries and the organization of my self as being particularly weak today and I do not want to have that organization further threatened." If the clinician responds to the initial statement only as a factual thing-of-action and physically keeps some distance with no further exploration of the situation, he or she will not know how the client views the reality of the moment. It may be that the client is experiencing himself or herself as more vulnerable strictly because the client does have a bad cold that has been sapping his or her energy. On the other hand, the client may really be wishing to convey, "I think I got this cold and these weak boundaries because you became a little too close to me last week, and that was very threatening to me so I want you to stay further away from me today." Or the client may mean, "Last week I wanted you to come closer to me and the fact that you did not was such a disappointment that I am not going to expose myself to that much pain again." Yet again, the message may be, "I think I got this cold and these weak boundaries because what we talked about last week necessitated so much reorganization of meaning in relation to myself that now my structure is still weak and cannot tolerate any more strain." Still another possibility is that the reason for the weak boundaries has nothing to do with the relationship with the worker, but rather with recent events in the life of the client outside the treatment situation. Further exploration, utilizing the cold as a possible metaphor for the state of the self, will give the worker considerable information as to how to proceed in the interview to follow.

Translated into theoretical terms, this example is an illustration of what Werner and Kaplan (1963) meant when they pointed out that in human functioning, language can be utilized purely as a sign or a signal that is intended to provide a direction for action to be taken. On the other hand, language can also be utilized in a symbolic fashion such that it actually stands for or represents something else. In any given communication, of course, both usages and purposes may pertain. In human communication it is often the case that messages of this sort are "intuitively" received without the person knowing on more than an impressionistic level how the knowledge about the interpersonal relationship was received. The achievement of skill in a clinical situation, however, involves being able to conceptualize such intuitions so that the worker can be clearer about the nature of the observational base of his or her perceptions in order to be surer of their accuracy.

Affects and Symbolization

Since the time of Aristotle, there has been a tendency to separate emotions from rationality in human thought. Affects have been thought of as irrational and, therefore, as not being in one's best interest in adaptive behavior. No doubt this strong tradition influenced Freud's initial formulation, in which he saw affects as derivatives of the instincts, as located in the id, and as a major factor in primary process thinking. Such a formulation certainly can help one understand the common enough human experience of finding that intensely experienced emotions at times can seem to threaten the organization of the self. Furthermore most people have found themselves doing things impulsively at times of strong feelings that they later sorely regretted.

Freud himself, however, found that his initial formulation of affects as located within the id and as part of the primary process was inadequate. In an examination of what he termed signal anxiety, Freud (1923) changed his theory by placing the affects as a part of the ego, and therefore as having adaptive qualities. Anxiety, after all, could alert the human being to situations of danger in both the external and internal worlds. The knowledge that these emotions provided could then give the individual clues as to how best to prepare for and deal with the circumstances that might be threatening. Although Freud did not achieve a fully satisfactory theory of affects, to some extent because he did not understand the primacy of action in relation to the unconscious, he did call attention to the importance of affectivity in life and laid down the groundwork for a revolution in the history of human thought that is now slowly becoming accepted. This revolution involves an understanding that affect and cognition are not really opposites, that emotions are not the enemies of rationality, and that feelings are knowledge about the well-being of the self.

Initial formulations about the nature of psychosis involved the idea that the person was flooded with too much affect in the form of primary process. Such an approach does not, however, fit very well with the commonly reported experience of persons who have recovered from acute psychotic episodes that the worst part of that state was that they were unable to feel much of anything at all. As Seton (1981) has pointed out, people like to experience emotions as these tell them they are alive and give them a sense of being human and of participating in the human community. A more current developmental approach to the problem would indicate that affects at a primitive level are still embedded in action schemas as well as that they are experienced as global and undifferentiated. The human experience of being overwhelmed by affective intensity is attributable to the failure of the self to be able to organize the affects in a manner in which they can provide a knowledge base from which the person can draw in order to operate adaptively. For affects to be maximally useful as knowledge, they must be utilized as both a signal and a symbol.

The original psychoanalytic theory contained contradictions as to what the nature of the healthy person's relationship to the unconscious actually was. Neurosis presumably was caused by the repression of unconcscious content. This would imply that a knowledge of the unconscious was a good thing and that repression should be avoided. However, psychosis was presumably too much knowledge of the unconscious with an absence of repression, an implication that knowledge of the unconscious was not such a good thing. It was difficult to know which point of view the theory really meant. It was essentially for this reason that the ego psychologists turned to explanatory concepts involving the notion of personality structure or organization. It has become increasingly clear, however, that the nature and meaning of "structure" have been left at too vague a level. A developmental approach with an emphasis on the importance of organization and symbolization not only fits the observational data much better, but is capable of providing a much more integrated framework for explanation.

A knowlege of the unconscious, defined not so much as a knowledge of specific inherited content but rather as of additional meanings and possibilities, is a highly desirable and adaptive thing. Winnicott (1978) was known to believe that one should make friends with one's unconscious and, in fact, wrote a poem:

> Let down your taproot
> to the centre of your soul
> Suck up the sap
> from the infinite source
> of your unconscious
> And
> Be Evergreen.

The actual experiencing of strong affects such as depression is not a particularly pleasant one. Persons who are experiencing this to a significant extent can become so overwhelmed by it that they may be quite nonfunctional for a time. This fact has led to the identification of depression as an illness. In many ways this is unfortunate since depression, as an affect, is a symptom, not an illness. In this sense it is comparable to physical pain, which is also unpleasant, and which may also be disabling, but which is not considered an illness itself. Like physical pain depression may have to be endured, and perhaps some medication may be necessary to make the person more comfortable during that time. Physical pain is, however, a signal that something is wrong. It tells the individual that he or she temporarily should interrupt physical activity until the cause of the pain is discovered and remedied. In a psychological sense, depression should serve the same function—it indicates that something is wrong and that the cause should be located and remedied.

Depression as a signal does not always indicate a psychological problem. It may be signaling a physical problem of which other symptoms are not yet evident. For this reason social workers who encounter individuals with severe depression should always consider the possibility of physical illness and advise a medical examination. In a similar sense, since the depression as an affect is not in and of itself an illness, the remedy for the problem may not be psychological treatment but a change in the external life circumstances with which the person is attempting to cope. If the person is reluctant to make changes in his or her life that would lead to better coping and adaptation, then the reasons for the reluctance to take appropriate action may need psychological treatment, but this should be identified as the problem, rather than the depression itself. In other words it can be said that depression as a signal serves a useful purpose, but for it to serve its total function, it then must be used as an object-of-contemplation and a symbol to discover the implied meaning and to abstract a reasonable course of action. This is true for both the client and the clinician.

Psychotherapy may help people identify choices in their lives that they have not previously recognized or it may provide them with the support necessary to carry out actions that will rectify a problem. It will, however, not substitute for those actions. This is the reason why clinical social work, as distinguished from pure psychotherapy, has always involved the possibility of an intervention directly into the "external" world of some clients who are assessed as being either temporarily or chronically unable to take those actions for themselves. In a similar sense, while clinical work may help people to cope better within a social organization, and perhaps to be more effective in taking steps toward the modification of an imperfect social order, it will not directly modify the social order itself. This is the reason why programs for changes in social organization and social policy are necessary. On the other hand, any good program for social policy should utilize clinical knowledge to achieve the best possible understanding of the potential effects of social policies on the individuals who make up the society.

To return to a considertion of affect, it can now be said that the ability to experience an affect, even if it is unpleasant, is an asset and not a liability. Zetzel (1970) pointed this out in a classic paper entitled "Depression and the Incapacity to Bear It." She was considering, among other things, data regarding the functioning of servicemen and veterans. Some men seemed to break down in the sense of having very strong and disabling affects during combat, but did not experience significant psychological or adjustment difficulties thereafter. Some men, for example, became depressed upon seeing their comrades killed on the battlefield. Other men performed much "better" on the battlefield and did not become depressed at the time, but later had significant problems in adjusting to civilian life. Zetzel concluded that the ability to experience affect was a psychological strength that was evidence of a higher level of development. One other reasonable conclusion, not directly reached by Zetzel, would be that war is not good for human beings.

If the experiencing of affect in a differentiated fashion is useful in assisting the individual in knowing how to function adaptively, then further questions in relation to how this capability develops must be addressed. If the expansion of the conscious is desirable, how does this normally occur? Although Freud may not have had what would now be considered a fully complete answer to this question due to the limitations of the state of knowledge during his lifetime, he did point in a general direction that is useful. He (Freud, 1915) suggested that the difference between a conscious representation and one that is unconscious was that the conscious representation has a word connected with it whereas an unconscious representation does not have a connected word. The expansion of the conscious, including that of affective life, is connected to the development of language.

An examination of Helen Keller's exact description of her experiences may assist in making the relevance of the relationship between affects and symbolization through language clearer. Keller (1903, p. 315) wrote:

We walked down the path to the well-house, attracted by the fragrance of the honeysuckle with which it was covered. Someone was drawing water and my teacher placed my hand under the spout. As the cool stream gushed over one hand, she spelled into the other the word water, first slowly, then rapidly. I stood still, my whole attention fixed upon the motions of her fingers. Suddenly, I felt a misty consciousness as of something forgotten—a thrill of returning thought; and somehow the mystery of language was revealed to me. I knew then that "w-a-t-e-r" meant the wonderful cool something that was flowing over my hand. That living word awakened my soul, gave it light, hope, joy, set it free! There were barriers still, it is true, but barriers that could in time be swept away. . . . I left the well-house eager to learn. Everything had a name, and each name gave birth to a new thought. As we returned to the house every object which I touched seemed to quiver with life. That was because I saw everything with the strange new sight that had come to me. On entering the door I remembered the doll I had broken. I felt my way to the hearth and picked up the pieces. I tried vainly to put them together. *Then my eyes filled with tears; for I realized what I had done, and for the first time I felt repentance and sorrow.* (Italics added)

What Keller was saying here is that the acquisition of the capacity to utilize symbols not only gave her the capacity to think new thoughts, but to experience new feelings as well. This should signal the possibility that the commonplace tendency to use the words "I think" and "I feel" interchangeably may not be the result of a lack of sophistication, but an intuitive insight that is more advanced than have been the theories into which an understanding of these variables has traditionally been placed.

Under what conditions in relation to the development of symbolization might a person not be able to utilize affects as knowledge in order to facilitate adaptive functioning and further growth and development? Werner and Kaplan have suggested that the capacity to symbolize in a mature fashion depends, among other things, on the differentiation between the addressor and the addressee. Certainly in an extreme case, in which the self and the human object are psychologically totally fused, there would be no reason for verbal communication at all. The other person would be able to know one's internal thoughts without the necessity for communication. There are, however, conditions in which the self and the human other may be only partially differentiated and which would cause difficulties. An example from clinical research should help to illustrate this.

Mrs. Ingram was the mother of a patient in a private psychiatric hospital for the long-term treatment of severely ill adolescents and young adults and was herself in treatment in relation to this problem. During that time she was asked to participate in a research project by taking a simple test. The test was a modified version of a Q-sort in which the subject was asked to order a series of 40 cards according to how he or she was feeling at the moment. The cards were of four different types: (1) simple drawings of facial expressions depicting affect; (2) adjectives directly expressive of affect, such as *delighted;* (3) adjectives expressing affect in a metaphorical manner, such as *silky;* and (4) expressive lines showing affect through soft, light curves for pleasant things and heavy, jagged angles for unpleasant things. There were ten cards of each of the four types, representing a scale from very pleasant to very unpleasant. Thus each subject had available cards from each of the four types with which to express any given feeling level. Results of the testing have been reported elsewhere (Saari, 1976). For purposes of illustration here, the manner of relating to the test itself is more important.

A woman in her 40s, who had completed two years of postgraduate study, Mrs. Ingram had been the older of two children in an upper-middle-class family. She described her brother as the preferred child in a family in which cunning, trickery, and lying were the normal modes of relating. Mrs. Ingram thought her refusal to go along with the family way of doing things caused her to be disliked by everyone. She saw anger as her only means of self-defense within the family. She described her childhood as lonely and unhappy. She supposedly was sick as a child and, therefore, kept at home most of the time, being tutored privately until age 10. At that age she took some psychological tests, which she claimed showed she was functioning intellectually at a college level. Her parents were delighted, but Mrs. Ingram felt devastated by this and dated a mistrust of psychiatry to that time.

At the age of 10, apparently around the time of the adoption of her brother, Mrs. Ingram began attending a private boarding school and did well academically. About 15 years after her marriage, Mrs. Ingram's brother, who had become a brilliant young professional but a drug addict, and whom Mrs. Ingram saw as charming, weak, and undependable like her father, committed suicide. Mrs. Ingram felt somehow responsible in that she had been unable to save him from himself. Mrs. Ingram and her mother, who reportedly also held her responsible for his death, stopped speaking to each other at that time.

Mrs. Ingram initially had been seen by the social worker who treated her, as a cold, hardened woman who was hostile, sarcastic, and aggressive, and who used these traits to keep people at a distance. Diagnostically she was considered to be borderline. Very gradually in treatment, Mrs. Ingram became less fearful that she would be blamed for her son's problems and became quite involved. She was described to the investigator as having a very bizarre way of expressing herself, which at times seemed very artistic and creative and at other times seemed crazy.

Mrs. Ingram's history indicated that she was kept at home during her childhood. While it is perhaps too easy to read into historical material interpretations a theoretical point of view would predict, it seems clear that Mrs. Ingram was not allowed to separate from her family as a young child, and this raises the possibility that self boundaries may not have been well formed. She had experienced being sent away to school as a traumatic event in her life, which indicates that she was not psychologically prepared for this and that it may have been a very abrupt separation. This separation also occurred at the time of her brother's adoption, and it can be speculated that this brother may have taken her place in filling a need for symbiotic attachment on the part of Mrs. Ingram's mother. That Mrs. Ingram was likely to have experienced a very globally differentiated anger over this separation seems confirmed by her later feeling of responsibility for the brother, whom she tried unsuccessfully to save from himself and, un-doubtedly, from herself as well. Mrs. Ingram described anger as her only form of self-defense within the family, an indication that she considered the family as threatening to her self organization in the sense of there being a pull toward too much closeness and from which she needed more interpsychic space. While Mrs. Ingram's symbolic and affective development may have been stunted, it was clear that her native intelligence was excellent.

In the testing situation, Mrs. Ingram struck the investigator as a pleasant, rather likeable woman who seemed to have some warmth but who also rather quickly gave the impression of being a little peculiar. She used very flowery, metaphorical language and her responses to questions often seemed tangential. When asked if her contacts with the hospital had been helpful, Mrs. Ingram embarked on a long description of how meaningful this had been to her. She described it as quite remarkable since in the past she had always thought that "shrinks" made a mess of things and she would not have given ten cents for the hospital at first. Here, however, she had not felt "handled" as she had in treatment contacts in the past and the hospital had given her the first sense of security she had had since her brother had committed suicide. She described her son at the time he came to the hospital as the "creature from the blue lagoon," implying that this was something dreadful.

Mrs. Ingram took at least twice as long to do the test as most people, seemed literally to be struggling with trying to structure it for herself, and seemed to have so much difficulty in doing so that it was painful to watch her. As she began the test, she pointed to several cards with direct adjectives on them and commented, "You know, these words do have a great deal of meaning for me, but those meanings would have nothing to do with your test." She described herself as a very visual person and said she could only use the word cards as she thought they should be used by matching them with a face. She proceeded to match each direct adjective with a face, taking great care over the fit of each pair. When she had finished this, she turned to the metaphoric words, which she said had no meaning for her in terms of feelings. She asked what *"light"* meant, saying that it had meaning for her in terms of art but not in this context. Similarly she thought *"moldy"* meant bread.

Initially Mrs. Ingram wanted to put all the cards with lines and metaphoric adjectives in the center category as having no meaning for her. She had avoided dealing with the expressive lines until the last, but it seemed to the investigator that the problem was not that they had no meaning for her, but rather that they made her very anxious. As she had too many cards in the category of having no meaning for her, she chose to move the line cards into other categories first, commenting as she did so on her great love for art. One line reminded her of the only math course in which she had ever done well. She claimed she could not add, but was very good at spatial relations. She continued for some time to describe her interest in art and some of her attempts at creative projects of her own. Though Mrs. Ingram had been assured that there was no right way to order the cards, her parting comment was that she hoped she had not failed the test too badly.

Mrs. Ingram indicated quite clearly that she had an inner life, which she experienced most clearly in visual forms and images. She claimed that she was good in art and spatial relations and this assertion was quite convincing. Therefore, it would appear that she had progressed beyond what Piaget considered to be the sensori-motor stage of development in which thoughts are embedded in actions. In addition it can be observed that she both was engaging in pointing behavior and was interested in the contemplation of her observations. However, words did not serve to capture or organize her perceptions very well for her. She could not explain fully what the lines meant for her and it was unclear as to what about the line card reminded her of her math course. The words remained embedded in the context in which she had learned them and could not be moved successfully to the context of the test without losing their meaning, a situation of which she was painfully aware. In a sense this is

87

reminiscent of Blanche's (Chapter 2) difficulty in being able to maintain a sense of meaning in her life in a social context different from the one in which she grew up.

The data about Mrs. Ingram's life history seeem to be in concert with the problems she had in the testing situation. There is no report of a major problem in an excess of impulsive action here. There are many indications that she did experience affects, but that these caused her considerable difficulty in relation to internally experienced pain. Mrs. Ingram certainly expressed herself through the use of words in her relationships with other people. However, because they did not seem to fit well with commonly used imagery, these words often made her seem bizarre or crazy. There was little ability to use the words in conjunction with a language that was based on social agreement.

Mrs. Ingram's life problems had been primarily in the area of a lack of confidence in her capacity to use the knowledge of her affects and her inner life to establish interpersonal relationships from which she could achieve a sense of effectance, security, and self-esteem. Mrs. Ingram's existing visual symbols had some usefulness for her. However, she could not connect these personal and individualized images to socially shared symbols. Thus she had a very limited ability to use the images to understand others in her environment or to use social feedback to reassure herself about her own worth. At times of stress, which occur in the lives of all people, it is necessary to be able to reassure oneself about one's own value. As Erikson (1964) has pointed out, frustration does not cause pathology but frustration without social meaning does.

As Mrs. Ingram's early childhood had been one of isolation from other children of her own age, she must have had a very limited opportunity to practice the use of words, images, and actions, and their interrelationships in order to understand common usage. In addition there were indications that she had been held in a very close psychological relationship with her mother. It may be postulated that her mother, probably having very poor self boundaries of her own, may have engaged with Mrs. Ingram in a world in which feelings and affects were observed, but that she also may have assumed that Mrs. Ingram's feelings were the same as hers rather than that Mrs. Ingram might have feelings of her own that were different. Under these circumstances the relationship between words and affects would have to remain confused, because there was too much confusion in relation to the precise nature of the feelings and of who was feeling them. It is a situation in which there has been insufficient psychological distance between the addressor and the addressee.

Since a failure to recognize that feelings and perceptions are different in different people would not facilitate the growth of a stable sense of self–other boundaries, Mrs. Ingram's basic reality testing would have been impaired. She might be expected to have difficulties in differentiating what was external from what was internal and in being able to maintain an intact sense of self. Thus she learned to utilize anger as a defense against her family and the world. This was adaptive for her in that she was able to maintain an interpsychological sense of space. It would not have been adaptive for her, however, in fostering further growth in an ability to organize her inner life and her sense of social meaningfulness through use of the knowledge that affects provide; such further growth would have been dependent upon the ability to share perceptions of both internal and external realities with another person. Mrs. Ingram could not do this because it would threaten the very existence of a sense of self.

If it is assumed that these dynamics are accurate in understanding Mrs. Ingram's lifelong problems, then it can readily be seen that the formation of a treatment relationship with Mrs. Ingram would be a step of critical importance. According to both the social worker and Mrs. Ingram, this step had been achieved by the time of the testing. Indeed Mrs. Ingram indicated that this had been a matter of no small relief to her. The achievement of the relationship itself, however, was only a beginning of the work that needed to be done. Mrs. Ingram also needed to learn, through the sharing of perceptions of her own inner life with a significant other, how to utilize language to assist in the organization of this life in order to experience it as predicatable and understandable. She also needed to be able to learn how to use her inner experience to imagine what the feeling of others in her social environment might be like in order to interpret with some reasonable degree of accuracy the feedback she received from them about the effects of her own behavior. Since Mrs. Ingram had described herself as a very visual person, it can be assumed that an examination of her perceptions of dream or fantasy images or of her art work would be likely to be fruitful.

Inadequate Differentiation Between the Object and Its Symbol

M rs. Ingram actually experienced a primary visual inner life, but one that remained chaotic and peculiarly individual such that it was not useful to her in coping with the environment. There is, however, a quite different problem that also results from stunted growth in the ability to symbolize. The case of Mr. Jackson, another parent who participated in the same research project, illustrates this.

A man in his early 60s, Mr. Jackson had completed college and earned a postgraduate professional degree. He described growing up in a house located on so much land that no one could enter except through a gate. He saw himself as having been very protected as a child and never having been allowed to be very active. He felt lonely and separated even from his family, whom he saw as formal, undemonstrative, and socially isolated. As a result he became an avid reader with an interest in intellectual pursuits.

To please his parents, Mr. Jackson went to college near home and then entered his father's business, at which he was successful. He continued to keep up the role of being the good son, but claimed never to have felt close to anyone in the family. A "playboy" before marriage, Mr. Jackson described himself as glad to settle down when he married. He saw his life since the marriage as stable and content. He continued his hobbies of reading and gardening. It seemed to his social worker, however, that he had little investment in his relationship with his wife and, though he became annoyed at times with his mother-in-law's intrusive and domineering ways, he generally seemed content to allow her to occupy the primary position in his wife's concerns and affections. Although very proud of his business accomplishments, he spoke very little of relationships with people. He asked of his children only that they not misbehave in public and seemed primarily involved with his son over attempts at keeping him out of legal difficulties. He was described as a man who was logical, distant, and very guarded and who, though pleasant and cooperative on the surface, seemed hostile underneath.

Like Mrs. Ingram, Mr. Jackson had a childhood during which he had little opportunity to develop communication skills through contacts with peers. In contrast to Mrs. Ingram, however, who gave the impression that she had to defend herself from too much involvement with her family, Mr. Jackson gave the impression that there was never very much real involvement with his family of origin and that he had not been very involved with his family of procreation either. Mr. Jackson's family, and Mr. Jackson himself, seemed to have been so isolated that not only must one enter through a gate to reach them, but it appeared that the gate to their emotional life was not made very apparent, if it existed at all. While Mrs. Ingram's social worker had considered her to be borderline from a diagnostic point of view, Mr. Jackson's worker considered him to be character disorder and did not think that the treatment in his situation had been very successful. Observations of Mr. Jackson's manner of relating to the testing situation provide a striking contrast to that of Mrs. Ingram.

In the testing situation, Mr. Jackson made it very clear that, while he did not think his contacts with the hospital had been very helpful to him, he also did not think he needed any help. He did not believe in "this communication stuff." Kids are too busy with homework, phone calls, and other activities to communicate with parents, and none of them ever do. His had been no different.

Throughout the testing he was quite seductive in manner, but seemed guarded, suspicious, and somewhat anxious underneath. He arranged the cards quickly and without difficulty, but had some problems understanding how many cards were in each category, even though this was clearly marked on instruction cards. This problem seemed primarily related to a desire to complete the test quickly. He commented that the lines meant nothing to him at all and put them all into the category marked "neither like how I feel nor unlike it." He said he had never liked cubism in art either and that some well-known art critics, with whom he used to be very friendly, told him that such things had no real meanings except whatever people saw in them, implying that there was really nothing there at all.

Following the test Mr. Jackson was shown eight additional cards and asked if he thought these might have added to the test. He indicated he did not think any of them would be an improvement, but proceeded to interpret each to the investigator. The two lines meant nothing to him, but one could be a doodle and the other a business graph. He also did not think *"wooden" meant anything regarding feeling except maybe a wooden expression on a face. He said he was "happy"* to be helpful to the investigator, *"anxious"* to do things so they would help her, and that we have a *"smooth"* relationship. He pointed to the smiling face, saying he felt like that but not like the other (a sad face).

When he had completed the test, he wanted to know what it was to be used for, but offered little in the way of observations about his own use of the cards. Instead he tried to get the investigator to tell him how another parent, whom he knew to have taken the test, had arranged them.

It would appear that the interpersonal relationships in Mr. Jackson's family were extremely distant and that as a child he may not have received much stimulation from them. Werner and Kaplan have noted that the young child spends considerable time in practicing naming in conjunction with pointing. Such behavior is particularly apparent at about 18 months of age when the child is first learning language. At that early stage, the behavior usually involves the identification of facial or body parts such as eyes, ears, and noses. Furthermore this is usually a game in which the child includes adults. Naming does, however, continue for some time, and at later stages involves the identification of objects that are more distant from the child, and ultimately things that are less concrete. Clearly this endeavor not only helps the child in the mastery of words that can be utilized, but also assists in calling to the child's attention aspects of the surroundings that he or she can then differentiate and learn more about.

Brown (1973) has shown how the normal parent helps the child to use language by conversing with the child in terms that are only slightly more sophisticated than the child's own utterances. In this process the adult conveys that the child's essential meaning has been understood while at the same time the child is challenged to refine that communication and its meaningfulness a little bit in each interaction. It now appears likely that the child who grows up in a human milieu in which the child's affective communications are ignored actually may not identify or develop affects at more than a very concrete and global level since distinctions with inner experience are not fostered.

Mr. Jackson, for example, indicated that he did not believe in communication between people and that he did not really think there was very much to communicate. He thought that symbols that communicated a feeling state in a very abstract way really meant nothing much at all and clearly was uninterested in them as having no meaning for him. It is of some interest that Mr. Jackson did not use any word at all to describe the feeling state conveyed by the facial expressions but pointed to them, behavior that Werner and Kaplan see as being very early in the development of symbolization in the child. Even in the testing situation, Mr. Jackson's manner of attempting to gain reassurance that he had performed acceptably was based on external signs—he wished to know how another parent had arranged the cards so that he could compare their arrangements. He did not look inside himself to check whether or not the symbols fit with his own internal experience.

Since affects are generally experienced in an intrapsychic realm, persons who do not have a distinctly experienced inner life may not be aware of the fact that others have a different experience. Many persons who have been diagnostically considered to be either character disordered or sociopathic have been known to claim that they had "conned" professionals into believing that they were doing better or were feeling in certain ways when in fact their communications meant little or nothing. Such persons are apt to believe that psychological treatment is meaningless or useless. Often this is said with some bravado, but it is a bravado that may be covering up a sensed inner deficit the person is loath to admit. Many of these people also learn to compensate for this deficit by paying considerable attention to and overvaluing external signs of meaning in human behavior and material signs of success in life rather than more internal satisfactions.

The belief that internal affective states are present from birth has been so generally widespread that it has been difficult, even for sophisticated professionals, to take seriously data that indicate that this may not be so. Because that is the case, perhaps another illustration of this phenomenon may be in order.

Kathy, a very severely ill schizophrenic young woman, was in the habit of making a facial grimace that seemed very bizarre but did involve raising the corners of her mouth. She did this periodically whenever talking with anyone, but it seemed disconnected and unrelated to the content of any interpersonal reactions. When a relationship had been established in a treatment situation, her worker inquired as to why Kathy did this, since it made her seem very strange. Kathy explained that when she was in second grade her teacher had sent a note home to her mother saying that there was something wrong with her as she never smiled. Her mother dealt with the situation by teaching Kathy how to smile. Kathy indicated that she did not want people to think there was anything wrong with her, so whenever she happened to think about it, she would smile. Kathy seemed to have no understanding that the smile should be related to an internal state.

Since infants normally develop a social smile by about 3 months of age, Kathy's failure to master even this achievement is indicative of very deep pathology. In her particular instance, it raises the possibility that there may have been a neurological problem. However, there was also severe pathology within her family and it should be noted that clearly her mother did not seem to think it necessary to indicate to Kathy that the smile had any particular affective meaning, which probably means that the mother's inner life was also very poorly developed. Searles (1960) has also noted that it is not at all uncommon for persons with severe schizophrenia to experience themselves and others in their environment as inanimate objects.

Mr. Jackson's difficulties do not, of course, appear to have been nearly so severe. Moreover, he demonstrated in his interpretations of the affective words he was shown after he had completed the test that he could place these words into the context of an appropriate sentence. However, such skills depend only on the memorization of the meaning of the word. This does not mean that the referent of the word is very clearly envisioned. For example, it is possible to learn the dictionary definition of a kangaroo without ever having seen one. It is not only likely but expectable that a resident of the United States might have a relatively vague sense of associations and of personal meanings attached to these animals. On the other hand, a resident of the Australian countryside would be expected to have many associations for such a word.

A Russian psychologist named Vygotsky (1962) demonstrated that children up to about the age of 7 normally think that a word is a property of an object and that adults can tell the word from the inspection of the object. In this type of thinking, there is no understanding that the word itself is actually arbitrary and that the usage is determined by social consensus. In Werner and Kaplan's terms, this is the result of a failure of an adequate psychological distancing between the object and the symbol that stands for it. They point out that a fusion of the object and its referent is common in primitive forms of magic. In voodoo, for example, the doll utilized in

93

ceremonies in which a spell is cast upon someone is considered to be not a symbolic representation of a person, but the actual person. Thus to harm the doll is also to harm the person directly.

Since affects are not concrete and are not directly observed in a concrete fashion, it is much easier for a person to utilize words regarding them within a framework that has been memorized but in which the word and the referent may still be somewhat fused. Piaget (1962) and, following Piaget, Santostephano (1980) have indicated that development in the child proceeds from actions to images to language. In the case of Mr. Jackson, there has been development of language, but the critical step of visual images has been skipped or shortened. His language, therefore, cannot be utilized to represent symbolically an inner life. Language, in its fullest sense, is social and cannot develop properly if the sense of connectedness to others is not present.

Whereas Mrs. Ingram needed to have more reassurance about the nature of her self–other boundaries in order to allow herself to risk the sharing of perceptions of an inner life that did exist, Mr. Jackson needed to have more of a sense of connectedness with others before he could even begin to develop a sense of an inner life. Although individuals such as Mr. Jackson have proved very difficult to treat, the indications so far have been that group situations in which there is some cooperative activity and mutual dependence may be useful, at least initially. This may, for example, help to explain the effectiveness of such programs as Alcoholics Anonymous.

7 Values as Conceptualized Affects

Freud's formulation regarding the superego as the heir to the Oedipus complex and as the seat of the conscience has probably been the single most controversial aspect of his theory. Even a very brief overview of the concepts involved demonstrates major problems as seen from today's perspectives. Criticism has not only come from persons outside the psychoanalytic movement, but from within as well. For example, Sandler (1960) pointed out that when an attempt was made at the Hampstead Clinic in England to operationalize psychoanalytic concepts for use in treatment, it was discovered that clinicians rarely used superego theory and that there was common confusion about the nature of the superego.

In orthodox psychoanalytic theory, the superego was considered to develop out of identifications with the father at the time of the resolution of the Oedipus complex. The father was seen as the representative of harsh reality and the identifications with him were motivated out of the desire to avoid punishment from him for the heinous crime of having desired the mother. Thus the pleasure principle, with its assumed patricidal and sexually rapacious features, was reluctantly relinquished in favor of the reality principle in order to obtain survival and social adaptation. In this conception, then, the child was essentially seen as a little savage who was beset by many primitive desires and who resided in a world that appeared to the child as equally vicious in that it was likely to respond with castration or death for the infraction of its rules.

Given these underlying assumptions about the nature of humanity and of society, the need for clear, simplistic, and even rigidly prescribed moral values would appear to be a necessity to ensure any sort of human community. It predicts a need for a law that is harsh but certain. However, it must be asked as to whether such an extreme view of humanity is indicated by actual data. Current infant observations (e.g., Parens, 1979) would appear instead to support a view that says that the human being has the potential for both good and evil, for constructive or destructive behavior, but is preordained for neither. Furthermore all indications are that infants do not come to terms with a human community after several years of life, but have an inborn need for it and become a part of it at least at the time of birth, if not before. Kohut (1971), who has been one of the most vocal critics of superego theory, has repeatedly pointed out that human beings are as much pulled by their ambitions as they are pushed by their desires.

In fact neither Freud nor early psychoanalysis was really prepared to be satisfied with the extreme view of human nature that a simple construction of instinct theory seemed to dictate and the conceptualization of the superego was modified by the addition of the ego ideal. The ego ideal was defined as the internal structure that derived from the fact that the child also loved the father, wanted to be like the father, and in turn normally was the recipient of much love from the father. Schafer (1960), in particular, tried to emphasize this aspect of the superego within the traditional formulation. Since the time of Schafer's paper, many others have agreed with him that Freud was drawing most of his observations from a population that was quite pathological and that he was himself operating within a traditionally paternalistic and authoritarian German culture. This background now appears to have permeated Freud's fundamental outlook, coloring much of his work and making psychoanalytic thinking more concerned with issues of authority than is necessary and useful.

Recently Ross (1982), among many others, has pointed out that Oedipus' murderous conduct and conflict can be understood only in the context of the fact that Laius, Oedipus' father, was himself a murderous man who had tried to kill his son. Freud, in his interpretations of the myth, ignored this background "detail." Loewald (1980) has noted that the Oedipus story does have some universal appeal since it relates to rivalry and conflict between generations as the younger one moves into adulthood and ascendancy over the older one. However, it appears that this has been overutilized and overinterpreted in a context that emphasized its more violent aspects. Mair (1982) also recently brought out the little known fact that Freud's formulation of the Oedipus complex came during the year following his own father's death. While it should not be assumed from this that Freud's feelings about his father were entirely negative, it does raise the possibility that at that time in his life Freud may have had a particular need to come to terms with the negative aspects of his relationship with his father.

Freud's concept of the superego has, of course, contained other problems. Freud did not believe that women, because their experience with the Oedipus complex was different from that of men, could develop truly mature superegos. [For a discussion of some of the technical problems involved here, see Schafer (1974)] This relates to the problem that Freud's whole psychology of women seems to have suffered from his point of view that feminine identity could be totally explained on the basis of a physical organ that was not there, an idea that today not only is unacceptable from the point of view of its sexist base, but also because it simply is poor theorizing.

The view that the conscience did not develop in the child prior to the time of the Oedipus complex has also had inadequacies in relation to understanding developmental deficits that were presumed to have roots in earlier stages. According to the original theory, true guilt could not exist until that stage. This has not provided an adequate explanation for the fact that far more severe self-critical and self-punitive behavior can be observed in persons who presumably have not psychologically reached the stage of the Oedipus complex than in those who presumably have. This has led to confusing attempts to define affects that might underlie the behavior of persons not assumed to have fully developed superegos as "shame" rather than "true guilt" (Piers & Singer, 1971). It has also led some theoreticians, especially Jacobson (1963), to formulate notions about earlier superego precursors.

Even more fundamentally, there are currently valid questions about the significance of a relationship between the development of a mature conscience and sexual behavior and/or oedipal conflicts. For example, the original theory would predict to an understanding that homosexuals, like women, could not possibly develop a mature superego or mature object relations. However, Spaulding (1982), for example, found that a group of admitted lesbians who scored very highly on a cognitively oriented test of object relations could be located. In addition, there are reports in the literature of observations of latency-aged children who were still struggling with problems of a classically oedipal nature but who nevertheless were found to have a "fully internalized and structured superego which was functioning autonomously" (Gillman, 1982; Holder, 1982).

A formulation that has so many inadequacies needs to be reconsidered and revised to achieve a better fit with the observed data. There have been many attempts to accomplish this. Interestingly some of the clues pointing toward a more useful reorganization derive from the arena of theory regarding symbolization, a phenomenon to which Freud himself called considerable attention in his early work regarding dreams and the unconscious.

Values and the Transitional Process

*C*ulture, according to traditional sociological theory, is a socially shared world view. In other terms it is a particular perspective related to the manner in which the observable data regarding the external world should be ordered and interpreted. Culture also has been normally considered to be transmitted socially, primarily within the family and through the medium of language. In his early work, Talcott Parsons was particularly concerned with the interrelationships between culture, affect, symbolization, and human interaction patterns. For example, he (Parsons, 1970, p. 29) said:

Culture, however, is a system of generalized symbols and their meanings. In order for the integration with affect, which constitutes internalization, to take place, the individual's own affective organization must achieve levels of generalization of a higher order. . . . In other words, the process of forming attachments is *in itself* inherently a process of generalization of affect. But this generalization in turn actually is in one major aspect the process of symbolization   of emotional meanings—that is, it is a process of the acquisition of a culture.

In practicing naming with a participating adult, the child gradually learns what aspects of the surrounding concrete reality are important enough to warrant his or her attention, thus orienting the child to the world view held by adults and older children. In fact Whorf (1956) developed a theory around the idea that language determined perception and thought in the sense that it provided the words for that which would be noticed. He pointed out, for example, that the Eskimo language provided numerous words for various types of snow whereas English provided very few. This is now not considered to be totally the case since the lack of a special word for the quality of wet snow does not prohibit the person from noticing this quality.

In a different sense, however, there is a connection between language and thought. Bruner (Bruner et al., 1967) has pointed out that this connection does not so much involve the existence of the words themselves, but involves the thought units that the words make possible through a system of categorization and abstraction. Words, at higher levels of abstraction, make it possible to define relationships between observed phenomena through the invention of categories that cannot be directly seen. For example, one may observe concretely a chair in an immediate sense. To understand, however, that there are many types of chairs that may look quite different and be made of different materials requires an ability to select an aspect of the concrete object *chair* that is common to a variety of other chairs. Also, to comprehend that chairs are also furniture requires yet another level of abstraction. And further, categories are not mutually exclusive. Thus some furniture may also belong to a category of things made of wood, other furniture may belong to things made of metal, and some furniture may be made of both wood and metal, belonging to both categories at the same time.

These categories of abstraction provide human beings with the structure within which they will organize their world. Singer (1965) found that parents of schizophrenic adolescents had marked difficulty with the capacity to abstract in a simple object-sorting test. This capacity is an advanced achievement which, in Werner and Kaplan's terms, requires considerable distancing between the four aspects of the communicational system, that is, among the addressor, the addressee, the object, and the object's referent. Abstraction, and the symbolization upon which it is built, is necessary for a fully adequate understanding of the world. It is a part of the advanced thinking process, beyond that of reality testing, to which Robbins and Sadow were referring in their concept of reality processing. In fact it is of such importance in human functioning that Rose (1980) has suggested that the true opposite of Freud's concept of repression is not sublimation but abstraction.

Abstraction does not, however, just assist the individual in comprehending the external world. It is essential for an understanding of affects and the internal world as well. Epstein (1973) has pointed out that an understanding of the self is really a theory of the self that must rely on abstraction for its adequacy. Neither Mr. Jackson nor Mrs. Ingram (Chapter 6) had achieved adequate concepts of themselves because neither could move perceptions flexibly outside the concrete context in which they had first been learned. Thus while they may technically, if tenuously, have achieved reality testing, they had not achieved reality processing.

Sociological theory has generally seen values as a major part of culture in the sense that they represent judgments about social reality (Durkheim, 1953). Affects, as defined by Basch and as they are being considered here, are judgments about the well-being of the self. There are, then, as Parsons recognized, interconnections between affects, values, and a sense of self since a truly adequate understanding of the well-being of the self must involve a judgment about the social reality within which that self operates. Furthermore an adequate understanding of social reality cannot be achieved without not only a highly differentiated sense of one's own inner life, but also the ability to transfer that understanding to a different context into a contemplation of what the inner lives of others might be like. A brief example may help to make this clearer.

A student social worker, placed in a residential treatment center for delinquents, had watched Larry's progress with pleasure as he seemed to be becoming very much more aware and considerate of the feelings of those around him. Since Larry had a history of stealing, the student decided to try to impress upon him the idea that stealing was wrong by telling him of her current distress over the fact that her own stereo set had recently been burglarized from her home. Initially Larry seemed upset over this news. Then, to the student's horror, he offered to solve the problem by stealing another stereo set for her. The student asked if Larry could not see that this would not solve the problem but would only make someone else feel as badly as she now did. "But," Larry replied, "I don't know that other person. I care about how you feel because I know you. How can you care about the feelings of someone you don't know?"

Having a mature set of values means not only making an assessment of the details of the reality context of the situation, but also knowing and caring about the feelings of someone one does not know.

It was inevitable that psychoanalytic theory would have difficulty with the concept of values so long as it posited a view of reality as an objective, factual given that could be known and ascertained if the distortions of the emotions were removed. Such an approach would indicate that there must also be absolute values that could be similarly ascertained if only the affects were removed. When examined in depth, almost all value systems are seen to involve complicated and often conflicting goals and points of view, all of which must be taken into consideration. There are rarely simple solutions to complex problems. The extreme opposite of a position that indicates that there are simple "right" answers to value questions would be that all values are relative, a position in which there is no organization and no attempt at it. Since neither society nor social work can afford to discount an approach that stands for the dignity and worth of each individual human being, this approach is not tenable for either. Furthermore common-sense experience would indicate that values not only are not devoid of affective connections, but hold such emotion-laden meaning that people have been willing to die for them and have been honored by their fellow humans for doing so.

A number of psychoanalytically oriented theoreticians are now seeing values of conceptualized affects (Krystal, 1977; Rosenblatt & Thickstun, 1977). This more developmental approach both is in more consonance with observed experiential data and offers a solution to the problem of total rigidity versus total relativism in the understanding of values. It also provides a means of reconciling the psychoanalytic perspective with both classical sociological theory and Piaget's cognitive psychology.

Values as well as affects, then, have a developmental course. Kohlberg (1964), drawing from Piaget's theory, has outlined such a developmental course in some detail. In its general outlines, Kohlberg's theory is a major contribution. However, Kohlberg simply adopted the framework within which these values developed from Piaget, who basically did not consider the family as a primary socializing unit and focused more on the notion that values were acquired through peer interactions. While peer interactions certainly must be considered to have an impact, there is little doubt that the primary socializing agency remains that of the family unit. Affects, values, and culture, then, can all be seen as outgrowths of the transitional process in which the capacity to symbolize also develops and then provides the structure for further development.

Culture has somewhat facetiously been described as "living with dead men's habits." At one level of abstraction, this is indeed the case, since it involves the inheritance, through language and a sharing of perceptions, of the meaning of data from the external world and of the actions that such meanings signal as appropriate. At another level of abstraction, however, culture also means "living with dead men's emotions" since it also involves the inheritance of data about the knowledge of the internal world of the self and of other human beings. Erikson has stressed the idea that individual identity invariably consists not only of knowledge of the internal world of the self, but also of the place of that self within the wider social group. What this means in clinical work is that a failure to recognize and deal with a person's culture and world view is a failure to recognize and credit that person's true identity, including the basis of his or her affective life. However, because data regarding both the inner and external world are filtered through the perceptual system and the cognitive organization of each individual, culture as viewed in relation to an individual cannot be considered simply an external given any more than can an inner life. Knowledge of the reality of both worlds is constructed in the mind over time and experience.

Values and the Adolescent Experiences

*P*iaget has noted that it is not until adolescence that the child is capable, in a problem-solving process, of imagining alternative possibilities or differences that are not immediately present (Piaget & Inhelder, 1973). This is seen in the fact that in adolescence a youngster does not literally have to manipulate external objects to be able to conceive of their potential relationships but can instead do this in his or her head. Thus it can be said that the normal adolescent has achieved a high degree of differentiation of thought or abstraction in Werner and Kaplan's terms. Thought is both hypothetical and deductive at this stage. Problem solving is less trial and error and is far more directed by preformed conceptualizations.

Viewed from this perspective, it can be seen that part of the normal adolescent's tendency to be critical of his or her family is based upon the fact that for the first time he or she has come to realize that the possibility of difference exists. Prior to adolescence the child is likely to assume, in spite even of an ability to observe concrete differences, that all families are pretty much the same. The young child who has been neglected or actively abused usually will show less anger about this than adults often suspect simply because the child does not have the capacity to process in a meaningful way the idea that things might have been different. The teenager, who has believed in his or her parents as a source of wisdom about the world and is unaware of the different quality of his or her changing thinking capacities, now is apt either silently or overtly to blame the parents for not having described the meaningful distinctions in the world that he or she now sees for the first time. The adolescent may think the parents or other adults are stupid and do not see what he or she sees. Parents, who are unaware that they have ever concealed such information, may be bewildered by or defensive about the implied criticisms.

Adolescent "rap" sessions are partly motivated by a new awareness that others may act or feel differently. Thus there is a need to compare affective reactions so as to gain a new measurement of the relative well-being of the internal self that is now motivated by potential differences not before considered. Okun and Sasfy (1977) have indicated that a true theory of the self cannot be constructed prior to the achievement of formal operations, the term Piaget used to describe the cognitive advance of the adolescent period. Thus adolescence becomes a time of experimentation with various possible roles and possible selves. It is a time when a more complex sense of identity is achieved. The monitoring of identity is, of course, another of the functions Freud attributed to the superego.

In Werner and Kaplan's terms, after the development of the ability to utilize true symbols, the further development of the ability to conceptualize can be seen in the increasing differentiation between the internal and external forms of words. In this differentiation the system of internal meanings becomes more elaborated while the external form becomes increasingly freed from its context such that a concept can be manipulated in the total absence of perceptions of a concrete referent. This final development does not take place before adolescence and can be seen, for example, to underlie the acquisition of a genuinely mature sense of values.

In psychoanalytic theory it has been said that the id has no sense of time. From this perspective it is also noted that the superego is greatly transformed in adolescence. If the superego is defined in Loewald's terms as the wished-for self of the future, it is certainly clear why this would be so. The conceptual mastery of time and process makes it possible for adolescents to conceive of themselves as being different but also to conceive of an ideal. Since their self concept is likely to suffer in the comparative affective evaluations based upon the ideal, a state of underlying self-criticism is apt to be characteristic of adolescents. It is also a time when ideals and ideologies, which are in fact quite novel to the adolescent, have great appeal. The normally developing adolescent also can be quite newly empathic since, having now constructed a theory of the self, he or she can also imagine such a theory operating in others. If action is conceptualized as the primal mode through which both affects and thoughts are differentiated, then a need for increased action at a time in life when normal development involves a reorganization of perceptions becomes understandable.

These descriptions of the characteristics of adolescence are not new, but they have often been explained in terms of sexual and object relations development. The existence of a convergence among the developmental lines is clear, but the significance of action in adolescence, apart from the well-known tendency toward acting out, appears to have been relatively neglected. In some ways this seems strange given the fact that action—and not just that of a sexual

103

nature—is so characteristic of that time in the life cycle. Blos (1962, p. 125) does note that "thinking as trial action is in adolescence constantly interfered with by the proclivity to action and acting out," but does not greatly expand upon what such action might have for further development. Normally adolescence is a time of increased action, but it is also a time of increased need for the sharing of perceptions of those actions and of other data with others.

Erikson has pointed out that fidelity is a particular concern of youth, but that, while it cannot emerge prior to that developmental stage, it is characterized then by a preoccupation with total commitment to an ideology or cause and that this becomes refined only later. He says (Erikson, 1964, pp. 225–226):

The adolescent learns to grasp the flux of time, and to anticipate the future in a coherent way, to perceive ideas and assent to ideals, to take—in short—an *ideological* position for which the younger child is cognitively not prepared. In adolescence, then, an ethical view is approximated but it remains susceptible to an alteration of impulsive judgment and odd rationalization.

The *true ethical sense of the young adult, finally, encompasses and goes beyond moral restraint and ideal vision, while insisting on concrete commitments to those intimate relationships and work associations by which man can hope to share a lifetime of productivity and competence.*

It can be seen, then, that one of the major tasks of late adolescence and early adulthood is the integration of values and action such that the real commitment to an ideological position, which can take place only through sustained, purposive, and selective action, can be achieved.

Sometimes the features of normal development and their significance can best be illustrated through an example in which deficiencies have distorted that development:

Maria's mother, Mrs. Thomas, was a woman in her middle 30s, of Hispanic background. Mrs. Thomas knew little of her own parents, having been raised in an orphanage from an early age. She reported having hated the impersonal and punitive care she recalled having received as a child. Her most vivid memory seemed to be of having been forced to sit outside in the front of the home on a cold winter day wrapped only in the damp bedsheet she had wet the night before. As soon as she was old enough to leave the orphanage, Mrs. Thomas had done so, essentially alone. An attractive and basically intelligent woman, Mrs. Thomas came to earn a living as a prostitute in a large city, a venture at which she was reasonably successful financially. In her early 20s, however, she found herself pregnant, with the father one of her clients though she did not know which one. Wishing to change her life and to keep her baby, Mrs. Thomas found an uneducated but steadily employed man who was willing to marry her and raise the then unborn Maria as his child.

The marriage was chaotic from the outset, marked by violent outbursts on Mrs. Thomas' part and by chronic complaints by her husband about her lack of homemaking skills. It nevertheless lasted for approximately six years and resulted in a second child, Don. Following the divorce Mr. Thomas continued to send support money for both children but kept little other contact with them. Mrs. Thomas' first contact with the agency came when Maria was 8, at which time Mrs. Thomas sought help because of her own perceived inability to care for the children. The home was found to be filthy and in utter chaos. Maria and Don had been severely abused, as a result of which Maria had a broken front tooth. A rather quiet child who tried to help at home, Maria was having fights with other children at school. Don, aged 6, was judged to be possibly schizophrenic. In accordance with Mrs. Thomas' desires, both children were placed in an institution. Mrs. Thomas was seen in weekly appointments for a period of several years during which she also obtained further education, secured a clerical job she liked, managed to stabilize her life considerably, and visited her children regularly at least once a week.

Mrs. Thomas' plan had been to take back both of her children as she felt ready to care for them. Thus when Maria was 13, she returned home; Don remained in placement. The mother–daughter relationship, however, had not gone well. Instead of being appreciative of what Mrs. Thomas understandably considered to be real achievements on her part in attempting to improve herself and the home, Maria had become angry and defiant, thwarting her mother's attempts to guide her. According to Mrs. Thomas, the girl was doing poorly in school, frequently truanting, ignoring parental curfew hours, drinking, and keeping undesirable company. Mrs. Thomas had become convinced that Maria would end up repeating her own mistakes and would become a prostitute. Thus when Maria was a little over 14 years old, Mrs. Thomas brought her to the agency, requesting that she be placed for a second time.

Faced with the prospect of a second placement, Maria was angry and defiant, but pleaded with her mother not to return her to an institution. As a result Mrs. Thomas relented on the threatened placement but informed Maria that while she could remain at home, she was now on her own, and that Mrs. Thomas would no longer take any responsibility for or interest in Maria's conduct. Mrs. Thomas, who had previously terminated her own individual treatment with another worker at a time when both had considered that she had achieved her major goals, angrily refused any further involvement in treatment and announced that Maria could do as she wished.

Several months later Maria returned to the agency alone, requesting placement for herself. She indicated that her mother had stuck to her resolve to be uninvolved with her and that own attempts to take care of herself were not working. She indicated that she had been with a group of youths who were smoking marijuana on the street when the police arrested some of them. She had escaped arrest but was so frightened by the close call that she began wandering the streets alone for hours in a daze, which she insisted was not from drug use but from her emotional state. She could not describe this state more than to indicate she had been "out of it." In this condition she had come very close to walking directly in front of a car and was saved when a policeman directing traffic literally pulled her away. What had then frightened her the most was that she was not sure whether or not she might have intended to step in the automobile's path as a way of taking her life.

Following this incident Maria realized she was near her father's house and went there, hoping that somehow he might help her. Her father and his second wife were superficially pleasant, fed her dinner, and drove her home. The father also, however, managed to convey to Maria that he had no intention of becoming more deeply involved with her and that she could not count on him for emotional support. Maria then decided that the only place left for her was the agency. When Mrs. Thomas was contacted about Maria's problems, she continued her stance that Maria's life was her own and that she would neither support nor oppose placement but would have nothing to do with arrangements or counseling.

Although Maria persisted in her request for placement and an appropriate facility about which Maria was initially enthusiastic was located, the heavy demand for adolescent group homes meant that there was a long waiting list. Thus for over a year Maria continued to live in her mother's home. During that time she kept treatment appointments regularly, her truancy ended, and her grades improved markedly. She was involved in several relatively minor rule infractions at school, mostly about smoking where this was not permitted and arguments with female classmates. Although angry at school officials over such disciplinary measures, she managed to negotiate for herself in these problems without undue defiance and in each ultimately accepted whatever restrictions were imposed on her rather calmly. Evenings and weekends, however, she continued to associate with other youth, most of whom were school dropouts who were involved, at least marginally, in gang activities. Maria had several brief romances with these young men, each time being certain that the one in question would give up gang activities and become stable and reliable for her. In each instance it also became clear that the individual's mother had some appeal for her, though she could never describe the woman in question in much detail or convey what she found appealing about her. Each mother was described as "neat" or "fantastic."

In her appointments Maria initially talked of her deep desires for her mother to care about her and of her coming loss in moving out of the home. "If I could have anyone in the world, I would choose my mother, but I know I can't have her." There was a flavor to Maria's talk about her mother as if she wanted to own an object, not that person's love. Her sadness over this loss seemed, however, appropriate and genuine. She often referred to her broken tooth, the obvious and concrete evidence of her difficulties with her mother from an early age. Although Maria knew very little of her mother's early life, she did know enough to be able to verbalize a recognition that the mother had tried but had little to give her.

Maria also talked of having received more affection from her father when she was a very young child. She recalled that he would come home and play with her, tossing her into the air and catching her. The father had played very roughly and most of the time he would throw her so high and so hard that her head would slam into the ceiling. "It hurt like hell and I would end up with a terrible headache, but I wanted it so much that I would beg him to do it again." Maria could not recall a time when her mother had been very affectionate but could remember having always wanted her to be so. As Maria became more and more capable of giving up her hopes for her family and showed less depression, she was encouraged to talk more about what she wanted for herself in the future. Based on her previous experiences in placement, Maria could seem to imagine what the group home might be like but had a hard time going beyond that. Her one constant goal was to earn and save enough money so that she could go to a dentist and have her front tooth fixed. (Unfortunately attempts on the part of her social worker to get funding for this at the time were unsuccessful.) Apart from her recognition that this was a way to undo her problems with her mother, Maria seemed to think that this flaw in her physical appearance would be the only thing that would stand in the way of her becoming a rock star.

The opening in the group home came exactly one week before Maria's 16th birthday, at which time she became legally of age. Unfortunately this seemed to encourage Maria to think that she could now make it on her own and she verbalized feeling that somehow her going into the placement would be a hostile criticism of her mother whereas just trying to stay at home would not be. Thus she turned down the placement when it was available. Within a few weeks, however, she provoked a major battle with her mother, subsequent to which she left home, and did not show up for school or treatment appointments, and her whereabouts could not be determined.

Approximately one year later, Maria appeared at the agency without an appointment. She said she had been supporting herself by traveling around the country with a group of other youths selling bogus magazine subscriptions while claiming that the profit would be used to provide college scholarships for disadvantaged but deserving minorities. She had no concern that she had been doing something that was illegal or that she had taken money on false pretexts, but was amazed how easily people were duped. She was extremely proud of how much money she had made and displayed her newly capped front tooth, noting that this was the first thing she had done with her money.

As Maria continued to talk, her underlying depression and lack of sense of direction became evident. She related that she had acquired a little dog, which she was now caring for and had named "Mommie." Maria noted that only the night before she had been in a bad mood due to a disagreement over where the group was to travel next and had violently slammed Mommie against a wall when the dog had annoyed her. She was surprised and very frightened that she could have done something like this even though the dog had not been injured. She noted that the dog had been frightened and cowed, and tried to be affectionate with her, very much as she recalled herself having done with her mother when she was a child. In spite of her obvious distress, Maria refused further contact at that time, indicating that she was leaving town shortly to go on with the group to solicit more magazine subscriptions, a way of life she was not ready to give up.

Maria returned to the agency one more time. At that point, some six months later, she indicated that she was pregnant by a young man with whom she claimed to have been very much in love, and who, she said, was planning to marry her. She claimed that he had been killed in a gang war in another city and that now she was alone. She had returned to the city where she had grown up hoping to find people who would help her in having and raising her child, but was very frightened about what would happen if her mother found out about her pregnancy. She refused to disclose where she was staying but made an appointment for further contacts, which she did not keep. Efforts to locate her were unsuccessful.

Although Mrs. Thomas experienced Maria's behavior as angry and rebellious, and as unappreciating of all that Mrs. Thomas had tried to do for a daughter about whom she cared as much as her own limited capacities allowed, what can be seen here is that Maria very much wanted her mother's love. Indeed the expression of the anger is in large part based on the recognition that things might have been different. Maria would not be so ardently seeking caring if she could not recognize that there was something out there that she could conceivably get and was not getting. Thus in Winnicott's (1975) sense the anger represents not despair, but a sense of hope on Maria's part. In her latency years, prior to the first placement, Maria had not yet recognized at a meaningful emotional level that this was the case, and so at that age had played the role of the good mother's helper in an attempt to win approval.

It may be postulated that in infancy anger for Maria may have served as a distancing mechanism in an interpersonal sense as it did, for example, in the case of Mrs. Hernstein (Chapter 5). Thus it may have helped to build up self–other boundaries. However, Maria's problems do not primarily relate to poorly formed interpersonal boundaries or a need to distance herself from others. Her problems instead relate to an environmental unavailability of others with whom she can merge temporarily to nourish the closeness side of the closeness/distance continuum. Maria's anger has functional value for her as it maintains a separate sense of self; there is no evidence that she is likely to become schizophrenic, for example. However, this separate sense of self, and the anger that reinforces it, also has a negative effect in that it keeps her from being able to get more of the caring she really wants from others, notably, but not exclusively, her mother, simply because it serves as an interpsychic distancer. At the same time, it must be recognized that too much immediate merging would threaten what little internal sense of self Maria has. From that perspective it can be seen that she has what may be described as a defensive need to retain her anger, a dynamic that may have played a part in her refusal of the placement.

Maria seemed to have longed primarily for love from a maternal object so that many of the young men with whom she became romantically involved seemed to be utilized by Maria as a means of achieving a connection with their mothers. Her life experience, however, had taught her that affection and financial support were more easily obtainable from men. Yet even here her experience with her father also taught her that to achieve this, she must also endure considerable physical pain. It is likely, therefore, that this explains some of her proclivity for young men of the type she found in gangs.

Having had little experience with emotionally nurturing relationships, Maria's affective life remained at a very global and concrete level. Although she had a general sense that her mother would have liked to be able to give her more, she could not use that information in an empathic sense to know how to get what she wanted from Mrs. Thomas. Her means of talking about her desires for her mother seemed to be at a level of owning her mother, almost as if she were an animal or a concrete object. Similarly she could not describe the mothers of the young men with whom she became involved other than in very general terms. Her presumed magazine customers, who had even less connection with her emotional needs, were not really experienced as people who might have feelings.

What is important to note here is that this inability to sense the emotional life of others is secondary to the globality with which she experienced her own affective life. She was uncertain as to whether or not she might have wanted to commit suicide. It is likely that when, under great stress, she suddenly found herself near her father's residence, she had no awareness of having intentionally walked in that direction. She was bewildered and frightened by the strong outburst of rage on her part when she slammed the dog across the room, an action she clearly had not anticipated and could not find acceptable. Her identification with the dog, however, can be understood through the concept of the transitional object; in other words this dog was partly experienced as herself, partly as her mother, and partly as a component of the concrete external world. It would appear that it was at this level of object relations that Maria could function.

Maria's long-range plans for herself do not seem to have been especially antisocial. She seemed to long for a settled, quiet, and respectable family life much as had her mother, with whom Maria had a shared culture, both in the sense of a world view of reality and an affective life. Neither, however, had known how to go about getting what she wanted for herself. Mrs. Thomas's prediction that Maria would end up repeating her own mistakes was not so far off, but this was not necessarily evidence that either was inherently bad. Instead both may be seen as attempting to utilize actions to grow through an "active reversal of the passively experienced." Since these attempts, without treatment intervention or other fortuitous life experiences that would supply conditions under which the symbolic capacities could grow, would be doomed to be maladaptive, they merely served to pass on the difficulties from one generation to the next.

With so little real sense of herself, Maria could not plan beyond what was concretely conceivable to her. She had some idea from the past of placement and a group home, an experience that apparently had not been totally negative for her, so she could manage to wait for that experience. She could similarly orient herself toward a goal that involved the changing of a concrete aspect of herself; that is, the capping of the tooth. This change, however, had magical overtones since her idea very clearly was that if her tooth were fixed, so also might be her past relationship with her mother and her future. Furthermore it can be pointed out that Maria's anger and rebelliousness seemed to surface at times when she had to deal with the notion of a future she could not imagine. Maria's anger and frustration in this sense can be seen to be evoked at times when the environment seemed to demand of her performance of which she simply was not capable. For example, Maria provoked the final argument with her mother when the future placement was no longer available, and she abused the dog when the group seemed confused about where it would travel. Maria was not capable of formulating an ideal she could use as a guide for her own future self or as a means of comprehending how her future might become different from what her mother's life had been.

Maria's experiences, therefore, seem to be at least as well, if not considerably more easily, explained through a theory that utilizes a concept of values as affects rather than a theory that relies upon a more orthodox concept of a superego that developed, or failed to develop, from an Oedipus complex. However, such a revised theoretical conception could not be reached without a prior base in and understanding that a rigid division between subjective and objective reality is false, as is a rigid separation between affect and cognition. Moreover, the newer theory also has to rest upon an understanding of the development of the symbolic capacities that simply did not exist in Freud's time.

8 Sensuality and the Development of Identity

Hartmann's (1958) revision of Freud's theory from one in which the neonate began with an id to one in which there was a primary undifferentiated matrix has been a change of critical significance. In relation to the development of a meaning system, Loewald (1980, p. 185) has noted:

According to modern developmental theory sensory perception in its initial stages is a global affair; there is no such thing as perception according to distinct sensory modalities in the beginnings of mental life. A thing, event, act, or experience given a word or words by the mother is one buzzing blooming confusion (Williams James) for the infant, and "the word" is part of that confusion.

Nevertheless, as Hartmann pointed out, that primary undifferentiated matrix does include the potentialities for a number of different functions. Along with language the potentialities include such things as perception, motility, intelligence, and physiologic functioning.

In a fundamental sense, the mind and the body are interrelated since both begin in the undifferentiated matrix that is present at the time of birth. Current research, primarily from disciplines other than social work, is rapidly discovering more about the nature of the undifferentiated matrix but has not yet been able to provide much information about the nature of the interrelationships between the various potentialities of the human infant at the time of birth. It is likely that the intricacies of these interrelationships will remain a mystery for some time to come. Until such knowledge is available, however, many of the precise relationships between the mind and the body, as well as of how these interact with the environment and how they affect the development of a meaning system, can not be fully comprehended. Therefore, a theory that attempts to link these elements must be considered to have a tentative nature. This condition necessitates caution, but nevertheless does not prohibit attempts at ordering and organizing available data into an explanatory system that can be used in clinical work.

The Meaning of Sexuality

*O*ne of psychoanalytic theory's major tenets has traditionally been that no particular behavior is, in and of itself, diagnostic. Instead the theory has emphasized that the motivation and meaning of that behavior must be understood in order to comprehend its function for the individual. Clinical experience has repeatedly demonstrated that this is the case with sexual behavior, just as with any other behavior. For example, the existence of heterosexual promiscuity in a client is not generally believed to be a reliable indicator of the level of personality organization of that person. Futhermore it is commonplace knowledge that sexuality may be utilized interpersonally to achieve a number of ends, ranging from the expression of intimacy and a genuine concern for the other person through an impersonal attempt at manipulation for material or other such gains to an expression of contempt or hatred.

In spite of this evidence, however, at least until the theory moved from a diagnostic framework that relied upon the stages of psychosexuality as primary indicators of the level of personality development to one that relied more heavily on the assessment of object relations, there was a contradictory tendency to treat sexual behavior as if it were a more direct indicator of health or pathology than other behaviors. Sexual behavior, as distinct from other types of behavior, was considered to have an explicit link to the contents of the unconscious. It was in a special class of its own.

Placing sexual behavior into this special class clearly created for psychoanalytic theory some awkward problems in relation to explanation. While the psychosexual line of development, when invoked to explain overt sexual dysfunctions or deviations, seemed at least reasonably comfortable for many therapists, it failed to explain why sexual dysfunctions did not occur in all persons with lower level personality organization. Adequate heterosexual performance in persons with severe psychological difficulties had to be explained as not being truly "genital" in a psychological sense and thus distinguished from sexuality, which was truly "genital." In a purely common-sense approach, it is difficult to understand how sexual intercourse could be more genital for some persons than for others since the behavior itself involves precisely the same activities and physical organs.

There has been a theoretical inconsistency here that would seem to be relatively easy to resolve simply by considering that sexual behavior, like all other behaviors, cannot be understood outside a framework that takes into account the meaning system or context within which such behaviors take place. There has been a reluctance on the part of analytic theorists, however, to rely totally on this seemingly apparent and simple resolution of the problem. The question, therefore, must be asked as to why this reluctance should have been so pervasive. It could be dismissed as an irrational desire to cling to Freud's conclusions about sexual behavior in spite of contradicting evidence. However, that explanation will not suffice since it is also demonstrable that many of Freud's insights about sensual behaviors in children, as well as about the importance of sexuality in human life, have much real merit.

The fact that sexuality has a special place in current human life and in all known human cultures throughout history has been so well documented that even an attempt at any literature reference pointing this out seems unnecessary. The difficulty lies not in making this observation, but rather in defining the nature of that special place. The changing assumptions about social role specifications for males and females has made this a highly controversial area. Certainly new data indicate that anatomy is not destiny in the narrow sense in which Freud tended to construe this. Clearly the cultural system within which any individual is raised will determine much of the meaning of sexual behavior, just as it does the meaning of any other behavior, but simply to leave the question at that level is inadequate.

In a biological sense, sexuality is, of course, critical for the human species in that it is, or at least has in the past, been essential for the perpetuation of the population. Freud's theories about sexuality certainly began from this knowledge, but included the assumption that sexuality also had a fundamental function in a psychological sense as well. It is now quite arguable that Freud's error was not in the conclusion that sexuality had a special function, but rather in the assumption that this special function was accompanied and dictated by specific meaning content. This position has been eloquently posited by Klein (1976) and is in concert with an understanding that Freud's fundamental error regarding the nature of the unconscious was that it held universal and static content rather than that the unconscious was a function or structure the content of which was constructed over time and experience with the environment.

Lichtenberg (1978) and others have pointed out that while the psychological world of the neonate is that of an undifferentiated matrix in which there is no initial ability to tell self from the surrounding environment, the ego is first and foremost a body ego. Sensations of pleasure and unpleasure are fundamentally rooted in the physical experiences of the individual. In a primordial state, there is no division between the mind and the body. Piaget's theory acknowledges this in his assumption that knowledge begins in action in a sensorimotor sense, and Werner and Kaplan do likewise in positing that the initial perceptions of the child are of a physiognomic nature. At a very basic level, the existence of the centering of the sensations of pleasure and pain in the body itself makes it possible for the child to construct, over time, a sense of separation from the surrounding environment and of the boundaries of the ego or of the self.

Basic kinesthetic feedback, for example, provides the infant with the knowledge of the placement of the parts of the body whereas there is no such feedback concerning the placement of parts of other objects in the environment. Touching the surface of one's own skin provides sensation in two different locations, the touching of the surface of another object provides such sensation in only one location. The experiencing of these basic sensations can be considered to be universal to the species, at least to the extent to which the physical equipment of the neonate is "normal." The tremendous significance of research such as that of Fraiberg (1977) into the formation of indentity or the construction of the self in those children who are congenitally blind or who may have other impairments lies in the very fact that the feedback these persons have about themselves and the world is either limited or different from that of children who are normal in a physical sense.

The centering of the self in a physical body does not, however, end with infancy. It is an experience that continues throughout life. Physical experiences, therefore, provide a basic foundation for the continual assertion and reaffirmation of the self as a separate object. That this is the case has certain important implications for social work clinicians. It means, for example, that illness or injury that alters the experience with the physical self will inevitably result in the necessity for a psychological reevaluation and reconstruction of the meaning of the self. Persons undergoing such experiences are both vulnerable to the formation of images of the self that may be less socially adaptive and simultaneously may be open to the formation of new self-images, which can conceivably be more socially adaptive than were the older ones. Additionally this fact provides a solid explanation for the utility of activity-oriented treatments for those individuals whose sense of self may be very transient or poorly formed. It is also, of course, the reason why persons with very severe psychological disturbances, such as the schizophrenias, frequently have distorted body images.

The formation of a body self is, then, a critical foundation for psychological health. However, the existence of bodily sensations does not dictate for the individual the meaning of those sensations. This was the critical implication of Bruch's (Bruch, 1969; Coddington & Bruch, 1970) work in relation to eating disorders when she discovered that even the meaning of sensations as basic as those of hunger must be learned. The physical sensations of hunger exist in cases of severe anorexia nervosa, but some who suffer from this disorder have not learned to interpret these sensations as meaning that they should eat. The meaning of these sensations is one the neonate knows only over the course of experience with an organizing and caretaking environment through which the infant can connect the sensation of hunger, the experience of being fed, and the sensation of satisfaction.

The physical sensations that accompany sexuality are, in a general sense, very much a part of a body image or a sense of the body self.

Bobby, a 7-year-old boy in a residential treatment center because of a schizophrenic condition, indicated to his social worker that he feared his penis would come off. Exploration of the boy's fears elicited the thought that a slight bruise on his toe meant that an infection would travel up his leg and cause a detachment of his penis. The worker indicated that he did not think this would happen, but Bobby insisted that it would. The worker calmly continued to maintain that it would not and suggested that Bobby test it out for himself by examining his penis at night in the shower to see if it was loose. Bobby indicated he would do so and did not later return to this precise concern.

This brief vignette shows a clear example of castration fear. Had the worker responded from a purely othodox psychoanalytic orientation, he might have in some way connected Bobby's fear with primitive desires of an oedipal nature. Here, however, the worker was operating on the assumption that the anxiety was connected, not with oedipal content, but with more fundamental fears about the integrity of the body, and its safety and durability over time. While only a context within which the worker knew this particular child would provide a knowledge of the level of meaning at which the child was struggling, Bobby's response appears to be an indication that the judgment was correct.

Why, however, should Bobby (and many others like him) have chosen to say that his penis was the part of him that he feared would come off? Why not his arm, his leg, or his head, for example? Lichtenberg (1978) suggests that certain bodily sensations are more intense that others. This intensity of sensations not only calls attention to certain parts of the body, but places them in the forefront of the individual's formation of an image of the physical self as well as of a psychological self. In the physically normal child, the sensations relating to those organs that are a part of sexual functioning could be expected to be more intense than those of most other parts of the body. The particular parts of the body that may involve intense sensations may change, however, over the course of physical maturation. This, essentially, is what Erikson (1950) has implied in his notion of the zones and modes in psychosocial development.

It is important to recognize that the physical body has a maturational timetable that is more or less preprogrammed from birth and is relatively universal within the species. Under circumstances that allow for physical health, this timetable will proceed relatively independently of the psychological development of the child. Thus the child will physically proceed to stages in which the genitalia will become of importance whether or not the psychological issues attendant to the oral stage have been resolved with any degree of satisfaction. In the adult, therefore, one does not see "fixation" at a particular psychosexual level of development. Rather one sees issues of content at all levels within a self, which itself has a particular level of differentiation and integration. Dependent upon the life experiences of the individual, conflicts over content at particular stages of psychosexual development may be more predominant than conflicts related to other stages.

It is also important to recognize that there are variations in the child's experiences with his or her body. In some children, especially those with severe illnesses or handicaps, these experiences may be atypical. Body and self images, therefore, may be as much determined by the intensity of experiences of repeated or prolonged pain as by sensations of a more sexual nature, even though sensual experiences can be presumed to be taking place at the same time. In other children life experiences with the coincidence of pleasurable sensations of a sexual nature with painful sensations of either a physical or, perhaps more commonly, a psychological nature may account for later themes of sadistic or masochistic behavior. Such a coincidence was apparent in the example of Maria (Chapter 7), who found that to have the pleasure of interaction with her father, whose tossing her into the air no doubt stimulated pleasurable sensual feelings, she also had to tolerate the pain of banging her head on the ceiling.

In summary, it can be said that the meaning of sexuality and the behavior that may be connected with it can be extremely variable, depending especially, but by no means exclusively, upon the life experiences of the individual—those experiences in early childhood that lay down patterns or themes that will be repeated in later life. Psychological development, physical maturation, and experiences in a particular environment or culture may be separable intellectually, but in the course of one's life, they occur simultaneously and therefore are inevitably intertwined and inseparable in relation to their contribution to the content of the meaning system that is ultimately constructed by the individual.

The Confirmation of Identity

*I*t has already been suggested (Chapter 6) that people like to experience feelings. The experiencing of affect makes them feel alive. It confirms a sense of existence. If, then, the earliest sensations of the neonate are those of a physical nature, it is not very strange to suppose that the experiencing of intense sensations within the body self could retain throughout life a function through which the fundamental sense of identity is confirmed. To be sure there are other means of confirming identity that rely on personality or identity structures developed in later stages of life. For instance, nonsexual interpersonal relationships and work provide numerous and constant opportunities for such confirmation. However, the experiencing of physical sensations remains as a basic alternative, which, while it does not require the more complex mechanisms of later development, may be productively utilized for the retention of a sense of identity and organization as a part of a repertoire of behaviors in the person, who has alternatives as well.

The assumption that sexuality performs a basic role in the confirmation of identity throughout life, furthermore, would appear to be in consonance with commonly observed phenomena. An increase in sexual activity following the loss of a psychologically meaningful object seems to serve the dual function of reassurance that existence without that object is possible and of provision of a potential way of reorganizing meaning structures and support systems to fill the hole in life that may have been created by the loss. It is now well established clinically that the female "hysteric" or the exhibitionistic "macho" male who flaunts sexuality in public usually has less self-confidence, in both actual sexual functioning and other areas, than does the person who may be less overtly "sexual." Clinically the hypothesis that sensuality can confirm existence of identity serves both as an explanation for Blanche's (Chapter 2) need to create for herself a scandalous reputation and as a rationale for the worker's decision not to challenge her exhibitionistic waiting room behavior. Blanche needed to be able to hold on to what sense of self she had. Another commonly observed phenomenon is a return to the overt expression of sexual concerns or activity in elderly individuals who are attempting to cope with a sense of self that is deteriorating physically and psychologically in other ways.

Since sexuality is not the only intense physical sensation experienced by the infant or young child, it is also not the only means of confirmation of existence available to the person who has developmental deficits. In cases of severe borderline pathology, pain, often of a self-inflicted nature through cutting or burning, may serve the same function. Persons with serious schizophrenic disorders frequently indicate that they cannot actually feel the physical pain accompanied by wounds, but know that they are still alive through the observation of the blood flow. In addition it is now becoming clear that one of the dynamics in some cases of anorexia nervosa or bulimia may be that the individual utilizes hunger spasms for the same purposes. Presumably the need for a fundamental confirmation of one's basic existence continues in all people throughout life. Sexuality, utilized in a manner that is socially nondestructive, may well be the healthiest avenue for meeting this need.

Mr. Norman, a 47-year-old married man with two grown children, was seen for treatment in conjunction with his request for assistance with a problem with erectile dysfunctioning. Diagnostic assessment ultimately indicated that the primary cause of this dysfunctioning was a medical one, with a base in some vascular problems. However, Mr. Norman also complained of some sense of chronic depression, marital problems, and irritability with others. He reported that he had been married for 26 years and that initially the marriage had been a happy one, but began deteriorating shortly after the birth of the second child. At that time Mr. Norman, usually regularly employed in a skilled blue-collar job, had been temporarily laid off. The resulting economic necessity led his wife to obtain a job. Mrs. Norman continued working past the time when he was recalled to work. Mr. Norman dated his initial erectile problems to this period of unemployment, but noted they had become worse over the years. Sexual activity between himself and his wife had become less satisfactory for him, and presumably for his wife as well. There had been several separations in the marriage, some of considerable duration, but the couple had reunited and remained so largely for economic and convenience reasons.

Initially Mr. Norman's worker indicated that the clinic would like to have his wife involved in the treatment as this was considered essential for providing assistance in helping them deal with the sexual aspects of their relationship. Mr. Norman resisted this idea, and when the worker persisted in the recommendation, he terminated his contact even though the medical treatment had not been completed. A few months later, Mr. Norman returned to the clinic to request the medical treatment, but still insisted that he did not want his wife to be involved. Mr. Norman did, however, agree to the idea of treatment for himself.

As Mr. Norman became more comfortable in his treatment relationship, he revealed that he had been an illegitimate child who was raised by an aunt with fundamentalist religious convictions. He had always felt rather like a male Cinderella, minus the fairy godmother and the handsome prince, in comparison with his cousins, who were the legitimate children of his aunt and uncle. Later in life he had sought out both of his natural parents but found that neither had much interest in him. Mr. Norman had left home as soon as he thought he could support himself and had married relatively young, partly as a means of securing a comfortable environment in which his basic daily needs could be met. He had been a reliable employee and a good provider for his family, but had assumed a rather passive role in all of his relationships, seemingly having assumed that he would always remain on the periphery of any important activities in life.

In relation to his sexual history, Mr. Norman indicated that he had actually never found relations with his wife totally satisfactory. As a young man, he had enjoyed intercourse with his wife, but this had not been sufficient. As a result he developed a habit of sneaking out of the house after she had fallen asleep and of seeking the services of a male prostitute from whom he would obtain oral stimulation and a second ejaculation. Mr. Norman had, however, worried about the possible consequences of a discovery of this homosexual behavior, and began to substitute isolated masturbatory activities. As his marital difficulties increased and intercourse with his wife became less frequent, these masturbatory activities increased and he acquired the habit of using a pair of his wife's panties to increase a sense of sexual stimulation.

In the treatment relationship, Mr. Norman indicated that he was interested and invested in an interaction that would make him feel less depressed and fundamentally less angry over what he perceived to have been his position in life from the time of his birth. He was also interested in continuing the treatment for his medical condition since his sexual life, while fundamentally an isolated one, was important to him. However, he had no wish to resume sexual activities with his wife or with any other person.

In consonance with other clinical data, not presented here, it was clear that Mr. Norman's sense of himself and his boundaries was not very secure or highly developed. As such his ability to utilize sexuality in an interpersonal manner was highly limited. In intimate relationships with other persons, he became too threatened about a loss of sense of self through a potential merger with the other person. In fact psychologically he seemed to function at a level at which the connection with others was preserved primarily through the concrete use of a transitional object in the form of his wife's panties. It is quite possible that Mr. Norman's need for the homosexual prostitute actually may have served as a means of reassuring himself of a sense of intactness after intercourse with his wife because of fears that this more interpersonal closeness had actually damaged his existence and separateness as an individual. Additionally it is important to note that, although Mr. Norman seems always to have utilized sexual activity as a fundamental confirmation of a sense of self in a somewhat impersonal manner, his more isolated sexuality and his erectile dysfunctioning seem to have begun at a time when his ability to confirm his identity through his work was lost to him.

Numerous psychoanalytic and other writers have described the psychological experience of orgasm as being that of a temporary merger with another person. Others have described it as an experience of a type of "temporary death" in which both the mind and the body seem to be out of control and/or nonexistent. This is experienced as pleasurable and peaceful by most people, but only if the person involved is confident that it will be a momentary and very transient experience, with other functioning and capacities returning shortly. The psychological experience of orgasm in interaction with another person and the merger it involves therefore can be risked only when the sense of the self is sufficiently sure of a return to an organized and reasonably nonchaotic state following such an interruption. Developmentally the degree of security of a sense of identity that can allow for brief but intense psychological mergers appears not to occur until some time in adolesence. This is the reason why it seems to be in the direction of the achievement of the utmost in psychological development and pleasure to suggest to adolescents that they postpone intercourse until they have achieved some degree of psychological stability.

Lichtenstein (1977), who has indicated a belief that sexuality plays a special role in human life because of its function in the confirmation of identity at a primitive level, has taken this thesis one step further. He puts forth the possibility that the fundamental conflict of identity that is experienced by all humans is one in which there is a simultaneous desire for both being and nonbeing, for existence and nonexistence, at the same time. It is in this manner that Lichtenstein interprets the value of Freud's (1920) death instinct. Such a possibility would also be consistent with the existentialist philosophy that has had considerable influence on therapeutic approaches in recent years. Furthermore it would be consistent with a theory of separation–individuation and object relations that supposes that the fear of annihilation through merger is the basic conflict of schizophrenic individuals in the need–fear dilemma. Lichtenstein has suggested that the desire for nonbeing is in fact far more defended against by most people in today's world than are sexual instincts. Loewald (1978) has approached a similar position in indicating that religion and the notion of a unity with a god of some sort are currently more repressed than is sexuality.

Whether or not Lichtenstein's thesis is fully accepted, it is suggestive of an explanation for the socially destructive usage of sexuality by some individuals. Freud based much of his theory on the observation of the apparent universality of the incest taboo in human civilizations. Current data indicate that, in spite of the powerful nature of such taboos, incest and other sexual forms of child abuse are common. Furthermore such experiences in childhood produce psychological damage which, while not insurmountable in later life, is usually quite serious. It may be asked, therefore, what is special about these experiences that makes them potentially so disruptive of growth processes and later functioning.

Rape, whether heterosexual or homosexual, is the basic confirmation of the sense of individual identity through the active, though perhaps unconscious, denial of the fundamental identity or psychological existence of the other person. It is the ultimate use of anger to affirm personal boundaries while denying boundary integrity to the person upon whom it is perpetrated. In some instances the intensity of the sensual sensation must be supplemented by the intensity of physical pain, which may be achieved through an identification of sorts with the pain inflicted upon the victim. In addition there is usually the necessity to confirm the effectancy of personal action and the separateness of the self through the noncompliance, or nonwilling compliance, on the part of the other individual. In instances where these conditions do not exist, the rapist may find that his behavior does not serve the psychological purposes for which it is intended. For example:

Mrs. Olson, whose sense of self was frequently only tenuous, had been through a particularly stressful day when she was accosted at night in a deserted area. Her assailant threatened her with a knife and announced that he was going to rape her. Flustered and confused but showing no sign of fear or anger, Mrs. Olson replied, "Oh, no, you can't do that. I don't have time for this." She proceeded to offer the contents of her wallet instead. The prospective rapist became so confused that he apologized for his intrusion and departed without the contents of the wallet. Mrs. Olson's response to the rapist, not one that would be socially expectable, did not fulfill the conditions under which the act of rape could offer satisfaction.

Many instances of incest or sexual abuse of children do not necessarily involve force or violence. However, these acts do tend to evoke strong sensual reactions in children while at the same time the seducer is usually oblivious to or unconcerned with the child's feelings. Thus the perpetrator is utilizing the child essentially as an inanimate object to be manipulated purely for satisfaction. This amounts to a fundamental denial of the psychological identity or existence of the child. Searles (1960) has eloquently documented the fact that many severely disturbed people tend to treat themselves and others as if they were inanimate objects. It is no wonder that children who have been abused often, as adults, treat both themselves and others as if they had no affective or inner life.

The Life Cycle and Its Stages

Although anatomy is not necessarily destiny in the narrow sense in which some interpretations of orthodox psychoanalytic theory have made this appear, there can be little question that the human being is indeed an organism that is equipped with certain inherent capacities and a biologically based maturational timetable. Normality—defined strictly in statistical terms as average, which may well be the only sense in which the term can have clarity of meaning—indicates, for example, that the child will learn to walk within a certain age range. On an individual basis, however, the range of deviations from that average may be quite wide. Furthermore these deviations may be determined by deficits in the physical equipment, which may have been present from birth or acquired later, may be related to limitations in the surrounding environment such as curtailments in the space necessary for practicing motility, or may result from an interaction of both physical and environmental factors.

Determining in precise terms the causes of apparent malfunctions in individual human beings repeatedly has proved extremely difficult. Such determination has often been complicated by naive approaches that have assumed single causation and have failed to recognize the highly complicated interaction of variables, which is, in fact, the case. A similar situation exists in the realm of understanding the nature of the precise differences between the sexes. Differences that may be related purely to genetic endowment are currently impossible to isolate since it is clearly demonstrable that infants are responded to differentially from the moment of birth according to their percieved sex. This differential response is not limited to parents, but includes all others in the environment. Furthermore, since science now makes it possible to know the sex of the child prior to the birth, a differential response that influences in some way the development of the child could be of potential importance even prior to birth. For example, a mother who prefers a male child might be less careful about nutritional requirements related to pregnancy if she knows she will have a female child.

In spite of the difficulties of pinpointing with any precision the exact differences between the sexes that may be related to physiologic differences, it seems likely that some do exist. Some of these differences may be related to genetically inherited tendencies. On the other hand, some of the differences will also be related to the differences that male and female children find in their body equipment. For example, anyone who has ever witnessed a male infant notice for the first time that the urinary flow proceeds from his own penis can attest to the fact that this seems to be a highly significant experience for him. It is, furthermore, an experience the female child does not have, at least in the same manner. Freud's error in this regard may not have been so much in the assumption that the body equipment was of great significance to the child, as in the assumption that the female child's development of self was determined by a sense of inferiority based on a lack of male equipment. It is much more sensible to suppose that the female child's sense of herself is determined by experiences with her own body that are different from, though not inferior to, those of the male child.

Assuming that the meaning of the child's bodily sensations is constructed actively in the mind of the child, then the meaning of gender differences to children may vary greatly within an overall norm that has been determined by social agreement. For example, in a society in which homosexuality is not accepted as healthy, a young child may find that sensual experiences related to homosexuality are not as translatable into social means of confirming identity as are sensual experiences related to heterosexuality. The absence of such responses on the part of others is then likely to cause the child to pay less attention to homosexual sensations as being of any importance. This will not eliminate homosexual sensations, but it can limit awareness of the sensations themselves and the development of a meaning system around them. In this manner a child comes to learn the "appropriate" use of sexuality within the society in the same manner as the child will learn the appropriate use of many other capacities. This is precisely Erikson's fundamental point in his cross-cultural examples in *Childhood and Society*.

Each society has role prescriptions that may or may not relate to issues of gender identity. If the society is at all attuned to the needs of its membership, these role prescriptions will vary according to individual capacities and to biological changes over the full range of the life cycle, thus taking into account not just sex but age as well. The confirmation of identity and sense of self-esteem through feedback from interpersonal and social sources would appear to be nearly as fundamental to the human being as is the confirmation of identity through the utilization of bodily sensations. Current infant research is dramatically reconfirming the importance of the social needs of the child so extensively that a survey of such research would be impossible here.

A consideration of societal role prescriptions and of the overall organization of the social context is, of course, essential for any professional whose goal is to increase social functioning. A society that requires the individual to be involved in paid employment in order to receive recognition but then does not provide opportunities for work to a significant number of persons will be fundamentally dysfunctional. In a similar sense, a society that wishes to limit the expansion of the population to ensure the survival and quality of life of the existing members will be dysfunctional if it does not simultaneously allow channels of confirmation of identity through sexuality that does not lead to procreation.. Discrimination, whether it is based on racism, sexism, ageism, or any other variable, *does* result in limited opportunities for the social confirmation of identity and, therefore, leads to individual dysfunctioning, a fact of which all social workers need to be acutely aware.

Just as clinical social work treatment will be ineffective with a physical illness such as a broken leg, however, clinical social work in and of itself will not, and cannot, cure major societal dysfunctions. This must be done by social policy experts together with various other professional groups in the society. Clinical social workers, as responsible citizens, need to participate in attempts to create an optimal fit between individual needs and the social organization.

Furthermore clinical social workers need to make available to the general public their special knowledge about the effects of social problems on individual, family, and group functioning. In addition clinical social workers have a responsibility to be involved in the planning of specific programs targeted to the membership of populations that may be suffering from social disorganization.

It may be of the utmost importance to the daily functioning of the clinical social worker to be aware that to interpret a problem caused by factors outside the client's control as a psychological problem is not only a denial of the client's identity, but is both socially and individually repressive. The possibility of such repression was illustrated in the case of Mrs. Cook (Chapters 3 and 4). It is in this sense that it is critically important for clinical workers to realize that, while they need to be aware of causal factors to ensure the selection of appropriate corrective measures, the interventions are, by and large, not intended to alter causal factors, but to foster the development, maintenance, and further growth of a meaning system through which the individual can alter his or her own behavior so as to make it more effective in social functioning.

To return to the interrelationships between sexuality and the development of the meaning system, it is important to take notice of the cognitive capabilities of the developing child at the specific points in time when important events in sexual development take place. According to Mahler (Mahler, et al., 1975), the child seems to achieve a solid sense of the two sexes and an awareness of which of these categories applies to him or her by about the age of 18 months. In a cognitive sense, the child at this time is primarily able to deal only with polar opposites as differences. It is, for example, also the age at which Spitz (1966) noted the emergence of the use of the negative in the child's insistent differentiation of self from mother. It is, therefore, likely that the existence of the two sexes and the child's awareness of these and the ability to differentiate into dualities interact with and reinforce each other in the mind of the child. For this reason a sense of a solid gender identity probably is linked in most cases with a developmental level in which object permanence and basic reality testing in the sense of a difference between the self and the other are also present.

The child at 18 months is, however, in the practicing stage, at time when, both socially and cognitively, the attention is primarily on the external world and on making distinctions and differentiations in that area. The internal world of representations through symbols is still in a very primitive state. The capacity to utilize images and thus to fantasize has not yet developed (see Piaget, 1962). The meaning of sexual differences at this stage therefore, must remain tied to the concretes of social roles in a literal, rigid, and external sense. At this psychological stage, then, sexual activity can provide a confirmation of an intact identity in the sense not just of primitive existence, but also of the fundamental separation of the self from the other. It remains, however, incapable of confirming identity in the sense of any more individuated or internal feelings.

In a similar vein, by the time of the phallic-urethral stage, the complexities of the external world are much more differentiated and the child is beginning to struggle with the necessity to problem solve in the world that involves more than just dualities. The child does not yet, however, know fully how to do this. Internal representations are present and developing, but not yet flexibly manipulable in the form of extensive fantasizing. Thus the child tends to resort to still relatively primitive mechanisms for influencing others, which may include the use of exhibitionism and power to obtain the desired sense of effectance in dealing with others. Clearly, sexual activity at this level would still be unable to take into consideration in any real sense the needs of the other person, although there would exist a need for that person in order to achieve a sense of influence.

As the capacity to fantasize develops further and can be utilized in a more flexible form to problem solve in an internal manner, as well as to imagine and cope with situations that deal with more than dualities (the oedipal stage), the child can utilize another person as a participant in that fantasy world. There is, here, far more of a sense of a real relationship with the sexual partner. However, since at this level the partnership is based on the acting out or role taking within a fantasy that is internal and individual to the person, it is essential that the partner share the same fantasy. When, in the course of the events of the daily lives of adults who have remained organized primarily at this stage, it becomes clear that the other person's fantasy may differ from the one the individual had in mind, relationship problems occur. Even at this stage, then, a full capacity to appreciate the true individuality of the other person, and therefore a truly intimate relationship, is not present.

During the latency years, a sense of competence as well as many new cognitive abilities develop. This allows the child to be able to take some distance from problem solving in the internal world and to attempt it in the external social world. It diminishes, therefore, the sense of the need for the other person to play such a puppet-like role in the fantasy life that may accompany the confirmation of the sense of identity through sexuality. Furthermore the achievements associated with this period contribute greatly to the individual's ability to achieve a confirmation of the self through avenues that may be other than sensual, and the need for reliance on a sensual confirmation of identity diminishes greatly. At the same time, this period makes it possible for the individual to achieve considerably more tolerance for the sharing of a sexual life with a partner whose fantasies may differ. This is the reason why, in working with adults with marital problems caused by a discovery that the fantasies and goals of the partners are not identical, a focus on increasing the working capacities and satisfactions from outside the marital relationship may actually result in an increase of sexual satisfaction within the marriage.

As has been mentioned previously, the consolidation of an identity that can endure over a projected sense of time and the future, along with the significant differentiation of the complexities of that identity that occurs in adolescence, makes it possible for the individual to tolerate the temporary psychological fusion with another person that is a part of a mutuality of orgasm. In addition this sense of identity makes it much more possible for the person to tolerate, indeed to appreciate, the differences in internal life between the self and the sexual mate. The ability to have a highly differentiated and abstracted affective life, which permits the comprehension of feelings in others different from one's own, is critical here.

It is, however, probably not until early adulthood when the capacity for the long-term sharing of an intimate life with a partner, including a commitment toward some shared goal in a mutually reinforcing manner, becomes possible. It appears that it is during this time that a sense of comfort with the coexistence of a variety of aspects of the self, newly differentiated and perceived during adolescence, is achieved. This comfort with identity complexity makes it possible to be comfortable with a sexuality that is well integrated within a life-style that includes many other variables, as well as to understand that some goals and aspects of the self may be shared with the life partner whereas others may not be.

The meaning of sexuality does not, of course, end with the establishment of a life partnership. Particularly in those individuals who choose to parent children, this is central to the achievement of the creativity that characterizes what Erikson has called the achievement of generativity in adult life. The content of the meaning of sexuality continues to evolve into further differentiation throughout life. It should be apparent, for example, that a major shift in life-style or life role, such as occurs with the birth of a child or the departure of children from the home, would necessitate the reintegration of the meaning content regarding the self as a whole, including that aspect of the self that deals with sensuality. In addition, of course, since no individual is likely to have fully settled all of the identity issues that may accompany ealier stages of development, these may be reworked and reorganized as life experience proceeds. It also should be emphasized that the achievement and maintenance of a lifetime sexual partnership are by no means the only route to creativity and generativity in life. Since life goals may indeed change with the course of events over time, the maintenance of an alliance with a partner is by no means evidence *per se* of health, and at times actually may be an impediment to further growth in the individuals involved.

While the content of the meaning system relative to sexuality in life does change over the course of adulthood, it is, at least at present, not possible to describe with any specificity what that content will be; beyond early adulthood this is extremely individual, based not just on events in life as seen from an environmental viewpoint, but also on the very complexity of the identity that may be achieved by those persons whose development has reached optimal levels. At present, however, it would appear that there may not be additional developmental changes in the *structure* of the meaning system beyond early adulthood. But this is a little explored area and one about which there may be much yet to learn.

A Clinical Application

Mrs. Porter sought treatment because of what she experienced as chaos in her personal life. A 42-year-old woman who had been quite successful within a demanding profession, Mrs. Porter had remained for some 15 years in a very unsatisfactory marriage, which had always been characterized by arguments with violent verbal attacks on the part of both partners. Two years prior to her entering treatment, Mrs. Porter's husband had hit her in the course of one of these arguments. Although she had not been badly hurt physically by this blow, Mrs. Porter considered this to be a literally life-threatening situation and had immediately separated from her husband. Mr. Porter had, however, continued to request a reconciliation and Mrs. Porter had been unable to give him a final and unambiguous negative answer even though she claimed that she did not love him and would under no circumstances consider living with him again. She claimed she wanted a divorce, but had taken no steps to initiate one. She could not understand why she had not been able to do this.

Shortly before the separation, Mrs. Porter had become involved in a homosexual affair with a single woman she had met through her work. Mrs. Porter indicated that the other woman had been the initiator of the sexual activities between them, but that she had found herself experiencing orgasm in a highly satisfying manner quite consistently in this relationship. In contrast, she noted, she had rarely achieved orgasm with her husband, and had never found that sexual relationship to be very satisfying to her. Thus, though she had not previously considered herself homosexual, she now decided that this must always have been the case and that it must have been a major factor contributing to the failure of the marriage. Since the separation Mrs. Porter had been living with her lesbian mate, but had found that, while the sexual relationship continued to be pleasurable, this relationship too was becoming more and more conflictual and was increasingly characterized by verbally abusive interchanges. Mrs. Porter was no longer convinced that she wanted this relationship either, but had taken no steps to end it. Meanwhile she continued to have dinner with her husband, though insisting on meeting him in public restaurants because she was physically afraid to be alone with him, on a regular once-a-week basis. She presented herself as being totally confused about what she really wanted.

A highly educated, intelligent, and articulate woman, Mrs. Porter seemed to enter her treatment with enthusiasm, feeling that it would be of great use to her. She presented a rather complete and detailed history of her background, replete with many "insights" into why she might be having her current problems. She was the elder of two daughters, her sister being three years younger. Mrs. Porter speculated that in some ways she thought her relationship with her current lover might be related to the fact that she always wanted to be closer to her sister than she had been. She recalled that as a young child she had wanted to take care of the baby sister, perhaps even wishing that this was her own child, and had been angry that her mother had discouraged such activity on her part. Later the younger sister would accuse her of wanting to control her or to flaunt the fact that she was older by being authoritarian and would refuse to have much to do with her. After her marriage Mrs. Porter had not especially wanted to have children, but had preferred to concentrate on her career. Mr. Porter had agreed with this, though at times he expressed the desire for children, and this was one of the many topics over which they argued. Mrs. Porter now wondered if perhaps she had really wanted children, but thought that her mother had given her a message that she would be a failure in this role. She talked, though in a highly intellectualized manner, about her anger at her mother over this.

Mrs. Porter reported numerous details of other childhood incidents she thought might be of significance in her current life. It appeared however, that she had actually come from a relatively stable background in a middle-class family that had high achievement aspirations for both daughters. Her father had been especially encouraging in wanting his daughters to obtain the college education he had himself been unable to complete because of limited financial resources. Mrs. Porter was 12 years old when her father suffered his first heart attack, and tearfully recalled how upsetting this had been to her. She had tried to take care of him during a period of recuperation and had spent considerable time with him. During this time, however, her father would often warn her that she should not neglect her studies on his account.

Though he recovered from the first attack, he had a second one about one year later, and died when Mrs. Porter was 13.

Subsequent to her father's death, Mrs. Porter's mother had concentrated on supporting her two daughters so that she could save enough to send them both to college. Her mother had refused to consider dating or remarriage even though both girls had, at times, expressed a hope that she would do so. Although the family was not poor and the mother's work, combined with income from a pension fund from the father, had provided enough to achieve these goals, Mrs. Porter often experienced her mother as being tired and emotionally distant from her. This was in some contrast to the mother's relationship with the younger daughter, which Mrs. Porter thought had been closer and less conflictual. Her mother was killed in an automobile accident shortly before Mrs. Porter's marriage, an incident she reported with relatively little show of emotion. At that time Mrs. Porter had completed both college and graduate school and had begun a career, living on her own. Thus, she indicated, her mother's death, though painful, had actually made little difference in her daily life.

During the first six months of treatment, Mrs. Porter seemed to be very involved in her attempts at self-understanding and reported finding the contact with her worker very helpful. In addition to reviewing her life, she talked of her current relationships with her husband and her female lover, which remained relatively unchanged. Mrs. Porter continued to have no significant difficulties on her job, at which she was quite successful. She did, however, increasingly complain of acute anxiety attacks that seemed to occur around the meetings with her husband. During these attacks she presumably would be unable to sleep or to engage in productive activity at home and was exceedingly irritable with her housemate. Her lover increasingly attributed these to her contact with her husband and began putting more and more pressure on her to stop seeing him.

Mrs. Porter at this time claimed that she herself felt relatively comfortable about her homosexual activities, but did not want anyone else to know of them. She seemed to think that to end her relationship with her husband, she would have to tell him of her homosexuality. This, she thought, was a shock with which he would have considerable difficulty in dealing. She indicated he knew that she was living with a roommate, but she thought he had no idea that there was a physical relationship involved. She was convinced that the only way to get him to understand the futility of their relationship was to tell him of her lover, but expressed herself as not wanting to hurt him that much. When she would explain her position to her lesbian friend, this woman would accuse her of being unable to face up to her own homosexuality. Mrs. Porter then increasingly began to wonder if this might not be the case, which made her even more conflicted. Was she, she wondered, really homosexual or not? And if she was, how did she really feel about it?

As this conflict rose to a height, Mrs. Porter began demanding that her worker solve it for her. Treatment, she began angrily asserting, was helping nothing at all. She had worked hard at relating all the facts of her background to the worker who must surely, by now, understand her and know what she should do. She pointed out that the worker had never really offered her anything in the way of valuable insights and that she was too distant and useless in helping her know how to solve her problems. Mrs. Porter's anger in the sessions became quite virulent. Finally she made a telephone call to the director of the clinic, insisting that she be assigned to another worker since this one was not helping her. Fortunately the director refused to approve a transfer, suggesting that Mrs. Porter would have to work out her problems directly with her assigned worker. (There was at this time an administrative decision to consider the possibility of a transfer if the situation did not improve within a maximum of two months, but Mrs. Porter was not told of this decision.)

In the session following her phone call, Mrs. Porter raged both at the worker for her lack of sensitivity and at the director for what she considered to be his bureaucratic rigidity. In the second session, however, she was considerably calmer. She almost playfully accused the worker of being a stubborn woman, wondered why the worker would still want to see her, and, sighing, said "Well, if I have to work with you, I will." She reported that she had decided to get an apartment of her own. She had informed her lover of her desire to be on her own for a while as she tried to make up her mind who she really was and what she really wanted. She had expected this woman to be angry, but instead found her to be quite understanding about the dilemma and wanting to retain a friendship.

In the weeks that followed, the sessions became filled with reports of apartment hunting, details of decorating it, and daily incidents relating to Mrs. Porter's work. Gradually there built a sense of intimacy about these reports and slowly Mrs. Porter seemed to be becoming somewhat seductive with the worker. In one session Mrs. Porter verbalized feeling that it was too bad that she had met the worker under professional circumstances since, if it had been otherwise, they might have been able to have a relationship that would surely be much more satisfying than that with either her husband or her lesbian friend and then her problems would be solved. During this time Mrs. Porter still had made no decision as to what she wished to do with either relationship, both of which were being maintained without sexual activity. However, she was also no longer having anxiety attacks and seemed to be gaining an increasing sense of comfort in living as she was.

At this point in the treatment, Mrs. Porter began talking of her mother in more positive terms. She recalled, for example, how hard her mother had worked to provide her and her sister with a good home and education after her father's death. She thought her mother must have been very lonely and tired at this time and that she must have missed her husband very much. Mrs. Porter talked of her own sadness that her mother seemed never to have dealt sufficiently with her father's death to be able to allow herself to remarry even though she was still relatively young and attractive and might well have done so. She also noted that just prior to her mother's death, her younger sister was graduating from college but seemed to have no interest in a career and was preparing to marry. Her mother had indicated to Mrs. Porter some pride in the fact that, in contrast to her sister, she had established herself in a good and satisfying career prior to getting married. She had, however, indicated a strong hope that Mrs. Porter would soon marry.

. It was at this point that Mrs. Porter came to one session in quite an agitated state, indicating that she had experienced a massive anxiety attack. However, Mrs. Porter now began recounting the story of her mother's death. It seemed that Mrs. Porter had been driving when the automobile accident in which her mother was killed had occurred. Mrs. Porter had been injured only slightly because the other car, which had been speeding through an intersection, had hit the side of the car in which her mother had been sitting. Although she was not technically at fault for the accident, she had often wondered if perhaps she might have been able to prevent the collision had she been paying more attention to her driving at the time. She recalled that she had been very preoccupied that night with some problems concerning the relationship with her current boyfriend, the man who was to become her husband less than a year later. She knew that she had been thinking of the possibility of ending this relationship and was wondering how her mother would react if she were told that Mrs. Porter had stopped seeing him. It seemed that the mother had liked this young man and had been assuming that Mrs. Porter would marry him whereas Mrs. Porter herself had not seen the relationship as being that serious and was not at all sure she wanted it to be so.

Her sister was born at a time in Mrs. Porter's life when in normal development the child is just beginning to achieve an ability to fantasize. Children at this time often utilize this budding capacity to help explain the complexities of the world and to make themselves feel better about their perceived lack of power relative to the adults in their world. Judging by Mrs. Porter's memories, it is indeed reasonable to assume that she may have wished herself to be a mother, even her sister's mother. The mother, however, discouraged this and the sister's later resentment of her attempt at caretaking probably did, as she believed, help to create in her a sense that she would be an inadequate mother. In this way Mrs. Porter denied herself the experience of having children, which, for adults, is another significant avenue for the confirmation of a basic identity with roots in the sexual experience.

Her mother, however, had not been the only one who had discouraged Mrs. Porter from utilizing sexuality as a means of identity confirmation. In early adolescence girls are just beginning to get some sense of themselves as potentially sexually attractive. When this development occurs, along with the physical changes that create conflict for most girls, it is usually of some importance that the father confirm for them that they can have attributes that could attract a sexual mate (Searles, 1959). It is likely that Mrs. Porter's ministrations to her ill father at that age had, in part, a goal of proving to herself and to her father that she could be an adequate and desirable mate without, however, raising the far-too-threatening possibility of an actual sexual relationship between them.

Once again, however, Mrs. Porter apparently experienced failure as her father, no doubt fully well-meaning, encouraged her to devote herself to her studies rather than to him. His subsequent death, and perhaps some feelings of guilt on Mrs. Porter's part that she was unable to save him, seems to have reinforced an idea that she could not be an adequately functioning and desirable female. The father's death not only robbed Mrs. Porter of the opportunity to work out this issue with him later, but also made her mother less available to her emotionally during the period of adolescence when a female role model would have been important.

It would appear that at the time of her mother's death, Mrs. Porter may have been experimenting with ways of solving the earlier issues through close relationships with women and some dating experiences with men, but had not really mastered the conflicts since she was still conflicted about ideas relative to marriage versus a career and was not yet serious about a permanent intimate relationship with any particular person. It may even have been that she needed to remourn the loss of her father, specifically in relation to the loss of his confirmation of her as a potentially attractive female. In an extremely unfortunate coincidence of events, then, Mrs. Porter had to cope with the possibility that not only might she not have been unable to save her father, but had perhaps also contributed to her mother's death, if not actually causing it. Mrs. Porter's marriage, within a short time following her mother's death, appears to have been a means of proving herself a good daughter by carrying out her mother's wishes, and of providing herself with emotional support during a difficult period of loss (including perhaps an attempt at the confirmation of self through sexual activity), as well as of repressing the now all-too-painful sense of herself as inadequate.

Mrs. Porter's marriage was doomed to failure from the beginning since it was, for her, a means of covering over or repressing a conflict that was too difficult for her to cope with. In this light it is not surprising that the arguments should have been experienced as violent—for Mrs. Porter anger had already proved to be potentially accompanied by the death of someone of great significance to her. Her fear that her husband actually might kill her when there appears to have been little reason to believe that he was that impulsive or dangerous was probably a projection on her part of a feeling that she deserved to be killed for her previous sins. At the same time, it is understandable that Mrs. Porter might have been incapable of ending the relationship with her husband since this would have reraised the issue she had attempted to avoid through the marriage, and also might have resulted in her contributing to her husband's demise should something happen to him after the marriage ended.

Apparently, as the discomfort in the marriage increased, the opportunity for a homosexual involvement could serve a number of purposes for Mrs Porter. It would provide her with some feeling of being acceptable to a female, thus mitigating the sense that she had been a disappointment to her mother and reinforcing her sense of herself as a good daughter while not directly reraising the issue of whether or not she actually killed her mother. It would be a means of going back emotionally to a situation in which there might be an opportunity to return to the "relatively homosexual" best-friend phase characteristic of the stage of development at which Mrs. Porter had been when her father became ill, and thereby perhaps a chance to rework actively the issues in her life at that time. It also would provide, of course, an opportunity to achieve a more consolidated identity as a female. This usually occurs in adolescence , but Mrs. Porter apparently had not acccomplished it, partially because of her mother's emotional distance at that time. In addition this affair seems to have taken place when Mrs. Porter was about 40 years old, an age at which most women become acutely aware that they soon no longer will be able to bear children, thus reraising the desire in Mrs. Porter to be an adequate mother to her younger sister.

If, however, the homosexual affair promised to solve some issues for Mrs. Porter, it raised others. The intimacy with another woman could not help but raise some of the problems in the relationship with her mother that had not been solved either. Thus it is not an accident that this relationship, too, became fraught with violent arguments that caused considerable anxiety for her. Mrs. Porter was now totally caught in a real dilemma. She could not end the relationship with her husband without the support of a relationship with a caring female, but she could not really tolerate a close relationship with a woman without that also becoming potentially murderous.

Within this context, then, it becomes easy to understand why it was important for Mrs. Porter to try to "kill" her female therapist through trying to fire her. It is also understandable why she was reassured and enabled by the worker's refusal to be killed. At that point Mrs. Porter seems to have been able to return to the stage she had been at when her mother had died—that is, of establishing for herself an independent life that revolved around her own apartment and her career. During this time it became abundantly clear in the treatment that another root of the arguments between Mrs. Porter and her husband had been her anger at his refusal to replicate in their relationship her image of her father. She saw her father as having a tremendous investment in her career, thus insulating her from the conflicts around her feeling of being unable to perform as a mother, a role she desired but feared because she assumed she would be a failure. In a cognitive sense, then, Mrs. Porter had been at a level at which she had attempted to utilize the partner as an actor in an internal drama without the capacity to recognize that the partner chosen might have more of a separate and individual identity than that which had been projected upon him.

From this perspective it should be clear that for Mrs. Porter the issue of whether she wished to live in a relationship that was homosexual or one that was heterosexual was secondary to other issues that surrounded the meaningfulness of the behavior in either role. So long as she had not dealt adequately with the conflicts concerning her identity and the role of sensuality in confirming that identity, she could not be comfortable in making either choice. This is the treatment issue rather than whether homosexuality is fundamentally pathological.

9 *The Structure of the Self*

Much of the content in previous chapters has been focused on aspects of the manner in which lines of development and maturation are now being conceptualized, as well as on how such knowledge is useful in treatment. A number of different lines, organized from various points of view (psychosexual, separation–individuation, affective, cognitive, moral, and narcissistic) have been formulated in psychodynamic theory. Although these lines have much in common and no doubt ultimately can be integrated with each other, such an attempt in any specific detail is beyond the scope of the present work. Furthermore the resolution of many of the current issues in such an ultimate integration will have to rest on further research into these processes as they occur in children. Such research is taking place so widely that it is very difficult for the clinician to keep abreast of it.

In spite of the difficulty for the clinician in remaining current in relation to information about the natural processes of maturation and development, this is critical knowledge. Clinical social work treatment is not a magical ritual through which the omniscient expert cures the patient. Indeed, to the extent to which it is at all appropriate to utilize the word "cure," this would have to be limited to a comprehension that clients "cure" themselves. The treatment process is an attempt to create the conditions under which impediments to social functioning can be removed and the maximal utilization of inherent growth processes can be fostered. It is for the purpose of creating an individualized favorable therapeutic environment that it is critical for the clinician to know as much as possible about the processes of development and maturation as well as about conditions that may lead to stopping, slowing, or distorting growth.

Understanding where the client is at present, however, cannot be achieved by a review of presumed historical events on any of these developmental lines. Even if it could be assumed that research had already succeeded in capturing all of the variables in the course of development (which is not the case), it would be impossible to obtain accurate data retrospectively about the multiplicity of influences in any individual's past. Instead there is here an assumption that the processes of maturation and development operate so as to build the structure of the self. The outcome of such processes—that is, the nature of the self structure—must be judged as it is observed to be functioning at the moment. It must be observed, therefore, within the interactions of the treatment process itself.

A clinician must have some conceptual system for the organizing of observations about the structure of the self and its presumed functioning. This conceptual system needs to function as a type of bridge between the presumed manner in which normal human functioning and growth occur and the manner in which the treatment system is expected to foster adaptation and growth. There is, however, no need to assume that this bridging function requires a concrete one-to-one relationship between the observational data and a specific treatment modality or technique. Indeed the clinician is advantaged if the bridge is wide enough to accommodate the possibility of a variety of means of intervention, allowing for more tailoring to the nature of the total picture of the client/worker/problem/agency/society relationships.

This chapter proposes a conceptual system for the structure of the self. It is not intended to be a formal diagnostic system in a medical sense. It is not an ordering of symptom clusters of that sort. Furthermore this model may or may not have a relationship to patterns of physiological or neurological functioning. It is not intended to record such data, but rather as a framework within which the clinician can organize psychological data that must be taken into consideration if a therapeutic relationship with a client is to be undertaken. Because human functioning will be quite different at three different levels of development of the structures of the self, the discussion will be divided into sections in accordance with those levels. However, this should not be interpreted to mean that an individual always operates only on one of these levels.

The total self may be divided into two parts. First there is what will here be referred to as the operational self—that part of the self that responds in the immediate sense to transactions with the external world. Its structure is that which underlies the current sense of an enduring identity as well as the current organization of perceptual data of both cognitive and affective natures. It represents the meaning system as it has been built to the present time, which must include, of necessity, the current recording of the meaning of past events. The operational self, therefore, would include aspects of the inner life that in the past may have been considered instinctual, sensual, cognitive, affective, and activity directing in the present. In traditional terms it might be said that this is the part of the self that has already been internalized. The level of development designated here as psychotic is primarily concerned with the basic construction of an operational self.

A human meaning system is, however, never complete. It is not possible for any person to reach the ideal in the development of such a system. Furthermore the demands, stresses, and changes of life, from both new experiences that might be considered external events and from different challenges over the course of the life span, require constant refinement of the meaning system. A meaning system that is static is, by definition, pathologic. The human being thus is constantly involved in attempts to refine the fundamental sense of self that is contained in the inner life in order to retain a sense of equilibrium, homeostasis, or adaptation. These attempts at refinement of the operational self involve the construction of new theories of the self and are located in the transitional self. The borderline level of functioning is that which is primarily concerned with the construction and basic functioning of a transitional self through which the operational self can be maintained and modified.

The third or neurotic level of functioning is primarily concerned with the articulation, refinement, and interrelationships of the substructures of the operational self which primarily determine the content of current self-understanding.

The Psychotic Level

*T*raditionally psychoanalytic theory has considered that what made the difference between psychosis and a healthier level of functioning was whether or not the individual had been able to achieve reality testing. Reality testing has been defined as the ability to know whether an impulse or a perception was originating from inside the self or from the outside. In the terms utilized here as the dimensions of the structure of the self, this can be translated into whether or not a demarcation of the boundaries of the operational self has occured. The critical question is whether or not the individual does know the self from the human other and from the external inanimate environment.

Without some at least tentative differentiation of the self from the environment, there is, quite literally, no possibility of a stable organization or of meaning. The environment, whether animate or inanimate, is experienced as composed of things-of-action that operate physiognomically as either immediate need gratifying or need frustrating for the individual. Language tends to be utilized as a series of signs or signals rather than more abstract symbols. What may pass as symbolic usage tends to be extremely concrete in the sense that the word or symbolic vehicle is fused with the object of reference. Furthermore there may be no need for any communication since there may be psychological fusion of the self with any other potential object in the environment.

In extreme instances in which there is a lack of demarcation, the sense of self must remain fragmented and/or amorphous. Thus it would be necessary to assume that such individuals must live in a world inhabited by a constant free-floating anxiety, a world in which nothing makes sense and nothing can be predicted. Hill (1955) has compared the experience of the individual with schizophrenia to the experience of returning to a parking lot after a long and tiring workday to find the car not in the space where it supposedly had been left. Under such circumstances the normal individual has a type of brief panic in which there is no way to orient the self. Hill points out, however, that for the nonschizophrenic individual, this is only a momentary experience that recedes as the person begins to form hypotheses about what may have occurred and to proceed with a plan to check these out. The psychotic individual has at best a limited capacity for such hypothesis formation and so may remain at the mercy of the anxiety.

But the question must be asked as to precisely how much the fragmented schizophrenic actually experiences this anxiety. There are some severely ill individuals who appear never to have developed the capacity to experience affects at all. Kathy (Chapter 6), for example, appeared not to know that a smile, for most people, is connected with an inner sensation of pleasure. In other psychotic individuals, it is quite clear that the experiencing of the disorganization and of a state of anxiety accompanying it is quite painfully acute. This can be observed, for example, in annihilation panic in relation to closeness/distance issues in interpersonal interactions. It appears that some people, such as Kathy, quite literally never had a very highly articulated inner life such that the self must then be experienced as a literal void or as something akin to a dead mass. On the other hand, it also appears that some people who have experienced the anxiety attendent to a disorganized state ultimately become burned out because of an inability to tolerate such pain over a sustained period. It may be that nature provides some comfort in allowing for a deadening of this sensation in time.

In the conceptualization of a notion of the demarcation of self boundaries, the theoretical analogy is a spatial one. Thus while the problem might reside in the fact that there has been no demarcation at all, it might also be that the demarcation had been faulty and is either over- or underinclusive. The phenomenon of overinclusiveness has been extensively documented in the literature on schizophrenia in terminology relating to symbiosis. Thus some other person, usually, but not exclusively, the one who has been in an early caretaking role, has been included within the self definition. Since this inclusion is actually a foreign body within the self, its existence often provides some friction and/or conflict within the self along with an attempt to eject that which is nonself. The ejection attempts may fail, however, as a result of a continuing inability to define the nonself.

In instances of overinclusiveness that result in a symbiotic relationship or a *folie à deux*, a meaning system may result, but the behavior based upon such a meaning system cannot be fully comprehended by the person because a significant part of its content derives from experiences not directly the person's own, but those of another person. Not infrequently here one may see an unconscious but quite concrete attempt to relive someone else's life (for example, the mother's) in the hope that such an enaction will provide the data necessary for reality testing and the definition of the foreign body versus the self.

Overinclusiveness in the delineation of the self boundaries generally leads to an inner life that exists, but is disorganized and chaotic within itself. This is so because the overinclusiveness usually involves a human object as part of the self definition. However, there are instances in which part of the inclusiveness is related to inanimate objects. Thus the self may be experienced as a machine or other concrete or lifeless thing. Searles (1960) has described a number of examples in which this has appeared to be the case in the group of schizophrenic patients with whom he has worked. In such instances it may be clear that the individual has some idea of the content of the self, but that this content is defined as relatively lifeless objects. Although this is, in fact, a different phenomenon, it frequently may be difficult to tell this situation from one in which there has been an underinclusion in the demarcation of the boundaries of the self, such that there is little content at all.

Underinclusiveness in the delineation of the self boundaries is evident in, for example, instances in which there is a relatively stable and enduring sense of the self, but in which a paranoid-type delusion persists. In such cases the person has excluded, on a relatively permanent basis, aspects of the self that must then be perceived as a part of the external world. It is important to recognize that this situation is different from one in which a description of projection is technically useful. In projection a quality of the self is disowned and is sent out through, over, or across an established boundary. In underinclusion the aspect of the self is not projected through the boundary. It is defined as never having been a part of the self at all.

A distinction between underinclusion and projection is clinically important to be able to comprehend the experience of the individual in relation to the urgency of the necessity to retain the distorted organizational perspective that results from the structural problems. In those cases in which the issue is truly the demarcation of the self boundaries, the person generally experiences the situation as being one in which any solution would have to involve an operation similar by analogy to pulling up the stakes of the self and shifting these to an entirely different position. Such a major move would appear to require the total reorganization of the entire meaning system for even a relatively small adjustment. Furthermore the chances of discovering that, once the stakes had been removed from the ground, it might not be possible to plant them again, would leave the individual with a permanent sense of boundarilessness, and thus in a chronic state of disorganization and anxiety. The relinquishment of a true psychotic delusion, therefore, is not easily accomplished, and challenging such a position in treatment is not likely to be a fruitful therapeutic intervention. The individual has too much to lose in the process to take a chance on any modifications.

If there are boundaries of the self in the psychotic, these are generally too rigid and impermeable to permit movement across them, such as would occur in the case of true projection as it typically has been described in the psychoanalytic literature. Projection—that is, pushing elements of the self out through or across previously delineated boundaries that remain in place—is a phenomenon that occurs in what is here considered a part of the borderline state. The psychotic individual does not experientially seem to know that movement across demarcated boundaries of the self is possible. Treatment of a psychotic individual with a delusion generally requires the reinforcement of the demarcation of the boundaries of the self such that adjustments in the over- or underinclusiveness can be made through the dimension of permeability. This can be done, but it is not easily accomplished, and accounts for much of the difficulty in treating such individuals.

It is presumably in the very early days of life that the child's first impressions of reality are formed. Although it is very difficult to know how such learning processes actually occur, it is important to have some notion of these processes. Freud's early theory relied heavily on an oral theme that assumed that the child simply "took in" or incorporated the qualities of the external world much as he or she took in the milk from the mother's breast. Unfortunately the assumptions behind such a model are not very different from those that underlie a rather simple associationist theory of learning. By analogy it can be seen that these models may be able to explain the surface actions of eating, but cannot be adequately extended to complex processes such as that of digestion, which ultimately are the crux of the problem.

Piaget's processes of assimilation and accommodation are much more adequate for providing an explanation of the infant's gradual accumulation of knowledge about the environment. However, Piaget neglected to credit the fact that the child is a social animal from the outset. The child, therefore, has two fundamental sources of feedback about the nature of reality. One concerns the information obtained through direct experience with the qualities of the environment and the other is the information obtained through communication with the human other. Both sources are extremely important to the child and both are operative from the very beginning of life. Communication between the child and the human other at the earliest stages of life is, of course, through action and affect rather than verbalization, but it is communication nonetheless. It is also important to understand that in caretaking activities in which the "good enough" mother meets the child's needs, she not only is providing the means for continued life, but she also is imparting critical information about that which is safe and pleasurable and that which is not.

Under the ideal circumstances, the two sources of feedback about the nature of reality confirm and build upon each other. The child is then able to learn how to differentiate himself or herself from both aspects of the environment—that is, the human other and the inanimate world. If, however, there is a constant and chronic disagreement between the two sources of feedback, this differentiation becomes increasingly problematic for the child. And if there is no means of confronting and reconciling these differences, then the child is faced with the classic "double bind," a situation in which the essential processing of information about basic reality cannot occur. To be sure it must be assumed that during the early days of life these processes take place around very simple issues, but they take place nevertheless. For example, the child may gather only very general impressions about the level of safety and comfort to be derived from nestling against the mother's body following feeding as well as about what this experience is like for the mother, but this is critical information all the same.

Attention needs to be called once again to the fact that the manner in which the environment will be experienced and the degree to which the information can be processed also depend on neurological and perhaps other physiological processes. The precise nature of these processes is not yet fully understood. Subtle individual differences between children in relation to mood or temperament may have major influences on the manner in which the world is experienced, is related to, and in turn responds. A determination that interpersonal psychological processes have not or are not proceeding as expected often may not provide any definitive data about causation. Psychological or psychosocial intervention may not correct problems that have been caused largely by neurological conditions. On the other hand, neurological causation in no way prohibits the utilization of psychosocial interventions in attempts at maximal development of whatever potential may exist.

The nature of reality is not initially processed or questioned by the infant. It is simply there. Since there are no boundaries between the self and the rest of the world, those qualities that are somewhat vaguely experienced as part of the environment are taken also to be a part of the self. No other possibilities are conceivable and the question is not even raised. Thus at a very primitive and preverbal level, the human being simply inherits the foundation for many of the qualities that will be perceived in the self and in the environment. The primary caretaker is, however, the major organizer of the meaning in this inheritance. Yet the inheritance itself is not solely biological, intrapsychic, or social—it is already a complex mixture of the interactions of all three. This inheritance, laid down as it is in the unconscious and later included within the boundaries of the demarcated self, is continued in action and affective patterns that may still be influential, but that may never be totally available for conscious thought, contemplation, or exploration.

It is important to note that reality—the nonhuman as well as the human environment—begins psychologically as a part of the individual and not as some foreign external element that has been imposed against the human being's will. Just as in the relationship with the human other, there needs to be some interpsychic distance in order to achieve maximal functioning, there also must be some psychological distance from the inanimate world. However, total autonomy or disconnection is neither possible nor desirable. The space between the individual and the external world, both animate and inanimate, must be shared and traversible for maximal functioning. As Winnicott (1971) has pointed out, it is within the psychological space between the self and the external world that the meaning system called culture develops.

The meaning system of the individual self has some independence of the meaning system of the surrounding culture. Thus while there is a fundamental relationship between the two, they are not identical. This is so because unless a totally symbiotic union is assumed to exist, the perspectives of the infant and the caretaker are never the same. The presumably healthy mother knows this and makes an attempt to imagine what any given experience may be like for her infant at a particular level of development so that her communications will be sufficiently close to that experience to be comprehensible to the child. She does not assume, however, that the child sees things precisely as she does. No matter how skilled the caretaker is in adapting communications to the perspective of the infant, there will always be some discrepancies between the feedback the child receives from direct interactions with the elements of the environment and that received from the human other. Such differences help the infant to learn how to draw the self–other boundaries if the differences can be presumed to be less than life-threatening in affective meaning. However, such differences must also be reconciled with each other.

The need for the reconciliation of the feedback from the two different sources helps to create the need for the development of the transitional self. This transitional self exists in the shared interpsychic space between the self and the human other. It is in this space that the individual creates a hypothesis about his or her own relationship to the environment in order to account for the data of experience. It is also in this shared space that the individual negotiates the social agreements that will dictate that which becomes "fact" about reality. It is, therefore, within this transitional space or transitional self that there exists the application of the meaning of tradition, culture, art, religion, and social organization. It is in this space that language and communication develop and perform their essential functions in life. And it is this transitional self wherein exists the potential for adaptation and the maintenance of a peaceful equilibrium between the individual and the environment.

From a purely conceptual point of view, the individual who

operates exclusively at a psychotic level would have an operational self that would be more or less organized and/or chaotic depending upon the state of progress made in the development of accurately demarcated self boundaries, but would have no transitional self at all. In actuality, of course, such a state is not likely to exist since it is not clear that a person could really survive physically without some degree of a transitional self. David's (Chapter 3) difficultites in comprehending the meaning of the check from his father is an example not only of the importance of his being able to create a meaning system, but also of the difficulty he experienced in trying to accomplish this and of the awkwardness of his attempts. It is also, unfortunately, an illustration of the highest level of adaptation of which he was capable. David experienced chronic problems in his relationships with others in his environment simply because most of the time he failed to recognize that events might have different meanings to him than to others. Under these circumstances he failed either to share his own meanings, which might have allowed others to understand him, or to ask others about what things meant to them. It is no wonder that David found himself living in a world that seemed to be depriving and unresponsive to his needs.

It was clear that, in part, David had a transitional self that was capable of forming hypotheses and checking these out. Unfortunately, however, that rather tentatively functioning meaning system could be shared only within the boundaries of his family system. It was not translatable to other social systems and thus could not assist David in transactions with and an adaptive relationship with a larger social system. Furthermore the conflicts relating to the establishment of a clear and consistent meaning system within his family were extreme. There were, for example, far too many areas in which David received messages that he simply was not allowed to raise questions. This is, of course, what he had assumed was the case when he discovered that his mother did not know of the check his father had sent him. Under these circumstances David was experiencing great difficulty in being able to utilize his rudimentary operational and transitional selves in the service of adaptation with the larger environment.

The Borderline Level

Whereas the demarcation of the boundary of the operational self is the major issue at a psychotic level, the establishment and functioning of the transitional self are the major issues at the borderline level. Some degree of permeability and flexibility in the boundaries of the operational self is essential to proper functioning. However, if the boundary is so permeable that almost anything can be allowed inside, not only can the current functioning become flooded with more stimulation or information than can be processed into the meaning system at any given time, but also the bulging self may threaten to burst its seams and thereby demolish the demarcation and the sense of any self at all. Conversely boundaries that are so impermeable that nothing can pass through them will be subject to very high stress rates from either internal or external pressures that cannot be modulated in small doses. Thus the experience can be that impermeable boundaries also may be in danger of collapse.

Probably only persons who are extremely and chronically psychotic do not function at times at a borderline level as this has been conceptualized here. It is, therefore, important to recognize that this structural level encompasses individuals with widely diverse characteristics and includes persons who might for all other intents and purposes be considered "normal." Fundamentally the person with borderline structure has boundaries that are demarcated and are relatively firmly in place. However, persons with borderline functioning are apt to behave in ways that betray a fear that the demarcation might collapse. At the very lowest levels of borderline functioning, some collapse may occur on occasions of stress. Normally such collapse is relatively short-lived, although long-term periods of regression can occur.

Tommy, a 17-year-old adolescent who functioned at a low borderline level, maintained a belief that he was inherently creative in some unique fashion. In part this belief served as his excuse for his failure to be able to achieve either socially or academically in spite of evidence that he was quite capable. A number of therapists had attempted to work with Tommy, but each had experienced active and severe rejection that was partially based on Tommy's conscious belief that if he allowed himself to become involved in therapy he would lose his creative abilities. Thus relationships with all workers were invariably quite stormy. It happened that, in an unusual period of relative calm during which Tommy and a new worker had elected to take a walk on a pleasant spring day, this worker mentioned his own pleasure in imagining pictures in the outlines of clouds. Tommy showed considerable excitement and amazement, asking, "Do you mean normal people do that too?" Tommy had believed that "normal people" were dominated by some sort of static rationality. The realization that did not have to be the case was the beginning of Tommy's willingness to participate in what became a successful treatment relationship.

In Tommy's case it was clear that what he considered to be his special creativeness was indeed his highest level of functioning. In developmental terms, however, it was still only an early beginning of the ability to imagine and to fantasize. What Tommy feared and believed to be characteristic of "normality" was in fact a more primitive level of functioning at which the meaning of reality would not be processed, but would instead simply be accepted. Tommy appeared to have acquired this picture of normality partially from interactions with a mother who discouraged the formation of operative self boundaries through a failure to recognize that Tommy's view of the world was not the same as hers. Thus Tommy had developed a practice of maintaining considerable interpsychic distance between himself and others to protect the demarcation of the self that he feared might collapse. Tommy's fundamental sense of self was thereby protected, but he was also prevented further development of the transitional self, which would have required some sharing of perceptions with a significant other.

Interpsychic space is important for the functioning of the individual. At times the operational self becomes overloaded in relation to the demands placed upon it and requires some rest or rebuilding. These demands may come from pressures originating either in the external environmental world or in the internal world of the operational self. The most obvious occurrence of a need for rebuilding is the recurring physical need for sleep. Physical illness is another example of a time when the operational self may need to withdraw to protect itself. However, social, familial, or other environmental demands including even change that has meanings presumed to be positive such as vacations or job promotions (see Overbeck, 1977) but that takes place too rapidly, may cause or contribute to a need for some restoration of the operational self. A complete diagnosis of the potentially multiple causation of a problem in the operational self quite frequently may be beyond the expertise of a social worker. Both diagnosis and treatment of a problem affecting the functioning of the operational self legitimately may require the cooperative team efforts of a wide variety of different professionals. However, the social worker's contribution to the team effort comes primarily, though not exclusively, through a knowledge of the functioning of the transitional self.

Once the operational self has fundamentally been formed, the maintenance of a sense of continued meaning and identity therein becomes the task of the transitional self. The transitional self monitors the two sources of feedback regarding the relationship of the operational self to reality, processes the newly available data into concepts or classes, and formulates hypotheses regarding the meaning of the data. One of the important things that Freud discovered was that once the operational self had withdrawn, the transitional self did not cease its labor. Thus, for example, in periods of rest through sleep, the transitional self may be carrying on through dreaming. But the primary function of the dream is not necessarily defined as instinctual drive discharge (Freud, 1900), although something of that sort may occur. Nor is the primary function that of wish fulfillment (Holt, 1976), although something of that sort also may occur. Rather the primary function of the dream is considered to be more broadly defined as the maintenance of an organizational system or a theory of meaning whereby the identity of the individual is maintained and protected.

As formulated here the transitional self serves as a kind of buffer between the operational self and the stresses of life. It increasingly takes on the organizational tasks initially performed by the primary caretaker. Some of its functioning is rather like that which has traditionally been attributed to the observing ego in that it serves to monitor the relative strengths and weaknesses of the self and the relative safety and danger of the environment. There is, however, an important characteristic of the transitional self that must be taken into consideration: it exclusively processes information that is feedback from the activities of the operational self. The transitional self does not intervene in the immediate interactions between the operational self and the external world. Its hypotheses, while they may anticipate and help the operational self prepare for the possibility of the recurrences of similar events in the future, are always about events that have already occurred. The functioning of the transitional self builds for the future, but is itself behind the times.

The adequacy of present adaptive functioning depends in large part on how well the transitional self has prepared the operational self for whatever life demands actually present themselves. Thus when one leaves work after a tiring day only to discover that the car is not where one expected it to be, it is the transitional self that permits the formation of a series of hypotheses about what might have gone wrong. The transitional self, therefore, can limit the affect of anxiety that emanated from the operational self's lack of preparedness for this event, but cannot prevent the experiencing of the affect itself. Furthermore the operational self must learn to have confidence in and to rely upon the transitional self in order for this to take place. The individual who relies purely upon immediate action not only will be more scattered in problem-solving activities, but also will be much more vulnerable to feelings of helplessness in relation to negotiating life tasks. The transitional self thus can be seen also to provide a shock absorber for the basic self-esteem of the operational self in instances of experienced failure.

The transitional self is, and must remain, fundamentally a social self. This is essential in order to retain a connection with both of the basic sources of feedback about reality. Throughout the phases of adulthood, it is the existence of the transitional self with its sharing of interpsychic space that permits the individual to experience a sense of Erikson's generativity. As an increasing awareness of the finiteness of the self develops in the later phases of life (Cohler, 1981), it is the transitional self that prepares the operational self for the inevitability of death. The person who has not had a sense of a shared self will be at a significant disadvantage in the face of this eventuality.

Mrs. Stone was a housewife in her middle 50s who sought medical treatment for a series of symptoms she experienced as extremely debilitating, but for which there seemed to be little organic basis. Mrs. Stone's children, with whom she had rather angry relationships, had grown up and left home. Although her marriage was technically intact, this too was a very troubled relationship. Ultimately Mrs. Stone was referred for social work treatment, a contact in which she related only minimally to the worker and was unable to consider the possibility of any actions she might take in her own behalf. Her communications centered almost exclusively around ruminations about possible illnesses and frequently contained the words "if I die." In the context of her treatment, it became clear that Mrs. Stone was unable to accept the fact that she would eventually die. Her refusal to allow any professionals to help her seemed a process through which she could convince herself of her own immortality through what she seemed to experience as a series of close calls in which her existence was threatened but over which she (and she alone) prevailed. Paradoxically, of course, through these maneuvers Mrs. Stone was propelling herself toward a psychotic state that ultimately did occur and in which she experienced a type of death of the self.

Since the transitional self must retain a connection with the environment in order to perform its functions, a transitional self is not possible prior to the time developmentally when at least some degree of object and person permanence has been achieved. If the individual cannot retain an image of the elements of the environment when the operational self has withdrawn temporarily from immediate inter-action with that environment, the task of the transitional self cannot be performed. It is for this reason that the capacity for representation and symbolization is the critical functional element of the transitional self.

Observations by child developmental specialists would seem to indicate that the child is able to achieve a reasonably firm demarcation of the boundaries of the operational self in the second year of life. Kagan (1983) notes that it is during the first half of the second year that the child becomes concerned with the standards of others as well as with the intactness of toys and other common objects. He interprets these findings to mean the achievement of a sense of self. In the scheme utilized here, the self is not considered to have been developed until the rudiments of both an operational and a transitional self have been achieved. This does not happen until around the age when traditionally the oedipal crisis has been considered to be solved. However, the disagreement with Kagan is definitional only.

In Mahler's terms the child in the second year is in the practicing stage in which there is a "love affair with the world." It may be assumed that one of the functions of this period of active and enthusiastic exploration is the confirmation, and therefore the firming up, of the operational self boundaries. Another development related to this period is the realization of sexual identity; thus a comprehension of the existence of the two sexes and a knowledge of membership in one of these two groups may be fundamental to a demarcation of the self boundaries. The precise interrelationship between the realization of sexual identity and the achievement of self boundaries is a technical issue that appears not to be clear at present. What is clear, however, is that developmentally the two take place at around the same time and probably reinforce each other.

It is during the second year of life that the oppositional tendencies become prominent (Spitz, 1966). Spitz, of course, supposed that this negative and often angry behavior was useful in the basic formation of a sense of self. As pointed out earlier, affects help in setting up the basic boundaries of the operational self. Anger also can help create the interpsychic space within which the transitional self will grow. Since this space must also be socially shared, however, the interpsychic space must be traversible. In other words, anger that creates space ideally should be balanced with a sense of interpersonal warmth or love that would reduce the space. An overabundance of either affect may be indicative of an individual who has difficulties with the establishment and maintenance of an appropriate space for the transitional self.

It is, of course, also during the second year of life that the utilization of language as a means of communication and of the sharing of perceptions begins to develop. Thus all of these achievements can be assumed to interact and interweave with each other in the further development of the symbolic ability that provides the mainstay for the transitional self.

CLINICAL APPLICATION

Recently there have been many attempts to refine diagnostic distinctions in the large "wastebasket" category of borderline functioning. Certainly there is no question about the diversity among the individuals who appear to function within what has been described as the broad dimensions of that development level. Viewing individuals from the point of view of the development and functioning of the operational and transitional selves seems to help in the achievement of some clarity about perceived differences within this large group. If one were describing the ideally adapted person, the picture would emerge as:

1. Boundaries of the operational self that are moderately permeable and capable of screening out information overload while admitting new data a pace consistent with the demands of the environmental pressure and the needs of the operational self.
2. Perceived qualities of the self and the primary significant other(s) that are within a range from the strongly positive to the mildly negative.
3. Interpsychic space in which the distance may vary from one moment to the next in accordance with the level of perceived safety and/or attractiveness of the immediate environment, but which is fundamentally traversible.
4. An operational self that has highly articulated elements, and an organization that is neither static nor overly fluid and that has parts that are syntonic with each other rather than conflicted.
5. A transitional self that participates in a sense of sharing with the human others in the environment and that is capable of highly abstract and symbolic functioning.
6. Although both nonessential and nonreliable as a determinant, in many cases a history consistent with the possibility that early caretaking figures were empathic but nonintrusive and supportive.

The advantage of these descriptive aspects of the self is not that they can be utilized to identify nonexistent ideal types, but that they can capture some elements of the various types of individuals within the borderline range of functioning in a manner that is related to both previous diagnostic categorizations and possible ranges or types of treatment strategies. An examination of some of the case examples presented in previous chapters should demonstrate the usefulness of the scheme in highlighting the range of similarities and differences among these individuals.

Mrs. Ingram (Chapter 6)

Mrs. Ingram communicated quite clearly that she expected both herself and others in her world to be basically pernicious in some vague manner. She appeared to have boundaries that were fundamentally highly permeable in quality, but which she protected through the consistent maintenance of considerable nontraversible interpsychic space between herself and others. Presumably because Mrs. Ingram did not employ an interpsychic defense rigidly until relatively late in her childhood development, her operational self was populated with a number of at least somewhat articulated parts. She did have some partially differentiated images of herself and of the qualities of others. However, largely because of the experienced rageful qualities of those object images, her inner life had become frozen into a static state of constant conflict and chaos.

Mrs. Ingram's transitional self had begun to develop but had not progressed beyond a fairly concrete level. Her primary difficulty, however, lay in the fact that she could not obtain feedback about reality from social resources without risking her sense of the stability of her operational self. Yet without such feedback, she also could not organize the chaos of her inner life.

This summary would indicate that in working with a woman like Mrs. Ingram, the most difficult issue probably would be in the area of the formation of a treatment relationship. Mrs. Ingram would be likely to be very frightened by such a possibility because of a potential threat to her operational self due to the permeability of her boundaries and the rageful quality of her object images. But she would also be likely to want such a treatment relationship in view of the experienced pain of the chaos in her operational self. Once a therapeutic relationship were established, as did in fact occur, it would be important not to frighten this woman with too much of a demand for interpsychic closeness. Therefore, too much direct focus on the details of her experienced affective life would be contraindicated.

Since one of Mrs. Ingram's major problems had been that of a lack of feedback about her perceptions of reality from human others, discussions within the treatment about external objects of interest to Mrs. Ingram could be expected to help develop her transitional self. In this manner the chaos in her operational self could be diminished without the necessity of placing too much direct strain on her need to guard her basic self organization and her overly permeable boundaries. Since it was known that Mrs. Ingram had a major interest in art, which must have served as an important medium for self-expression for her, showing an interest in the meaning of art objects would appear to be a natural way in which to approach the work with her. At least initially, however, a focus on the technical aspects of artistic productions might be safer than too much emphasis on their affective and expressive qualities.

Under most circumstances a woman such as Mrs. Ingram would probably be diagnosed simply as typically borderline.

Blanche (Chapter 2)

The boundaries of Blanche's operational self worked reasonably well for her except at times of stress and alcohol consumption. However, she was unable to experience her life as having meaning either for herself or for anyone else. Blanche's early life apparently had been relatively free of human others who had a genuine interest in her inner affective life or in sharing perceptions of inner experiences. Blanche had attempted to compensate for this lack in her life by reading about the experiences and lives of fictional characters. In the process she had developed a transitional self of sorts in that she could imagine a variety of possible human dilemmas and even participate to some extent in acting these out. Her world remained full of two-dimensional people, however, who did not actually have real feelings, but only acted-out roles. This, of course, included herself. Her characters remained fictional.

Blanche's transitional self was highly developed in its capacity to imagine the possible or to invent human scenarios, but she could not relate these scenarios to the content of the operational self. The transitional self failed in its function of nurturing the operational self. Blanche's interpsychic space was not traversible, but remained relatively constant and static. Thus her operational self was not threatened to a major extent with chaos or pain, but simply remained undeveloped and static. Although Blanche could imitate life, she had difficulty in actually living it. The problem in working with Blanche, therefore, would not be in involving her in going through the motions of treatment, but rather in experiencing those motions as having affective meaning. The danger would be that she once again could act out a role without actually participating in sharing perceptions of the affective meaning of those actions with significant others.

Blanche probably would be diagnosed as having a narcissistic personality disorder.

The Structure of the Self

Mr. Jackson (Chapter 6)

Mr. Jackson's boundaries appeared to be quite impermeable. There was a sense that he had had little genuine involvement with any other human being throughout the course of his lifetime. While it is possible that Mr. Jackson may have had more of an inner life than he had chosen to share, this seemed rather unlikely. Instead it appeared that he really did have a very undifferentiated inner experience and that, while he had a little curiosity about what the experience of other human beings was like, for the most part he had been able to convince himself that people who talked of such experiences were somehow imagining things that were unreal and unimportant.

Thus Mr. Jackson had firm operational self boundaries, but minimal development of an experiential component of that operational self and minimal development of a transitional self. Objects seemed to have a rather negative quality, though his inner life seemed to be fairly nonconflictual for him. He had, however, apparently achieved sufficient skill in imitating "appropriate" social behavior that he had never been directly in conflict with his environment in any major way. Mr. Jackson would be extremely difficult to treat through any methodology yet developed. He did not especially want treatment for himself and would not have sought any contact were it not for his son's difficulties with society. Experience with individuals with self structures similar to Mr. Jackson's seems to indicate that when treatment is necessary because of society's demands, an approach utilizing a total social milieu setting in which a basic relaxation of the impermeable operational boundary can occur is most likely to work. In such a setting, a focus on an active social participation coupled with a sharing of the meaning of such activities would be the approach most likely to have an effect.

It is presumed that under most circumstances Mr. Jackson would be diagnosed as having a severe character disorder. Similar personality structure has often been considered antisocial or sociopathic.

Maria (Chapter 7)

As an adolescent Maria's operational self boundaries had not yet become rigidly set in any one pattern. Thus the qualities of her boundaries could vary considerably from time to time. Maria seemed headed for a not-too-distant future, however, when her boundaries probably would be fairly consistently impermeable. At the time of her involvement in treatment, it was clear that when Maria allowed herself to become involved with another person, she could not regulate how much of that person to allow inside her boundaries. She therefore moved rapidly from overinvolvement with one person to overinvolvement with another, each time hoping to resolve her problems in some manner she could only vaguely comprehend. The fact that she preserved an image of her mother as a good object in spite of a history of abuse indicated both that Maria had managed to extract some good things from her generally very deprived environment and that she still had a sense of hope.

Unfortunately the structure of Maria's self, in both its operational and transitional aspects, was retarded in its development. Her representational capacities thus were not likely to be able to help her construct a sufficiently complex theory of her self, either to prepare her operational self for adaptive coping in the present or to protect her from severe blows to her self-esteem when the inevitable failures occurred. With her limited capacities, then, it appeared likely that she would be forced to settle for a self-protective conclusion that the environment was all bad and an adjustment in which her interpsychic distance would become less traversable and her operational self boundaries less permeable.

Although Maria probably also would be diagnosed eventually as having a character disorder or potentially an antisocial or sociopathic personality disorder, it was clear that she would probably always retain a more highly developed self than Mr. Jackson. While Mr. Jackson's early caretaking figures appear to have been primarily neglecting, thus not encouraging the taking in of any images of human objects, Maria's mother had been actively abusive, which had stimulated some impressions of external human objects, even if these were negative ones. Thus Maria's operational self and her inner life had become somewhat more differentiated than his, albeit also more conflicted. Therefore the possibilities for future constructive involvement with other human beings, within or outside of a formal therapeutic arrangement, would seem more hopeful for her.

Mr. and Mrs. Flynn (Chapter 4)

Mr. and Mrs. Flynn both appeared to have boundaries of the operational self that were moderately permeable and an interpsychic space that was reasonably flexible and traversable. Furthermore, although the qualities of their internal objects were mildly negative in some respects, they were not extremely so. In other words, Mr. and Mrs. Flynn did not have personality structures which, by traditional standards, would warrant a diagnosis involving an illness. Such people have often been troublesome to some clinicians, who expect them to behave in whatever manner the clinician deems they should through superficial techniques that are little more than advice or suggestion giving. There is even a school of thought that advocates not thinking of contacts with such clients as treatment. However, these "nontreatment" approaches frequently fail to work in the simple rational manner that had been anticipated and the clinician then feels somehow "duped." The result is often a diagnosis of something of the order of infantile or schizoid personality, which is mostly reflective of the clinician's anger at the clients.

The problem becomes that, although the environment of the Flynns had been relatively benign, it had also not been a highly stimulating one. As a result their operational selves were quite stable, but prepared only for functioning in a relatively stable and predictable environment. Similarly their transitional selves were not highly developed, but retained some qualities of concrete and magical thinking. Unfortunately life had presented them with a problem, in the form of their son's chronic and severe maladjustment, with which they were not equipped to deal. In the face of such environmental stress, they began to react by protectively creating more interpsychic distance and limiting the functioning of their transitional selves even more. In the sense that contact with the Flynns needed to be focused on helping them further develop their transitional selves and learn how to trust their own perceptions of reality even in the face of a difficult situation, it very much needs to be considered treatment.

Although the Flynns might not be considered to have typical "borderline personalities" in a diagnostic sense, they might be seen as functioning at a generalized borderline level. Clearly the treatment goal needed to be the further development of their transitional selves. Given the very real strengths of these people, however, work with them generally can be relatively uncomplicated.

The Neurotic Level

At the higher levels of borderline functioning, the boundaries of the individual become increasingly more capable of maintaining a reasonable degree of equilibrium through both a stable demarcation and a flexible permeability. Under these conditions the differentiation and integration of an articulated inner life are fostered. The concept of the self becomes more secure as its general features endure over time. This concept is also able to expand its dimensions gradually, as well as to become more articulated through increasingly refined differentiation and integration. At the neurotic level of functioning, the security and permeability of the boundaries of the self are not the major issues. At this point the construction of the self system is fundamentally complete. The primary issue then becomes that of the differentiation and articulation of subsystems within the self.

Ideals in any area of life or development are rarely attained in actuality. This seems to be particularly true in relation to human functioning. Furthermore the setting up of a "highest" level of functioning creates conditions under which such a level potentially can be utilized in a punitive manner through expectations that individuals who do not reach that level are somehow less deserving of respect than those who do—or who purport to have done so, which is probably more often the case. It is important to understand that functioning at a neurotic level in no way guarantees the individual happiness, comfort, or achievement as measured by material success or the admiration of others. Social work values clearly hold that the dignity of the human being is inherent in the organism and is not a quality that can be achieved. Experience in clinical work normally serves as a strong reinforcement of the old Greek idea that the nobility of humankind lies not in the outcome of the struggle, but in the quality of the struggle itself.

Throughout his work Freud was consistently preoccupied with the notion of intrapsychic conflict. There is some reason to believe that at times he may have seen psychoanalysis as a means whereby the conflict of humanity ultimately could be lessened. Yet the observations of human functioning that Freud's theories made possible seem to have led to the conclusion that conflict is both ubiquitous and essentially neutral. Depending upon the circumstances conflict may lead to a "regression," to a reinforcement of the status quo, or to growth through the realization of the existence of a challenge to be mastered. Neurotic functioning does not build a shelter from conflict. Instead it provides for the in-depth experiencing of the richness of life with all of its vicissitudes. Furthermore neurotic functioning does not guarantee control over the events of one's life. Rather it maximizes one's ability to distinguish between that which can be determined by the self and that which cannot be. It sharpens the individual's overall awareness of his or her own role in the drama of humanity.

In postulating the achievement of genitality as the ideal end point of development, even Erikson (1963), whose work has done so much to integrate Freud's theories with concepts of a social human being, provides a goal that may not be desirable for all individuals. Mutual orgasm, for example, may be an enriching experience, but not only is it difficult to achieve consistently in the best of relationships, but it may not even be relevant to the life-styles chosen by some. The concept of neurotic functioning as a highly differentiated and integrated inner life does not preclude the desirability of a satisfying sexual life, but also does not limit a measurement of health to that one aspect of an individual's total existence.

Mahler's work has been highly influential in recent years and she, too, has provided an ideal end point for development—that of object constancy. This concept is very much related to the manner in which the articulation of an inner life is conceived here. Because of the manner in which Mahler conceptualizes the development process and the libidinal drive, however, in her work there is some implication that at the highest levels of functioning it is necessary for the individual to love or to feel a positive affect toward the primary caretaker in early life. Mahler may never have intended such an interpretation, but clarifying this point seems important since, should this be the case, it either would preclude the possibility of those whose relationships with caretakers were essentially negative from attaining neurotic functioning, or signal that persons who had negative early experiences should strive to achieve a personal fondness for those caretakers. Fortunately neither of these two conditions needs to be the case. Rather the person at the neurotic level of functioning would more readily recognize that the caretakers were complex human beings who were themselves attempting, with perhaps variable degrees of success, to achieve an adequate meaning system in an environment that might or might not have been favorable for such a venture.

Mead (1934), whose sociological theories are well worth review in relation to clinical social work treatment, postulated that there are as many selves as there are social roles. The mature individual is aware of many aspects of the self that become prominent to various degrees in transactions with different individuals and in different social situations. In fact at times there may appear to be conflicts between the requirements of the various roles and of the selves. It can, for example, appear conflictual to perform both as a loving son or daughter and as a competent professional or businessperson. The existence of such conflicts in a fundamentally sound self structure has been recognized as the existence of "true ambivalence." The mature individual must cope with such conflicts so that a variety of discrete parts of the self can come into play as these are appropriate to the environment of the moment.

159

It is interesting that in psychoanalysis there is a term for identity diffusion, introduced by Erikson, but there has been relatively little mention of the existence of identity complexity. It is nevertheless clinically demonstrable that the neurotic person experiences himself or herself as not knowing who he or she is, not because of identity diffusion, but because of identity complexity. The complaint from the client may be the same, but the inner state to which the client would be referring would be quite different at the two levels of functioning.

In a related issue, it is common for clinicians to say that after some treatment, a client finally has come to terms with a significant other as that object "really was." Such a statement might be made, for example, about Mrs. Porter's ideas about her mother in the later stages of the treatment outlined in Chapter 8. Yet, because of identity complexity and of the necessarily limited perspective that human beings have, it is unlikely that anyone knows who he or she or anyone else "really is." The concept of a "real object" in that sense is illusionary. A more accurate way, then, of describing what Mrs. Porter is actually capable of doing following some growth in the treatment process is as seeing the possibility that mother had been a complex person, with a broader range of more articulated qualities than had been noticed before. Neither Mrs. Porter nor her social worker could know who her mother "really was" in any final sense.

10 *The Self and the Maintenance of Identity*

The maintenance of identity is the primary task of the self. Identity maintenance involves a maximal utilization of the inborn potential of the organism. Since it is assumed that the organism has what Hartmann referred to as a "pleasure in functioning," this maintenance of identity is pleasurable in and of itself and serves as its own goal. The goal is achieved through the development of a progression of increasingly more complex—that is, more highly articulated and integrated—organizational structures. Inherent in the organism is a fundamental psychological relationship with the environment, both the animate and the inanimate. Thus as Erikson has so often stressed, an identity outside of membership and participation in a social group is not possible. Neither, however, is the maintenance of identity possible without a constant interrelationship with the rest of reality. Since these fundamental relationships do exist, by definition any therapeutic intervention that contributes to the self's maintenance of its identity or the organizational capacities underlying its meaning system also increases the possibility of adaptive social functioning.

Thought as Action

*U*nfortunately too often thought has been treated as if it were a thing with substance. In this sense thought has been regarded as the opposite of action, as if these two elements were mutually exclusive. It is important, as Piaget has particularly emphasized, to recognize that thought is action. It is only through the utilization of the processes of symbolization, such as language, that thinking can lead to the production of an external thing with substance, such as the printed word. Although Freud described thought as "internalized action," he also seemed to assume that thought preceded action, at least in the sense of an unconscious with content that had motivational consequences and of an image of the rational person as behaving in accord with a scientifically verifiable reality. Today it is quite clear that since thought itself is composed of action patterns, thought with specific content must develop out of initial primitive action schemata.

The primary unconscious of the individual is related to actions and events that occurred prior to the time when the capacity to organize and categorize meaning was possible. Infant observations and studies make it clear that the events of the first year and a half or so of life, prior to the basic formation of the operational self and its boundaries, are in many regards critical for later functioning. The infant seems to engage in attempts to construct a meaning system soon after birth. Later in life, however, the individual has no direct access to these events since they have not been organized into a representational memory system. It is important to understand that the primary unconscious does not come into being because of repression due to the primitivity of instincts. It comes into being because of the lack of a functioning meaning system within which to record the data. In spite of the fact that interactions with the environment at this early age are not recorded as content in a representational memory system, these interactions do have significant influence on the basic shaping of the primary patterns of action and affect that underlie thought. Since these patterns are the foundation upon which the operational self will continue to build, they will influence behavior for the rest of the individual's life.

The human environment is exceedingly rich in information that might be recorded in the memorial system. It is, of course, not possible for the individual to pay attention to everything. Selective perception, therefore, means that from the outset of life, and throughout its duration, each person will have been exposed to far more than he or she may realize. For example, young children may not know details of their parents' political opinions, not because they have not heard them discussed, but because they have not yet acquired a system of meaning within which such discussions would seem important. The child thus is quite likely to "tune out" such discussions and pay attention to other things that may be occurring simultaneously in the environment.

Other available data may not be recorded because the individual does not recognize that the data have any meaning. Piaget's explanation is that a person can assimilate data only into preexisting schemata. Thus the person may ignore masses of data that the cognitive structure has not been prepared to receive. These data may have, in fact, no recording in the memory system at all—even in an unconscious sense. Therefore, not all of the events that take place during the early months of life will be influential in the modification of basic action patterns. It would be, of course, quite impossible for the individual, or therapist, to know with any certainty which specific early environmental transactions may have been influential and which may have gone by unrecorded.

Not all of that which has been considered unconscious is acquired during the first 18 months of life, however. The existence of a meaning system that makes conscious thought a possibility does not guarantee that all events will be recorded therein. This remains true throughout life, even if the meaning system itself is a quite sophisticated one. Any single life experience, therefore, may have no effect on the meaning system, or it may simultaneously affect any or all existing levels of organization from the most primitive unconscious action pattern, through fantasy (which may be either conscious or unconscious), to highly abstract conscious and analytical thinking. In this manner the unconscious memory fund is growing throughout life.

While recognizing that there may be several levels of organization of the meaning system, it is important to understand that there are several different types of situations in which an individual may come to have limitations upon his or her consciously available fund of knowledge. There is such a thing as simple forgetting. For example, the social worker who had been a good student in a calculus class in college is, after a few years, likely to find that the knowledge acquired in that class is no longer available. Social workers rarely need calculus in the performance of their daily work and a failure to exercise the thoughts involved in that knowledge arena eventually will lead to their loss. The material may be relearned with more ease than it was initially, but it probably will need to be restudied in some detail.

In addition to passive forgetting, there also may be an active exclusion from the conscious memory system because of the affective significance of a particular piece of information. This would be what Freud meant by the defense mechanisms of repression, denial, and isolation. Mrs. Porter (Chapter 8), for instance, seemed unaware of the significance of the particular circumstances of her mother's death. It was not that, had one known to ask her about the details of her mother's death, Mrs. Porter could not have given these. She had failed, however, to integrate these details into the meaning system of her own theory of herself because of the intensely traumatic and disorganizing nature of the potential meaning. Thus the details of the death remained somewhat isolated in the functioning of the operational self and were, in fact, rarely actively recalled.

In yet another circumstance, data may never be recorded in the memory system because the individual may avoid any situation in which information related to a particular subject might be encountered. Orthodox psychoanalytic theory has utilized this explanation for most cases of learning disability, and it can be shown, in some instances, to have been the problem. Tommy (Chapter 9), for example, essentially avoided further learning in school in large part because he consciously believed that such learning would rob him of his cherished kernel of imagination rather than that it actually might help him expand that imagination. It is important to remember, however, that although some type of avoidance or denial may be the cause of a learning problem, there also can be a number of other causes, some of which may be neurologically based.

Orthodox psychoanalytic theory rested on a foundation in which influences from unconscious fantasies were fundamentally responsible for the determination of most behavior patterns. Freud linked his idea of repression, which was the element essentially considered to be a part of all defenses, with a notion of a meaning system in his article on "The Unconscious" (1914b). There he noted that what made the difference between something that is conscious and something that is not had to do with whether or not the idea of a thing was connected with a word. In Freud's day linguistics and an understanding of the symbolic capacity had not developed to the extent it has at present. Thus it is now possible to outline a somewhat more complex comprehension of the functioning of the unconscious and memory systems that has different assumptions than those Freud utilized, but is nevertheless not entirely different than what he seems to have envisioned.

Although repression can be understood in linguistic terms, Klein (1976) has taken a broader and seemingly more useful viewpoint of this concept. Klein claims that it is not inconsistent with Freud's thinking to consider repression to be simply a "limitation of function." In this conception repression would include not just the avoidance of behavior in terms of internal thinking, but in terms of external types of action as well. Repression, as the fundamental of pathology, then would be seen as anything that interfered with the development and utilization of the maximum potential of the organism as a whole. Repression could be anything that prevented the achievement of a very highly developed meaning or identity system.

In a position with some similarities to Klein's, Rose (1974) has pointed out that analysis can be utilized as a defense against life itself. He argues essentially that it is possible to utilize in a somewhat obsessive manner a constant fruitless examination of the various possibilities of inner life at the expense of taking any type of risk or action in the external living situation. This type of repression inadvertently can be encouraged by therapists so long as one assumes that thought with content precedes action and is more rational than action, as well as that pleasure, and presumably normality, equals a state of rest or a lack of tension.

Mr. Hernstein (see Chapter 5) was a highly intelligent and well-educated man who had spent many years in analysis. When seen individually this very articulate man seemed initially to be the picture of mental health. He could discuss in great detail his own perceptions of any situation, always including a wide range of his inner thoughts and feelings. Therefore, it seemed reasonable to agree with him that the severe problems in his marriage must be due to the pathology of his rather pathetic wife, whom he saw himself as having tried to help over a period of some years. When seen together with his wife, however, a very different picture of Mr. Hernstein emerged. Each time Mrs. Hernstein would try to get her husband to commit himself to some course of action, he would reply "I don't know. I haven't analyzed that yet." It did not take long to recognize that Mrs. Hernstein's rage at her husband was not solely the expression of some earlier unfortunate deprivation in her life, but had some connection with his current behavior toward her.

Health, as envisioned by Rose and as it is being considered here, instead presumably would be characterized by some reasonable balance of action in the internal world of contemplation and action in the external world of the environment. In another of his works, Rose (1980) has also suggested that the integration of all action into a meaning system is of importance. Indeed he has suggested that the opposite of repression should be considered to be, not sublimation, but abstraction. It would appear that fully adaptive human functioning may involve a constantly repeating cycle in which there is activity in the external world (carried on through the operational self), a contemplation of that action (carried on primarily in the transitional self, but then related to the contents of the operational self), and a repeated action by the operational self.

Just as there are several different ways in which information may fail to become a part of an organized conscious meaning system, there are also several different ways in which the recall of information may occur. There is a type of memory that frequently has been referred to as "enactive." Such memory is fundamentally unconscious and involves action patterns that have not been integrated into a representational system. As such these action patterns cannot be utilized by the individual as a part of thinking process that involves content. However, these patterns do have an effect upon behavior. Perhaps the most obvious example of enactive memory may be that of anniversary reactions in which a person may find himself or herself in a mood and carrying out behaviors that may be appropriate to an event that occurred on that date in some previous year. Yet the person may have no conscious awareness of the significance of the date, or perhaps of the fact that the event that took place on that date had a significant effect on that person.

There are, however, other related situations in which one sees the expression in action of potential content that has not been recorded into a more developmentally advanced representational system.

Edgar, a boy in late adolescence, was referred with his family by their lawyer for evaluation and possible treatment after Edgar's involvement in several serious robberies. Edgar acknowledged his guilt and could describe the robberies in detail, but had no explanation for why he had done this. It did not appear to be a matter of much concern to him. His parents had no explanation either and saw things as fine at home, but literally could not describe in affective terms the nature of family relationships. Edgar could only say that he wanted to leave home and live on his own. His parents indicated that they did not care whether he left or not, only that he not disgrace them in the community, regardless of where he lived.

After a number of frustrating and apparently futile attempts to get the family members to talk and to relate to one another, the social worker asked Edgar to place himself and his family in the interviewing room according to how he saw them in relation to each other. Edgar carefully put all members of the family at one end of the room and himself in a corner at the opposite end. Commenting that he had separated himself from the others, the therapist asked Edgar how it felt there. Edgar pointed to the running air conditioner in front of which he had positioned himself, and said "cold." He seemed genuinely surprised at the social worker's comment that cold might also have something to do with his feelings about his relationship to his family.

Edgar's "feeling system" could be expressed through actions. He had a language vocabulary, but the two seem not to have been connected for him. Therefore, his inner life was not accessible to conscious deliberation or consideration, but remained embedded in more primitive mechanisms of action patterns and enactive memory.

In addition to enactive memory, there is evocative memory. This has sometimes been considered a "passive" rather than an "active" memory system in that the individual may not be capable of directly recalling content from this system by pure will, but if there are reminders in the current environment that are associated with the content of the memory system, then recall may occur. This type of memory seems most frequently to involve events the meaning of which were integrated at the level of fantasy or imagery systems. It is a somewhat more highly developed form of memory.

Mrs. Allen's case (Chapter 4) illustrates the utilization of both enactive and evocative memory as well as representational memory. Her fingering of the ring was an action pattern that in and of itself probably had some meaning for Mrs. Allen, and that served as a form of primitive communication to the worker. However, the meaning of the friendship rings to Mrs. Allen also seems to have been determined by an unconscious association to the meaning of the baby ring. The recall of the meaning of the baby ring was based upon evocative memory since, once Mrs. Allen had been reminded of the presence of the baby ring, she was able to make a connection the worker could have known nothing about. Once this connection had been made, Mrs. Allen could then proceed to call upon data from her conscious representational memory to interpret for herself the meaning of the friendship rings. Another example of evocative memory in treatment is that of Blanche (Chapter 2), who appeared to recall the significance of all of the extended family and friends who were a part of her childhood only when she had become a part of a parents' group.

Events that have been recorded in the meaning system at a fully symbolic level utilizing language normally will be more available through simple forms of direct representational recall. In other words, they will exist at a conscious level of the mind. This does not, however, guarantee that all of the possible meanings of such occurrences will have been recognized. For example, a person may have an image of a parent as weak in relation to a particular event but as strong in relation to another particular event. If a person functioning at an essentially borderline level were to become aware of a potential contradiction here, that person might have to deny the reality of either one or the other perception—an operation Kernberg has called splitting. On the other hand, contradictions in the parental image may continue to coexist without any recognition of the inconsistency or raising of such questions. A person with a capacity to utilize representational thinking at a neurotic level may be able to solve the problem of the apparent contradiction by considering the possibility of greater complexity in the parent's personality such that the questions "Weak in relation to what?" and "Strong in relation to what?" become possible. Thus representational memory is essentially what makes identity complexity possible.

The Role of the Human Other in Internalization

A n understanding of the nature and construction of personality structures is at the crux of an understanding of how treatment works. Yet this is an area that has been marked by theoretical confusion from the very beginning of psychoanalytic theory. In even a superficial review of the writing surrounding this topic, one encounters an array of concepts related to incorporation, introjection, primary and secondary internalizations, projections and externalizations, imitation, and indentification, to say nothing of defensive and adaptive identifications as well as narcissistic, self, id, superego, and ego identifications. Various writers have used these terms with quite different meanings, sometimes without specifying their own definitions, and sometimes with apparent failure to recognize that usages varied and contradicted each other.

There are a variety of reasons for the extensive confusion regarding the manner in which the structures of the personality develop. One of the major reasons for the multitude of concepts has been a recognition of the fact that the interactions of the person with the environment have fundamental differences at different levels of symbolic capability. Thus the process of further development is qualitatively different for children at different ages and for adults. Furthermore it may be quite different for two individuals, both of the same age, but who have had varying successes with the tasks in previous stages of life. In general, however, there has been a recognition of varying stages or levels and attempts have been made to encompass these in the theory.

Relatively speaking, there may have been more neglect of the complexity of the roles that the human caretaking other plays in the development of the offspring. At one extreme the theory has almost assumed that the female of the species, simply because of her biological inheritance, should somehow magically and globally know how to perform as a "good enough mother," whatever that may be. At another extreme there have been numerous attempts to educate mothers into ways in which they "should" perform as mothers, with most of these models being insufficiently complex and flexible so that those parents who followed the models in concrete and literal terms frequently found themselves ending up as "failures" in spite of considerable effort to do otherwise. Additionally until relatively recently there has been little organized attempt in psychoanalytic or other "clinical" spheres to deal systematically with roles, influences, and potential contributions to adaptive development on the part of fathers, siblings, or other members of the extended family or social milieu.

This criticism remains valid in spite of the pioneering and often beautifully articulate work of such individuals as Escalona (1968), Brody (1956), Bowlby (1969), Spitz (1965), Mahler (1969), and Fraiberg (1977). On the one hand, there is a need for much more information about the interpsychic dimensions of development; on the other hand, there is a serious need for more sophisticated ways of integrating the observational data from such studies into theories of treatment. There is at present a sense that the potential utility of developmental understanding in a comprehension of the dynamics of treatment is just beginning. There is probably a wide range of conceptual ways in which developmental data and treatment processes can be interrelated that have not yet been discovered. It is, however, quite clear that a translation of the characteristics of a childhood developmental stage into the characteristics of adult functioning in a concrete manner as explanatory variables is grossly insufficient.

In early infancy the human other serves at least four distinct psychological functions for the child. These are apart from but interwoven with the physical functions without which the child could not survive in a physical sense. Yet without the psychological functions, the child would not survive either. The four functions are: (1) as the psychological organizer of the environment with which the child is initially fused in a global and undifferentiated manner; (2) as the provider of feedback about the qualities of the self, the nature of the environment, and the interrelationships of the two; (3) as a thing-of-action in the external world of action and interaction; and (4) as a sharer of perceptions of the external world.

Obviously these functions do not take place independently of each other in specific behaviors, but are highly interconnected and are probably occurring simultaneously most of the time. It is important to realize that the human being never outgrows the need for other humans to fulfill these functions. What seems to shift at different stages in life is the relative primacy of need for different functions and the degrees of flexibility with which these functions can be met by different individuals. However, there is probably an infinite number of variational degrees to which different significant others may participate in these roles, as well as an infinite number of various degrees to which a child may respond interactionally. When combined with a recognition of the changing character of other environmental factors, these conditions account, along with variations in inherited physiological and/or neurological capacities, for the production of human individuality.

PSYCHOLOGICAL ORGANIZER OF THE ENVIRONMENT

This is the relationship that Mahler (1969) has identified as that of infantile symbiosis and included in her theory as an early stage in development. There is little question that in early infancy the need for the human other to function in this fashion is great, and that it normally diminishes considerably as the child matures. It is, however, an error to suppose that the "normal" human being ever outgrows the need for a symbiotic mode of relating to the environment, both animate and inanimate. Prior to the time of the establishment of basic self-other boundaries, this may be the primary mode of relating and may be engaged in fully with only one other human being. Thereafter a symbiotic mode of relating will ordinarily continue, potentially with a range of significant others and for varying periods of time, some of which may last for no more than a few seconds. Furthermore in adulthood experiences of group "mergers" are not uncommon.

Although the primacy of anxiety as the initial affect and the need for a stimulus barrier have been exaggerated in some of the early psychoanalytic literature, the importance of the soothing effect of a psychological fusion with the environment in the early stages of life (and at times thereafter) should not be underestimated. Such soothing probably initially derives from the appropriately timed, and therefore empathic, physical ministrations of the caretaker and from moments of pure physical closeness during periods of relaxation in which even the back-and-forth motions of breathing become coordinated. The comfort of such psychological union, also seems to be communicated across physical space in the utilization of the eyes and through the soft but enveloping tones of the mother's voice. It seems likely that much of the early babbling of the child may be an attempt to provide himself or herself with the same reassurance that comes from hearing the mother's voice.

It is important to understand that symbiosis is not limited to relationships in which there is or has been physical or sensual contact. To be sure the existence of some sort of sensual contact may heighten the intensity of a merger experience, as in moments of sexual union, or even of the sense of fundamental peace with the universe that may come during a moment of relaxation in the warmth of the sun. But pure physical closeness or contact in no way guarantees the experience of psychological symbiosis, nor does its absence prevent it. Brief merger experiences throughout life seem to function as very primitive and basic ways of confirming identity and existence. However, the permanent or prolonged fusion with another person generally becomes a type of death through the loss of individual identity and the production of a psychotic state. As such these experiences have tremendously powerful effects that may be both desired and feared.

Merger experiences commonly leave the nonpsychotic participant with a sense of a psychological high. Renewed energy and creativity frequently accompany the experience. For that reason some revivalist religions, and indeed some popular but faddist therapies, thrive on the dramatic production of these experiences. Unfortunately many of these religious or therapeutic groups pay no further attention to the translation of these experiences into the routines of the daily lives of the individuals involved. Thus tremendous numbers of persons have actually been psychologically damaged through the utilization of techniques that induced a sense of unity with humankind or the world in general through undermining the stability of the boundary of the operational self. While merger experiences in later life may contribute greatly to psychological growth, they can do so only if the experience itself is relatively short-lived, and if at least some parts of the qualities of the experience can later be processed through a functioning transitional self. A prolonged return to a fused state is a return to a basically psychotic mode of functioning.

Some of the basic qualities attributed to the self and/or to the world in general are not actually constructed in Piaget's sense, but rather are acquired or imprinted into unconscious action patterns through merger experiences. Much of this unconscious material comes from the days of early infancy, but it is continually supplemented by fusion experiences throughout life. This internalized material is not normally accessible to conscious attempts at recall, but may play a prominent role in shaping behavior in the form of enactive memory. The content of this primary unconscious will include material that is primitive in an instinctual or bodily sense. Primitive material, however, is by no means all of the content of the unconscious. Furthermore the unconscious may include some aspects the individual may find painful or unpleasant to know about himself or herself. On the other hand, much of it may be quite a pleasant discovery. In any event the individual whose functioning is in harmony with these unconsciously acquired aspects of the operational self is likely to be much more productive. The primary unconscious is not automatically an enemy, and most commonly serves as an invaluable friend.

PROVIDER OF FEEDBACK

The human other is, from the outset, a major provider of feedback about the qualities of the self, the nature of the environment, and the interrelationships between the two. In the very early stages of infancy, this feedback frequently will take place through primitive action and affective patterns. For example, a mother who is tense or anxious will communicate these affects as appropriate assessments of the environment while one who is happy and relaxed will communicate a different attitude. While the infant will have only global and very indistinct ways of understanding these communications, they nevertheless will have an effect upon that infant, his or her state of comfort with the world, and his or her assumptions about the self.

The nature of the feedback from the human other not only will provide information about the inanimate world, but also about the nature of the self. Thus the child will be most likely to come to think of himself or herself as having the qualities that are most frequently identified by the human other as attributable to the child. In other words the human other provides a "mirroring" function for the child in the senses that both Kohut (1971) and Cooley (1956) have outlined. The feedback received in this interchange will have considerable influence on how the individual comes to view himself or herself in relation to issues of competence and self-esteem.

Throughout life feedback from the human other is of major importance in the capacity of the individual to make conscious, and presumably adaptive, choices for behavior. As the individual matures, this feedback is received from an increasingly wide variety of human sources. Prioritizing the weights that will be given to information from different sources can be a problem. However, even more fundamentally there will be great differences in the ability of the individual to utilize any human feedback at all. The capacity to process information through the transitional self, and ultimately to integrate it into the operational self, will depend upon the state of the self boundaries, the relative stages of development of the two parts of the self, and the degree of interpsychic space that exists at any given moment.

As indicated in Chapter 9, each individual tends to have a range of interpsychic space within which he or she tends to function. For some individuals this range is relatively limited; for others it is quite wide and flexible. In addition the degree of interpsychic space that exists at any given time depends not only on the overall quality of the relationship with the particular person or group, but also on the nature of the affective climate within that relationship at the moment. The monitoring of interpsychic space is normally done, of course, in accordance with how secure the boundaries of the operational self are experienced as being.

There are, then, at least three different conditions that may negatively impact upon the overall ability of a given individual to utilize feedback from the human other. There may be an environmental failure, in which there is an insufficiency of feedback because of a lack of human others as providers. There may be a physical reason why the particular individual cannot process feedback as well as others. Finally, the early human environment may have been perceived as being so pernicious as to encourage the premature formation of impermeable boundaries of the operational self and the setting up of a pattern of rigidly held interpsychic distance such that input from others is typically resisted rather than evaluated and integrated.

A THING-OF-ACTION IN THE EXTERNAL WORLD

For the infant the human other is not initially fully distinguished from the rest of the environment. Infant research is increasingly demonstrating the neonate's ability to respond differentially to significant human others. While this is assuredly the case, the human being also plays a role in which that person is simply another object, not yet considered to have feelings of its own, upon which action can be taken. Babies may experiment with hitting, kicking, biting, pulling hair, and a variety of other acts of miniviolence with essentially no comprehension that the object of these acts might in any way object to such treatment. In these early explorations of the world, the child is merely testing out a capacity to manipulate the environment and the child's powers of effectance (White, 1963). The human other is treated very much as part of the inanimate world. In interactions with the human being as a thing-of-action, the child receives direct feedback about his or her effectiveness in the world in the same manner as in his or her interactions with inanimate objects.

Humans, of course, behave differently than purely inanimate objects in that they can and do respond with movements initiated by their own independent motivations. Such reactions may cause these objects to be more attractive as objects over which to gain some sense of ascendancy and power. Furthermore the existence of independent movements no doubt assists in stimulating awareness of separation. Increasingly, of course, the normal child learns that animate objects have both affective systems and physical sensitivities. But there can be little doubt about the fact that at times throughout life all human beings continue to relate to others as if they were in fact devoid of human feelings; that is, they simply utilize others as things-of-action upon which manipulation skills can be tested. Searles (1960) has pointed out that treating the self as if it were an inanimate thing is also common.

The manipulation of another human being for the purpose of testing out one's own skill in doing so may not necessarily involve any hostile or destructive intent (Parens, 1979). Indeed it may cause no harm at all, and can lead, in fact, to improvement in the human environment. Much "altruistic" behavior is partially based on attempts at testing the power of one's ability to affect the environment, both animate and inanimate. In general, however, social workers and other members of the helping professions have tended to think of this type of human interaction as pathological and not to recognize its prevalence and potentially constructive results. These constructive results, however, probably depend on the simultaneous recognition of the existence of feelings in others. Individuals who continue throughout life to fail to recognize the existence and extent of affective systems in themselves and others are deeply deficient individuals who frequently will be destructive to those around them.

There may be many reasons why social workers have failed to pay sufficient attention to the possibility of a relationship with a human other as a "thing-of-action," including an idealistic attempt to deny the extent of the exploitive potentiality and actuality in human relationships. One other reason for a failure to pay much attention to this type of behavior may be that it has been thought to have limited usefulness or place in therapeutic relationships. Behavior in which the external world, whether animate or inanimate, is merely utilized as a thing-of-action does not lead directly to internalization (Werner & Kaplan, 1963). However, the utilization of another human being as a thing-of-action may be a part of an enactive memory pattern that subsequently can be contemplated, thus making it conscious.

A SHARER OF PERCEPTIONS OF THE EXTERNAL WORLD

Werner and Kaplan have pointed out that in order for there to be development of the capacity to symbolize, the infant must shift his or her basic attitude toward the external world as a thing-of-action to that of an object-of-contemplation. This contemplation is here considered to be a function of the transitional self, not of the operational self. The sharing of perceptions of an external world, therefore, is presumed to occur only to a minimal extent during the earliest months of the child's life and begins to become prominent only after there has been some self–other differentiation. It is through the sharing of perceptions with human others that most internalization takes place. As the child develops a distinct and separate inner life, it becomes possible for the object-of-contemplation to be that of the inner life as well as of the external world. At the higher levels of development, the contemplation can be shared with an imaginary other or within the self. However, the human being never outgrows this need for interpersonal sharing and most internalization and learning occur in a social context.

The sharing of perceptions in a contemplative sense takes place normally between two (or more) transitional selves. In most healthy sharing, there is a recognition that the perceptions of the external world are not precisely the same. However, in spite of the fact that in a technical sense there are always differences in the points of view of two different human beings, there are commonly pulls toward fusion and therefore attempts to deny or ignore differences. Thus the experience may be that the perceptions are identical—that the transitional selves are merged. Such mergers of transitional selves are part of normal everyday experience and are normally experienced as pleasant and comfortable, but without the powerful intensity of the merger of two operational selves. The strain on the boundaries of the operational self thus is considerably less. It is the merger of transitional selves that provides us with the ongoing sense of participation in a human community.

In normal human interaction, there are also times when there is a clear recognition of the differences of perception between individuals. The development of the capacity for object relations can be viewed as a gradual increase in the ability of the transitional self to process these differences—from the polarity or splitting of the severely borderline individual to the comprehension of complexity characteristic of the neurotic individual. Under normal conditions the growth of the transitional self is stimulated by its exercise. The regular back-and-forth movements between mergers and differentiations of transitional selves in the context of an ongoing human relationship are a major part of what promotes healthy, adaptive social functioning. It is for this reason that long-term intimate relationships with other human beings are healthy.

Just as in the utilization of feedback from the human other, the ability to share contemplative perceptions will depend on the state of the self boundaries, the relative stages of development of the two parts of the self, and the degree of interpsychic space that exists at any given moment. In fact it is legitimate to wonder if there are differences between the human other as a source of feedback about the self and as a sharer of perceptions. In many ways these functions are similar, but there are at least two important differences. First, the human other may actively provide feedback that is never contemplated. This may happen because of nonparticipation by either of the two parties. Second, while the object-of-contemplation may be that of the self or of an affective state, it may also be a part of the external inanimate world. Of course, in the sense that the transitional self maintains a relationship with the inanimate world, to contemplate the external world is to some extent also to contemplate the self.

Minicycles of Action Underlying Maintenance and Growth

A human meaning system is never complete and an identity that is static is by definition pathologic. Changing external conditions demand constant refinement and reorganization of the structures of the individual. In addition, of course, adjustments are necessitated by changing demands and needs in the progression through the various stages of one's life. As a result identity must be constantly redefined and reorganized and the underlying meaning system must be constantly exercised simply to remain, relatively speaking, in place. As the basic identity system continues to function in order to maintain itself, however, the possibility of additional growth is always a possible outcome. Thus, although Maria (Chapter 7) knew that she could not have her mother's love in the way in which she wanted it, she carried on a search for another woman who might more completely meet her needs. Although Blanche had declared herself to be beyond help, such proved not to be the case. The attempt at growth is, of course, a part of the "pleasure in functioning" and the push toward the utilization of maximum potential that is presumed to be an inborn characteristic of the human being.

The circumstances of life are such that the human being never faces precisely the same situation twice. Thus the challenge to meet the new is an everyday occurrence even though the differences between events and situations from one day to the next may be quite small. As indicated in Chapter 9, it is the operational self that determines the interaction with the environment in the present. The operational self can do so only to the extent to which its various facets have been developed up until that time. Thus, for example, in coping with Patrick's bringing *Mad Magazine* to the dinner table, Mr. and Mrs. Flynn (Chapter 4) had to rely on expectations that he would respect parental authority even if he were angry at them. When he did not conform to these expectations, their range of choices for other problem-solving behavior was limited.

Once, however, the immediate interaction with Patrick had taken place, the Flynns' transactional selves could come into play in an attempt to evaluate what had happened and gone awry. Here the feedback about the effectiveness of their attempts at parenting came directly from interactions with Patrick, although they were also receiving feedback from the school authorities that indicated that Patrick was not progressing well there either. In the Flynns' meaning system, the feedback they received from these interactions with the environment meant that they were not able to function as good authority figures. Other options for meaning were not conceivable to them. They were threatened with images of themselves as inadequate and powerless children. Such a meaning caused their transitional selves to evaluate conditions as potentially dangerous.

When the transitional self evaluates conditions as potentially dangerous and the transitional self is overwhelmed, as occurred in the case of the Flynns, the tendency of the transitional self is to pull back into the operational self in order to buttress the boundaries of the operational self and to protect the integrity of the fundamental organization of meaning within that more primary structure. The Flynns, therefore, created more interpsychic distance between themselves and others in their environment, utilizing a disguised anger to do so. In this manner the Flynns became even less capable of processing feedback than they normally would have been. This diminution of capacity was the result of the attempted isolation from participation in the sharing of perceptions of reality—a form of repression, in Klein's terms, since it can be seen as a means of adaptation through limitation.

In classical treatment terminology, it might be said that the Flynns had regressed in the face of environmental stress. Use of the concept of regression can be seen to be an accurate description of the situation, but it is not necessarily the most useful way to describe the events. There is too much of a temptation, once having noted the regression, to leave the analysis at that. To do so is to miss critical dimensions of what was actually transpiring. The judgment by the Flynns' transitional selves that they were both overwhelmed by the seeming enormity of their problem had increased their feeling of being like inadequate and powerless children. Their history indicated that a tendency to feel this way was an unresolved problem for both Mr. and Mrs. Flynn, an area of vulnerability that had been created by the ethnic and familial culture in which they had been raised. An examination of the Flynns' subsequent behavior reveals their attempt to remedy this problem.

Mr. and Mrs. Flynn's symbolic or representational systems had not progressed to the point that their transitional selves could deal with their dilemma through a contemplative sharing with each other of their perceptions of the problem. Coping in a direct sense with the feelings of being powerless children was not possible for them. Instead they needed to solve the problem through action and enactive memory rather than representational memory. They needed to live through an active reversal of that which had been passively experienced. Thus the more inadequate the Flynns felt, the more they scapegoated Patrick by treating him in the manner in which they themselves had felt treated, the more they encouraged Sean to do so as well, and the more Patrick reacted through an increased disorganization. The way in which the Flynns were attempting to solve the problem was creating a destructive vicious circle in which the problem was increased.

The Flynns' first worker, though accurate in assessing this couple as individuals who were relatively free of major personality disturbances, failed to give credence to the power of the human being's attempts to solve problems and thereby failed to assess accurately the couple's relationship needs. The provision of expert advice, while intended to be useful to them, simply set up another situation in which the Flynns, through transference, could attempt to act out and thereby both demonstrate and potentially solve their feelings of inadequacy and anger at parental figures. The first worker's failure to recognize the underlying attempts at solutions amounted to a lack of attunement in the treatment situation. This situation was, of course, also simply a further extension of the vicious circle that had already been in progress with Patrick prior to the beginning of treatment.

It might be supposed that the Flynns' first worker had a need to present herself as omniscient and authoritative. A form of counter-transference might have been operative here. It is, however, important not simply to move the authority problem to another level and blame the worker for a lack of knowledge about the dynamics of human growth. It can often be difficult for workers to watch the demonstration of what may appear to be very destructive behavior if they do not have a clear comprehension of the possible functions of such demonstrations. For example, at one point during the treatment with Mr. and Mrs. Flynn, Mrs. Flynn got out of her chair and literally acted out in a mocking manner the pathetic way in which she had seen Patrick attempt to play baseball with some neighborhood children. If one failed to comprehend that this behavior on her part was a means of dealing, through an identification with Patrick, with her own sense of inadequacy, one would be angry and indignant at Mrs. Flynn's lack of empathy with and her scapegoating of her own child. To be therapeutic the worker must recognize that a shared contemplation of the features and attending affects of the action must follow it. Here, therefore, the worker needed to engage Mrs. Flynn in a reflective discussion of how Patrick might feel in such baseball games, knowing full well that Mrs. Flynn would talk about how she herself had at times felt.

In generalizing from the treatment experience with the Flynns and with other clients, it becomes possible to say that when, in the attempt to maintain identity and meaning systems, the transitional self cannot easily decipher the meaning of the feedback received, there is a repetition in the form of a type of minicycle of the original path of the developmental process. This minicycle functions for the person as an attempt to repair the deficit in the operational self that is causing the problem. In other terms the normal problem-solving attempt involves the processing, through the memorial system of the transitional self, of the effects of the past on the present so as to prepare the operational self for the events of the future. This processing is not a regression, though it may include the involvement of action patterns characteristic of previous stages. Instead this minicycle is very much a part of current adaptive functioning.

Current problem-solving behaviors, however, normally require a growth-promoting relationship with at least one human other to be successful. In the absence of such a relationship, problem-solving attempts may become endless repetitions of the same nonproductive action patterns, or may become vicious circles of self-destruction in which true regression rather than growth may be the outcome.

11 *Reality Processing in a Therapeutic Relationship*

The relationship has always been considered fundamental to treatment effectiveness in clinical social work. Social workers seem to be able to achieve a considerable degree of agreement in the recognition of those practitioners who have skill in attaining therapeutic relationships and to know, in particular treatment enterprises, whether or not a helpful relationship is operating. Primarily through supervision social workers have taught each other to utilize a type of relationship that has its own distinct qualities. Yet it has been inordinately difficult to obtain agreement or definition as to how the relationship is, in fact, expected to be helpful to the client.

An underlying, unarticulated assumption in some formulations regarding treatment has been that therapeutic effectiveness rests simply on the provision of unconditional positive regard for the client. Only a few social workers, however, have openly espoused this point of view, and it involves a number of problems. First, if this were all that is necessary, then the client must be in trouble because others in the environment had not cared enough. This is not only a highly simplistic formulation, but it is also an unnecessary and unreasonable accusation of the significant others in the client's life. Furthermore such a formulation would make it appear that clinical social work requires no particular knowledge, skill, or training—and that anyone who cares about other human beings should be able to provide adequate treatment. Experience has demonstrated, of course, that excellent clinical social work is a highly demanding task that requires many years of dedicated work and study.

The opposite view from the foregoing model is that of the therapist as a "blank screen," which derived from the early days of orthodox psychoanalysis. Here the therapist is seen as and objective an unemotional scientist, devoid of distorting affects, who remains a detached observer and occasionally makes interpretations in relation to the meaning of the pathology that the patient displays and projects onto the therapist via the transference. Although a few social workers have been attracted to this model, it has never been generally accepted in social work circles. As noted earlier the "blank screen" understanding of the nature of the relationship was part of a total formulation for treatment, which, while it had a kind of internal consistency, involved an understanding of cognition and of the unconscious that no longer is tenable in the light of current knowledge. At present even very few psychoanalysts espouse such a model.

Recently, in the midst of the popularity of object relations and Mahler's work, a formulation has emerged of the therapist as a parent figure who assists the client essentially in repairing the deficits from an unsatisfactory growth process through a type of return to the stage at which the deficit occurred. The difficulties with this model are by no means as severe as with the other two. It does, however, have several weaknesses: (1) it can imply more of a criticism of the original parents than may be useful; (2) it has been utilized in formulations based on purely linear schemes of development and causation in which the client is almost literally assumed to regress to a certain stage of early childhood and to function in that manner, thus requiring the therapist to act as the parent of a child of that age; (3) it retains a somewhat authoritarian and patriarchal (or matriarchal) cast whereby the therapist is expected to model more adequate functioning, which then will be internalized by the client. In this manner the reparenting model places too much authority and responsibility on the therapist, giving too little credit to the client's own functioning, initiative, and capacities.

A fourth view of the treatment relationship is probably most closely identified with the work of Franz Alexander (Alexander & French, 1946). This is the notion of the therapist as the provider of a "corrective emotional experience." In this conception the therapist determines just what it is that the client needs in order to reverse the effects of a psychological trauma. The clinician then actively undertakes to provide that element so that the client can reexperience and essentially undo the problems acquired in the past. This model was, during Alexander's lifetime, very popular with social workers, and still seems to retain considerable appeal in the profession. It also, however, requires the assumption of an essentially authoritarian or reparenting type of relationship within the treatment.

The articulation of the idea of a more egalitarian relationship in the treatment enterprise seems to have been primarily the contribution of the existential therapists. Here the therapist is seen essentially as a type of "fellow traveler" on a road of life that is sometimes bumpy and hilly. Such a formulation has had much appeal for many social workers who tend to be cognizant of their own inadequacies and problems with life. However, within this model it has been more difficult to formulate precisely how the relationship functions therapeutically other than through the achievement of unconditional positive regard. There has been a tendency in professional circles to view the endorsement of such egalitarianism as also espousing the benefits of simple fusion or merger experiences.

From a sociological point of view, it is interesting that psychoanalytic theory, as focused as it has been upon the family as a basic unit, has paid so little attention to the importance of sibling relationships. In comparing this with the tremendous emphasis that the father/son struggles of the Oedipus complex have been given, and which more recently also has been placed on mother/daughter relationships, the lack of attention to sibling relationships becomes even more striking. What begins to emerge is that the emphasis on hierarchical models of organization and authoritarian relationships in current Western culture have somewhat precluded the perception of the possibility of a type of relationship that involved role differentiation without status differentiation.

The psychoanalytic assumption of the human being as basically seeking a lack of tension as a pleasurable state has led to a correlary assumption of a fundamental need for dependency that has affected formulations relating to the treatment relationship in ways that have not been useful. If it is true that the human being needs at times to be actively problem solving and at other times to be passively receptive, then it is likely that a truly helpful therapeutic relationship should be based on a model in which both modes of operation on the part of the client are conceivable and permissible. Searles (1975) has pointed out that even quite severely ill individuals have a need to feel that they have the ability to have constructive influences on the persons with whom they interact. When it is true that clinicians of all professions grow psychologically themselves as a result of the participation in treatment relationships, it seems unnecessary and unwise to formulate a model of the treatment relationship that denies this fact or refuses the client any possibility of a recognition of contributions to the therapist.

In spite of the models of treatment found in the literature, social work treatment relationships quite commonly have been egalitarian in their nature. Examples such as that of Mrs. Cook and the Flynns, in which clients have been allowed or encouraged to utilize their own expertise in treatment, are not rare. Furthermore there is reason to believe that Blanche is by no means the only client who discovered that she could gain courage in facing her own imperfections through experiences in which an imperfection on the part of the clinician was revealed. This does not, of course, mean that imperfections or their revelation on the part of a clinician should be created for the purpose of demonstration to the client. Clinicians are human beings and their imperfections, if recognition is not defended against in some unnecessary manner, normally will be sufficiently available when needed.

The question can arise as to whether a model for the treatment relationship that implies that the client and the clinician are status equivalent detracts from the professional quality of the relationship. By no means is this the case. The hallmark of a professional relationship is that it is purposeful and goal directed. The goal itself is, of course, that of the client and must be identified as such within the treatment agreement. However, it is the responsibility of the professional to assume the monitoring of the goal directedness of the relationship. Thus the most basic reason that information about the social worker's personal life is not an appropriate focus for discussion is not that the client in some manner will be contaminated by such information or that it is inappropriate for the client to wonder about such things, but that such information is usually tangential and distracting to the task at hand—a task about which the worker should be very serious and the client has every reason to expect the worker to be.

A conception of the professional relationship as egalitarian but goal directed means that there is less pressure on the social worker to be omniscient. Such a relationship also makes it more necessary for there to be a mutually agreed upon and articulated goal for the treatment. In spite of social work's traditional insistence that the client must have self-determination, a view of the treatment relationship as having a significant authoritarian base has led workers at times to be less than ideally communicative to clients concerning what was involved in the treatment process. This, of course, has been problematic for the social worker since the profession itself has not achieved total agreement about what in a particular treatment works. A mystique about treatment, however, does not promote the establishment of and participation in a cooperative venture that is ideal for the achievement of a desirable outcome.

In recent years there has been some emphasis in social work on the idea of the setting of a contract. In many circles this has been thought of in specific, concrete, and somewhat legalistic terms. At the other extreme, there have been those who have resisted the idea of a negotiated goal on the basis that it is not possible to predict just what specific concrete achievements can be accomplished, particularly prior to an extensive period of diagnostic observation. A middle-ground position on these issues is both possible and desirable.

The concept of the establishment of a working alliance appears to be more useful terminology in social work treatment than is that of setting a contract. The idea of a contract has connotations of a guarantee on the part of the worker. In treatment there can be no outcome guarantees. Furthermore the achievement of any outcome invariably will depend as much, if not more, on the work of the client than on the skill of the clinician. Also, as the client comes to understand the nature of the treatment process, the client's goals are apt to shift. It is, however, usually possible to agree upon general goals in language that is understandable to the client, but that also can be reviewed and modified as treatment proceeds.

The idea of a working alliance also has connotations of an agreement between two or more persons as to the roles each is to play. Too commonly in past treatment it has been assumed that clients automatically should know how to conduct themselves so as to gain its maximal benefits. Particularly for clients who have been deprived, either emotionally or socially, this is frequently not the case, as they have not had the opportunity to learn the general parameters of expected behavior in such relationships. To have expectations for behavior that are not articulated and yet for which the client is held accountable is certainly not therapeutic, and may be interpersonally repressive.

The idea of a working alliance is self-evident in many ways and can appear quite easy to accomplish, until it is recognized that many people who are in need of treatment require that treatment simply because of their difficulties in forming and maintaining a working alliance with anyone. Problem-solving behavior and the utilization of human relationships in ways that will lead to growth are by no means confined to treatment relationships. Indeed it is to be assumed that most human growth does not occur within treatment relationships and that therapy generally should be considered only when the circumstances of daily life are such that normal growth and adaptation are not taking place. For example, had Mr. and Mrs. Flynn been able to share perceptions with each other sufficiently to be able to identify a variety of possible parental strategies and to cope with the problems that Patrick presented them, treatment would not have been required. Helping Mr. and Mrs. Flynn develop such a sustaining relationship with each other and to learn how to use it were the major achievements of the treatment.

An understanding of the structure and functioning of the operational and transitional selves, such as outlined in Chapter 9, indicates not only that ambivalence is ubiquitous in human relationships, but also that there are a variety of ways in which less than ideal circumstances can interfere with the capacity to engage in and utilize human relationships for growth production. While hard work is required to maintain a working alliance in any relationship, therapeutic or otherwise, in some extreme situations the achievement of even a tentative alliance may require considerable time and effort.

The Underwood family's existence for many years had been extremely chaotic, literally filled with chronic fears of and violent episodes with each other. None of them seemed capable of forming much of a picture of what they themselves were like as people, and they certainly could not predict behavior on the part of others in the family. Mrs. Underwood and both of the two children had been repeatedly hospitalized for short periods of time. By the time Sarah, the elder child, was 20 years old, these three family members accounted for approximately 50 admissions to mental hospitals among them. Only Mr. Underwood had managed to remain out of a hospital. Yet it soon became clear that, in some ways, he was the most feared member of this severely ill and highly paranoid family. He managed to maintain an image of health through the necessity for someone to play the role of doctor in the family system, dispensing the necessary medicine, organizing the details of whatever was needed for treatment or educational programs, and attempting to maintain some surface semblance of safety and order. Since this required his full-time attention, no family member had any consistent external relationships and everyone in the family was very isolated socially. In spite of their literal terror of each other, they also clung to each other, largely out of a sense of shame in the face of what they expected the outside world would think of them and a certainty that none of them could survive in that outside world alone.

Upon Sarah's admission to a long-term treatment center for the severely disturbed, Mr. and Mrs. Underwood gave almost no family history other than the dates and places of previous hospitalizations. Mrs. Underwood came across as an extremely fragile woman, likely to erupt into flagrant psychosis at any moment, while Mr. Underwood appeared to be highly resistant and contemptuous. It quickly became clear that none of these people were capable of maintaining any sort of individual operational self boundaries and, in pooling their resources, could maintain even minimal functioning only through the rigid structuring of a very impermeable boundary around the entire family group. It was also discovered that Mr. Underwood could not relinquish his role as doctor for the entire family without all experiencing this as a dire threat to their survival. Therefore, it was essential to allow him to continue to participate as a sort of consultant about any medication prescibed for Sarah, simply to keep her in the hospital.

The early weeks of Sarah's hospitalization were filled with crises in the family with Mr. Underwood constantly behaving as if he believed that the hospital staff was collectively and individually responsible for these problems. It required an inordinate amount of patience on the part of the entire hospital staff, and especially the family's social worker, to resist the temptation to respond with a similar fury and contempt. Meanwhile records from previous hospitalizations, which had been requested, began to document the regularity of the pattern being played out. At one treatment center after another, the Underwoods had begged for help and relief from the strain and terror involved in having to live with whichever of the family members was at the time the most upset. However, as soon as the admission had taken place, the family would collectively behave as if it were the professionals themselves who had created all of the problems. Typically institutions would attempt to obtain a history upon or shortly after admission, only to be totally thwarted in this endeavor. Soon the family would remove the family member, convinced that the professionals they had encountered were incompetent, or the professionals would remove themselves from the scene by declaring the family to be impossible to treat.

The example of the Underwood family is an extreme. However, the problem here becomes that, although the family could outwardly agree to a treatment goal and a working alliance, the very difficulties that brought them into treatment prevented them from being able to make use of it. Although the clinician should always pay attention to the necessity of articulating for the client the nature of the role relationships in treatment, the generalized goals of the treatment endeavor and the means to be used to achieve them, it cannot always be assumed that these words, at least in their concrete form, hold the same meaning for the client. Mr. and Mrs. Underwood presented themselves and their children over and over again for treatment, yet seemed unable to follow through with any attempts made by professionals on their behalf.

Very gradually, as the Underwood family began to recognize that Mr. Underwood was being allowed to continue in his role as doctor, at least to some extent, that the social worker had backed off from demanding the production of a family history, and that the staff was not returning Mr. Underwood's hostility, the family began to allow the beginning of a highly tenuous working alliance. Movement in this direction was, of course, very slow and filled with repeated crises in which the nature of the relationship between the family and the social worker was tested and retested. Nevertheless Mr. and Mrs. Underwood very gradually began to be able to acknowledge more and more of their own state of confusion, chaos, terror, and shame. The worker made no attempts at any "interpretations" here, but simply accepted the facts of the situation as they were presented. Information about current treatment attempts or considerations was offerred before the Underwoods asked for it, whenever possible. On occasion the worker made offers of specific concrete help in alleviating in small ways some of the strain involved in their everyday lives.

It took nearly a year and a half, but in time Mr. and Mrs. Underwood could directly acknowledge that part of the reason why admissions to hospitals had always been so difficult for them was that they quite literally had no sense of their own family history and, therefore, could not produce one. They experienced the request for one as a demand that they humiliate themselves. Indeed an exploration of this area uncovered the reality that they could offer dates and isolated facts about their individual and collective experiences, but no one in the entire family was capable of putting this into any sort of a process with a beginning, a middle, and an end, and with a meaningful sequence of events that might have influences upon each other.

At this point in the treatment, the worker offered to help the Underwoods review their lives so that they could gain some sense of order. This offer was enthusiastically accepted by all four members of the family, and for a considerable period of time, weekly family meetings were devoted to a literal review of the events of the family history. A written chart was maintained and revised or updated each week as the Underwoods strove to organize for themselves some sense of what their lives, separately and together, had been like. No attempt was made to discuss or arrive at any agreement about the meaning of events. Instead the work focused much more literally and concretely on the "facts," a level of functioning much closer to that of which these people were capable. Even this was, of course, a slow and painful endeavor, still subject to interruption by crises, but it was nevertheless a task to which each family member, in his/or her own way, became highly dedicated.

A sense of time as a process is an advanced conceptual achievement—one that the Underwoods had by no means achieved. Without this understanding they could not really be expected to comprehend the notion of a working alliance or of a treatment process in the same manner in which the clinician presumably would have meant this. While this family is indeed an extreme example, a limitation in relation to the capacity to understand the treatment process is found with many clients. It was, for example, pointed out that Maria (Chapter 7) had little ability to think about her own future or to conceive of ways in which to work toward the goals she had set for herself. No doubt many clients have been considered untreatable because the demands of the treatment process itself were not adjusted to the level at which the clients could perform. A comprehension of the functioning of the operational and transitional selves, as well as of the role of affect as a mediator of interpsychic space, should alert the social worker to the fact that hostility from the client may be a sign that the client is being asked to perform a task that is beyond his or her psychological capabilities.

If the client's conceptual capacities do not enable the client to understand fully the meaning of a working alliance, how can any treatment be expected to take place with clients who have significant deficits? The formulation of the nature of the human being proposed here holds that there is an inherent push in all individuals toward development and the achievement of maximum potential. It is with this aspect of the client that the clinician must make an agreement. Therefore, while the client should be expected to make a verbal and conscious commitment to a working alliance, the clinician must be aware that some clients cannot be expected to comprehend the full meaning of such a contract for themselves and their meaning systems. Furthermore the clinician must be aware that the maintenance of any working relationship will depend on its effects on the functioning of the operational self and its experienced security. If the organization of the identity or meaning system seems to the client to be seriously threatened by the treatment experience, the client will withdraw from treatment.

As the Underwoods began meeting with each other to review their past, many memories were stimulated that involved very strong emotional reactions from the family members. These were, of course, the very feelings with which the family had been unable to cope without violence while living together. Seeing the family together meant that transference reactions would be centered more within the relationships between family members than on the worker as is the case in individual treatment. It then became the worker's role to ensure the goal directedness of the work and a reasonable degree of safety during the treatment encounters. Although Sarah was very highly invested in the process of the historical reconstruction, at times this raised issues she indicated she was not yet quite ready to handle. Thus she needed to be able to have permission not to attend family meetings on occasion. At other times Sarah felt that she wanted to attend meetings, but feared that she needed to participate in a discussion of an issue, and then might lose her self-control and physically attack someone during the meeting. It became part of the worker's role to set limits and to help Sarah identify when she was under too much strain as well as to take any other necessary measures to prevent physical violence. Other family members also needed to retain a choice as to how much strain on the organization of their self systems they could tolerate at any given time.

As has already been noted, the situation with the Underwoods was an extreme; however, limit-setting behavior on the part of the social worker, such as typically happens with children, adolescents, or delinquents, may be necessary at some point in nearly any treatment enterprise. In the past interventions of this type have usually been conceptualized as appropriate because of dependency needs or authority conflicts on the part of the client. This has often been located in a theoretical framework that viewed humankind as beginning fundamentally as primitive savages who needed to compromise with the demands of a harsh social reality in order to be appropriately socialized. The perspective that has been proposed here, however, would emphasize that limit-setting behavior is necessary at times during treatment, though for quite different reasons. Issues of reward and punishment, though they may be legitimate concerns for other segments of the social order, are not appropriate in the therapeutic relationship.

One of the social worker's primary professional responsibilities is the maintenance of the focus on the goal-directed nature of the relationship. Within the role as the monitor of the goal directedness, the worker must convey a belief that the client can achieve a future that is worth an investment of time and energy. Appropriate limit setting is, therefore, properly seen as a part of keeping the client focused on the achievement of that which ultimately will be more satisfying and fulfilling for his or her own functioning in life in the long run. The clinician must recognize, however, that while there is some professional responsibility for the establishment and maintenance of conditions that are most likely to result in psychological growth for the client, the client ultimately must make his or her own choices for behavior and must take responsibility for the results of any actions. The worker cannot and should not assume this responsibility.

Limit setting at times is essential in treatment, but precisely how this translates into concrete specific behaviors within which the clinician acts the role of maintaining goal directedness and yet expects that the client will retain ultimate control and responsibility for his or her own behavior is not always easy to determine. This is, and must remain, a judgment issue concerning which there never will be precise certainty for workers in some situations, and there probably always will be some disagreement among professionals as to what is necessary in individual situations. Issues relating to the protection of civil rights as well as those of professional responsibility may be involved. Since ultimate certainty about such issues is not totally achievable in all situations, the only generalizable resolution may well be a recognition that an open professional dialog with the continuing expression of all opinions may be the best way in which to guard against the most serious danger—that of any final resolution based on a simplistic interpretation of the issues involved.

This formulation purposefully has emphasized that clients, even those who function with very severe developmental deficits or emotional disturbances, must be treated as being responsible for their own behavior and for the results of their actions. The issue then becomes: "What constitutes responsibility?" Again to some extent this is a judgment issue that has to be resolved in individual contexts. It is perhaps sufficiently important here, however, to repeat the notion that social work treatment is not concerned with issues of reward and punishment, but rather with a dedication to the achievement of the maximal utilization of human potential—a potential that must be built upon an acceptance of whatever limitations have existed in the past and exist in the present. Each individual must come to terms with his or her own identity in whatever way possible.

The members of the Underwood family were functioning at a fundamentally psychotic level. Appropriate treatment goals in relation to the formation of their meaning systems, therefore, meant a focus on the construction and strengthening of the boundaries of their operational selves. In relation to action, these people functioned at the level of equating feelings and thoughts with action in a magical way. Thus, in relationship to each other, they needed to learn that to think or feel in an angry way with one another did not necessarily hurt the other person, whereas taking action against that person might. Part of the therapeutic reason for the limit setting in this instance, then, was to help them experience and understand this.

The Underwoods dealt with the world primarily as "things-of-action," as things that consisted of signals and signs. As such these things could not participate in the construction of transitional selves. Treatment, therefore, must encourage the transformation of the attitude toward the world into one in which there simply will be a contemplation of it. This involves patience and a willingness to accept conditions as they are without immediate action. Although the social worker may perform any of the four functions of the human other as outlined in Chapter 10 during the course of treatment, the worker primarily serves as a contemplative sharer of perceptions. This is the function that most commonly is not adequately performed by others in the client's natural environment. For some clients, such as the Underwoods, the possibility of behavior such as the contemplative sharing of perceptions may not even be known to them or be a part of their previous experience. Clients with problems as severe as those of the Underwoods are, however, by no means the only ones who may need assistance in the utilization of elements of the external world as objects-of-contemplation rather than as things-of-action.

Contemplative behavior makes sense only in a time process. The very utilization of contemplation implies the existence of a time process in the sense that one contemplates the events or creations of the past with the underlying assumption that this has something to do with a future. It is perhaps paradoxical, but nevertheless true, that the person who seems to engage in constant action, presumably to prepare for the future, often has little faith in or experience of a future as an actuality. It is for this reason that the worker frequently must begin a treatment process with helping the client gradually learn how to participate in contemplative sharing. This behavior is the beginning, not only of preparing for a future, but of the ability to conceive of one as possible.

The contemplative sharing of perceptions must be understood by the worker as an active process. It is not simply doing nothing. A time process means that if there is a past, there must also be a present and a future. Since the future cannot be achieved unless it is built on the foundation of the past, the acceptance and examination of the client as that person has been in the past are also a statement of a belief that the person has a future that can be different than the present. An active engagement in the sharing of perceptions is, therefore, an active statement on the part of the worker of belief that the client can change—can be more than he or she is at present. It is this challenge, this belief in self, that the client needs in order to engage in the hard work of preparing for that future. Yet this contemplation does not necessarily have to set specific concrete goals the client may experience as overwhelming, too demanding, or infantilizing through requiring too little.

While the contemplation of action may be the ultimate goal, frequently the action itself must be allowed to occur first so that it can be examined. Traditionally psychoanalysis prohibited action in the treatment setting itself, and attempted to discourage analysands from making major life changes during the course of treatment. Action, at least other than engaging in the free-association process of the treatment, was seen primarily as "acting out." In this manner psychoanalytic treatment essentially failed to deal adequately with the place of action in life. The demand that the patient meet these requirements also placed very real limits upon how much the patient could engage in enactive memory as a part of the transference and the treatment. Thus classic psychoanalysis could not be effective as a treatment modality except for individuals with very highly developed symbolic systems who could utilize visual and verbal modes of memory with some ease. It is no wonder, then, that psychoanalysis has had to reconsider its techniques in order to treat persons who may not have reached a neurotic level of functioning.

Transference

*A*lthough in parts of Freud's writing it appears that he may have intended some different interpretations of transference, this concept traditionally seems to have been understood as the projection of qualities of relationships from the past onto the therapeutic relationship. Frequently that which has been noted as transference has been that which has interfered with a working alliance or has been pathological, as, for example, in the Underwoods' viewing of the hospital staff as being dangerous to them. While positive qualities have been viewed also as transference, especially when these have clearly implied a grandiose view of the therapist, issues about positive transferences usually have been considered to be less of a problem than those of a negative nature. In part this has been true, no doubt, because therapists have preferred to think of themselves in positive terms. Therefore the client's behaving as if the clinician were seen in a positive light was not necessarily viewed as a "transference distortion" from the past but rather as a "reality" of the present. It has further been considered that the clinician's interpretations of the transference "distortions" and the "realities" of the present have accounted for the effectiveness of the treatment.

From a theoretical point of view, this formulation of the treatment presents some difficulties. It involves the assumption that there is a knowable objective "reality" in relation to the qualities of the therapist as well as of the external world. Furthermore it puts the therapist in the position of being the interpreter of that reality. The very idea that the therapist should be able to know what qualities he or she is displaying at any given time makes an unrealistic demand of the clinician. The implication is that the clinician is capable of achieving an objective sense of self. While certainly professional training involves the achievement of much self-awareness (a valued and necessary quality for any therapist), an objectivity about the functioning of the self even within the limits of a professional relationship, is unachievable.

So long as the effectiveness of treatment is considered to depend upon the capacity of the clinician to distinguish between a transference from the past and an objectivity about present reality, as well as to be able to interpret or define for the client the nature of that reality, there always will have to be a pull toward a consideration of the nature of the treatment relationship as authoritarian and as seeing the clinician as capable of near-omniscience. The clinician who is truly self-aware and honest is also aware that no amount of training and/or personal therapy will permit the worker to achieve this kind of personal self-knowledge. It is no wonder, then, that conscientious clinicians who have wished to see themselves as capable of helping others, but have been aware of their own limitations as human beings, have wished for an explication of the treatment enterprise that either would ensure that the client knew nothing about them as people, or that the effectiveness of the treatment depended upon something other than the achievement of perfection in the relationship.

Kohut's (1980) formulation of the therapist as the self object— that is, as the new object that is actively transformed by the client into that which is needed to complete the self—is a step in the direction of a solution to the problems outlined. Kohut viewed the human being as never outgrowing the need for self objects, thus placing more emphasis on the healthy aspects of the utilization of human relations than simply on pathology. However, to date the formulations from the Kohutian school of self psychology do not yet appear to have addressed the issues in relation to the meaning of reality in as much depth as would be desirable for clinical social work.

Individual knowledge of any reality, understood as constructed through the human being's experiences with the environment, both animate and inanimate, is inevitably individual and subjective. Since knowledge is constructed, the content of the meaning system normally will differ from one individual to another in ways that not only are not pathological, but that in fact define that particular person's individual identity. The nuances of meaning about the self, the external world, and the interrelationships between the two are what provide each person with a depth of experience, with a sense of being alive, and with an actual or potential satisfaction that can make life seem worth living. This same meaning system is that which makes it possible for the person to function in an adaptive social manner while retaining a choice as to his or her own behavior.

Experiences with the external world that have, for one reason or another, affected the person but that have not been integrated into a sophisticated and highly developed meaning system constitute the content of the individual's unconscious. The recognition and ownership of that unconscious allows the person to continue to build an increasingly more differentiated and integrated meaning system within which to comprehend the world. For example, it was when Mrs. Porter (Chapter 8) was able to recognize and deal with her "repressed" feelings about the circumstances of her mother's death that she was able to resume the normal developmental course that was interrupted by that event. It is important to understand that the issue for the treatment and the client is not the "factuality" of the events of the past, but rather, the meaning of these events for the present and future, which affects the degree to which the client is able to interact fully with the environment of the present.

For Mrs. Porter the meaning of the circumstances of her mother's death was recorded in a memorial system that apparently was accessible only through action. This meant that it was necessary for her to reexperience in an active fashion that which had been passively experienced previously. Thus, through the relationship with the worker, Mrs. Porter reenacted a situation in which symbolically she attempted to "murder" the unsatisfying parts of her mother—that is, to fire the worker. It was only following the failure of this action that Mrs. Porter could begin to resolve her present dilemmas in relation to her husband, her lover, and her current life situation in order to make some informed decisions about her wishes for her future life-style. With regard to the nature of the function the worker played for Mrs. Porter, it might be said that the worker served first as a "thing-of-action" whom the client could manipulate in order to reenact a scene from the past. Subsequently the worker also served as a sharer of perceptions as Mrs. Porter began to contemplate her own actions and to abstract meaning from them.

In the case of Mrs. Porter, the content of the repressed meaning had to do with negative feelings about her mother. Repression in the sense of the need for limitation of functioning, because the meaning is too overwhelming or powerful for the organizational of the self to process, may also be caused by positive feelings.

Mrs. Vincenti was a young housewife and mother who presented herself for treatment, saying that she did not seem to be able to perform adequately as either a wife or a mother though she loved her husband and her two young children. She thought she simply was not good enough for them. The description she supplied of her family made it seem as if there were no severe psychological pathology present in any of the other family members. Upon the worker's request at the time of the evaluation, Mr. Vincenti kept an appointment and appeared to be a very pleasant and responsible young man who presented himself as not being at all fundamentally unhappy with his wife and as quite baffled as to why she was so depressed. He indicated a willingness to involve himself in any treatment program that would help her. However, Mrs. Vincenti continued to insist that the problem was hers alone and that she wished to have individual treatment.

For some time Mrs. Vincenti kept weekly appointments quite regularly. She developed a routine during these interviews whereby she detailed some incident in which she thought she had performed inadequately at home and then began to talk of how abused and neglected she had been by her own presumably dreadful mother, who had died following a rather brief illness during Mrs. Vincenti's late adolescence. Mrs. Vincenti would spend most of the hour in tears, for which she brought her own facial tissues, over how impossible it was for her to be a good wife and mother when she had had such a terrible model. Throughout this time Mrs. Vincenti seemed not to experience any psychological relief as a result of the expression of this emotion, nor did her situation at home appear to have improved.

Finally the worker began to experience a sense that there was something that seemed both boring and insignificant about Mrs. Vincenti's constant complaints about her mother. Thus the worker began gently to question whether her mother had really been that terrible. Mrs. Vincenti's initial reaction was to become quite angry at the worker's presumed disbelief of her statements, which was followed by an intense sobbing that seemed to be far more genuine than had the tears that had been so frequently displayed. In the long run, it turned out that Mrs. Vincenti had very deep feelings of love for her mother, which she had been unable to admit to herself or to her mother at the time of her mother's death. She had been unable to accept her husband's genuine caring in part because she thought anyone who could be so unresponsive and ungrateful for another's love did not deserve it.

The organization of the operational self is normally very strained by many physical, social, and cognitive changes during adolescence. Because of this the individual typically needs to keep more inter-psychic distance from truly significant others in order to guard against a feared merging experience. Mrs. Vincenti had lost her mother through death at a time when it had been extremely difficult for her to allow herself to acknowledge how much she cared for her. In this instance, then, the experienced threat to the boundaries of the operational self had been a positive rather than negative emotion. The resulting failure to be able to admit to herself the importance of her mother had prevented Mrs. Vincenti from being able to mourn the loss adequately. There actually had been a number of clues to the worker that this might have been the case, and Mrs. Vincenti's obvious refusal to accept even facial tissues from the worker, even though she knew these were available, had been one of them. Mrs. Vincenti had been living out her own inability to accept help from her mother during her adolescence.

Both Mrs. Porter and Mrs. Vincenti were women who functioned at a fairly highly developed psychological level most of the time, thus nearing or reaching what might be considered a neurotic level. The examples of their relationships with their workers are somewhat typical of what has been reported in the literature as transference patterns in treatment. What is important to note here is that, although in both situations the clients were repeating important experiences with their mothers, in neither did the worker have any way of knowing the nature of the content that had been repressed, except as communicated by the client. The point is that the worker may be able to discern the level of differentiation or complexity in the structure of the symbolic or meaning system of the individual, but only the client can provide the nature of the content.

In entering the treatment situation and relationship, the client encounters a new environment and a new person. It is, therefore, to be expected that the client will attempt to integrate this new situation into his or her meaning system. As this takes place, the worker will see an example of the functioning of the transitional self in action unfold. The worker may not know, and undoubtedly will never know, the historical "factuality" of the client's past, and cannot know anything other than what is directly communicated by the client about the content of the client's meaning system. However, in observing the manner in which client's self structure organizes itself to accommodate this new situation, the worker can, through observation, learn a great deal about the relative development of the client's operational and transitional selves. It is, in fact, the operation of the minicycle of action intended to maintain the meaning system and the personal identity that it underlies that has in the past been labeled as transference.

Viewed in this light, transference not only is present in all relationships, but is normal and healthy. Its presence in relation to all human others is fundamental for the effectiveness of marital, family, and group treatment, as well as for individual treatment. In all of these modalities, the individuals are constantly demonstrating the manner in which their meaning systems operate. Different techniques may be employed to encourage maximum growth in the client systems and groupings, but the functioning of the self systems remains the same. In general the major shift of the clinician between individual

197

treatment and one that includes more than one person at a time involves the utilization of multiple transferences in order to provide growth-promoting opportunities for the clients.

The therapist, having evoked the action of the self systems. In the treatment environment, can make the details of the manner in which the client meaning system operates become more obvious through a failure to respond in a manner the client has come to expect in normal social interactions. For example, the clinician can learn something about the client's relative resourcefulness in hypothesis formation and the relative stability of the dimension of interpsychic space through a refusal to participate mutually in an interpersonal discussion. The failure to respond as the client has come to expect, however, will place a strain on the functioning of the self system. Since such a strain may not be in tune with the conditions the individual needs in order to foster further development, there well may be a tension between how much the clinician needs to know and how much strain the self system can tolerate in any given therapeutic enterprise.

Tracking the Client's Meaning System

In treatment the role of the clinical social worker is not only to monitor the goal directedness of the work, but also to provide, as far as is reasonable and possible, a human environment for the client that will encourage the maintenance, repair, and/or development of the client's meaning system. To provide this encouraging environment, the clinician will need to remain constantly aware of the relative state of the client's transitional and operational selves. Remaining aware of the state of the client's self involves a type of continuing "diagnostic assessment." This is not a one-time overview that is then expected to be static throughout the treatment, nor does it consist simply of the assignment of one of a series of labels that have been invented for professional convenience and communication. Such categorization systems have their place and importance in the educational, ethical, and knowledge-building segments of professional organization. But in the actual work with any given client, a much more highly differentiated and refined comprehension of that particular individual is necessary.

Existing categorization systems in which are found this type of refined comprehension of the state of the self of the individual are less than ideal in their power to capture the individual's characteristics.

For this reason detailed knowledge of the functioning of the self on the part of the clinician frequently has been considered to be "intuition." Unfortunately there has been far too much of a tendency, even in the social work profession, to consider clinical practice as somehow less than ideally scientific because of its reliance on intuition. Far too little attention has been paid to the fact that intuition is simply knowledge that has not been processed sufficiently to make it consciously analyzable. Intuition is not some sort of instinctually based, magical affect. This is true, of course, specifically because affect itself is not an incomprehensible given, but is an active judgment on the part of the self about its own current safety and security.

The ability to comprehend the functioning of another person's self system has generally been referred to as empathy. This has been considered an essential ingredient of all therapeutic endeavors, a statement about which there would be little controversy in any school of clinical thought. There has been some controversy, however, about how one defines empathy and whether or not it can be learned or taught. The idea that affect is a type of knowledge means that empathy is observationally based. It also means that the elements that underlie empathic knowledge are capable of conceptualization and communication in some system of categorization. Therefore the actuality that an ideal system for such categorization has not yet been achieved should serve as an intellectual challenge rather than as an area of despair for clinicians.

In psychoanalytic psychotherapy the formulation of the empathic process that traditionally has been the most influential is that of Greenson (1960). This and several similar formulations essentially describe a process in which the therapist, through a type of identification with the patient, actively attempts to comprehend the details of how a person in the situation the patient is describing (including the emotions the patient has articulated) would ordinarily feel. The therapist allows himself or herself to imagine what this affective state would feel like and then gears any therapeutic interventions in accordance with that feeling state.

The primary difficulty with Greenson's and other models of the empathic process has been the presence to some degree of an assumption that there was a "right," "normal," or "expectable" way to feel about a particular situation that could be discerned by the therapist. If the patient did not report feeling this way, the therapist would assume that some defense such as denial was operating. Current theory, of course, would indicate that there is no normal way in which to feel. Health or pathology cannot be based solely on the content of the affective state. Furthermore the therapist cannot assume that a feeling state exists but is denied unless there is direct observational evidence of it. This does not mean that the clinician cannot formulate hypotheses about how a client may feel on the basis of knowledge of the dimensions of commonly reported affective states. However, such hypotheses should be confirmed in a more direct manner through overt behavior or verbal report by the client. The clinician cannot assume some special insight into the content of the individual client's feeling state.

In the empathic process—that is, in the process of tracking the functioning of the operational and transitional selves of the client— the social worker must pay serious attention to the overt meaning of any content communicated by the client. Such content is, however, only one part of the necessary and available data. The fact that the transitional self of the client is constantly monitoring and feeding back to the operational self data about the relationship between the individual and the external environment means that content will always carry latent meanings about this relationship, including the manner in which the client/worker relationship is being experienced. Furthermore both action and affective patterns will give clues as to the relative need for interpsychic space at any given time.

Since the nature of the communicational patterns between two transitional selves frequently not only is in the modes of action and affective patterns but also is in states of brief mergers, some of the data the clinician will receive about the state of the client's self will have been both transmitted and received unconsciously. This invariably means that the affective state of the clinician will also be a source of data for use in hypothesis formation about the nature of the client's affective state. At times the clinician will experience affects that originated in the client but which that person was unable to discern or articulate. At other times, however, the clinician may be experiencing feelings that are not necessarily those of the client but are legitimate feelings of the client's significant other in some reenactment of an event from the past that is being restaged through the transference.

In the client's attempts to achieve active mastery over that which has been passively experienced, the worker may be required temporarily to play out the roles of a number of different individuals, which the client unconsciously may assign through the transference. Thus the worker will function as a thing-of-action to be utilized in the process of an attempt at capturing content from the unconscious through enactive memory. In fact part of the treatment contract involves some degree of willingness on the part of the clinician to be utilized in this fashion. For example, in both the Porter and Vincenti cases, the worker symbolically became the client's mother. In these instances the workers simply allowed the unfolding of the transference to take place. Neither the client nor the clinician may know precisely the content or nature of the play that will be enacted until the action itself has occurred and can be examined. In other instances, such as in the worker's learning about hockey from Mr. and Mrs. Flynn, the worker may have some conscious awareness of what role he or she is playing, and actually may be instrumental in suggesting to the client the possibility of the selected focus. In marital, family, or group therapy, the clinician's attention is frequently engaged in an attempt at understanding how the multiple clients are utilizing their relationships with each other in order to meet the relative needs of their operational and transitional selves.

Overall treatment planning must take place with some comprehension of the general outlines of the client's self system and of those features that may need strengthening or stimulation to increase the likelihood of improved social functioning. In addition to this, however, critical judgments about the delicate issues of the precise nature and timing of particular interventions depend on the clinician's ability to remain in empathic touch with the state of the client's self as well as with the probable nature of the current action of the transference. Collecting, sorting, and interpreting all of these data, as well as monitoring the current treatment interactions with the client, are a demanding, and frequently exhausting, task. It requires a high level of technical skill built into a refined and complex identity system within the personality of the clinician.

It is important for the worker to make judgments about the inner affective life of the client in an observational framework. At the same time, the way in which any individual initially knows about the existence of an inner life in human beings and about the potential depth and range of feeling states is through a knowledge of his or her own inner life. It is for this reason that the person who is to become a clinician needs to have as highly differentiated and integrated a meaning system as possible prior to undertaking the treatment of another human being. Therefore some individuals whose inherent psychological makeup and/or life experience has fostered the development of a complex identity system will begin professional life with more "natural" talent than others.

The treatment itself involves the conscious and disciplined exercise of the transitional self of the worker. Assuming that the beginning worker allows himself or herself to engage in a meaningful manner with clients and has sufficient supervisory assistance in comprehending the nature of the interactions involved, initial strain but eventual growth and strengthening of the transitional self of the worker are expectable side effects of such work. Personal growth of the worker need not be denied in professional circles, nor is there any reason to hide this from clients. Furthermore the possibility that such self-fulfillment may be one of the attractive features of the profession for social workers should not require any apology.

The goal of the therapy is, however, the provision of a growth-producing environment for the client. Indeed the professional social worker not only guarantees the assumption of the monitoring of the purposiveness of the work, but also contracts to rent out, as it were, aspects of his or her self to the client for this purpose. Therefore, while the clinician may grow as a side effect of the work, it is a violation of the treatment agreement for the clinician to substitute personal goals for those of the client. The client is allowed, at least within reasonable limits, to utilize the worker as a "thing-of-action." This utilization is a critical part of the service provided by the professional. The professional, being as human as the client is, may have some personal need to assist another human being in order to foster personal growth. The social worker, however, has no right to use a client to fulfill these needs and must look to other relationships for such assistance.

The critical difference between a professional relationship and a personal one is that in a personal relationship there is an assumption of a mutually shared attempt at the satisfaction of each other's legitimate needs for human contact. In a professional relationship, the worker agrees to forgo in this particular instance the rights to such mutuality. There must be, of course, some limits upon the extent to which the client may use the worker as a "thing-of-action." For example, the ultimate physical, psychological, and professional safety of the worker must be ensured. To pay maximum attention to the monitoring of the self system of the client, the worker must learn to forgo to some extent the monitoring of the worker's own self system and its goals during the treatment contact itself. The worker can afford to limit attention to his or her own well-being only if the physical and organizational setting of the treatment provides some basic assurances that this is a reasonable thing to do.

Countertransference, seen here as an undesirable element in treatment, may then be defined as a breach of the treatment agreement in the abuse or neglect of the monitoring of the purposiveness of the therapeutic endeavor, in the failure to monitor empathically the state of the client's self system, or in the utilization of the professional self for the purpose of client growth. From this point of view, a revelation of some aspect or quality of the clinician's personal self does not automatically qualify as countertransference. In fact a countertransference reaction easily might result in the worker's failure to respond to a client's legitimate need for a sense connection with the worker through information about some aspect of the worker's life. For example, particularly in working with relatively disturbed clients, it is important for them to be assured that the worker is capable of appropriate self-care and has not been injured by angry thoughts. If, therefore, events in the course of the worker's personal life cause observable injuries or unusual degrees of strain that might temporarily result in worker distractability, it may be of critical importance for the worker to share this information to assure the stability of the boundaries of the client's operational self. The simple provision of such information, of course, must be distinguished from the expectation that the client will then become the source of soothing or support for the worker.

The experienced worker learns that the overt content of the communicational focus of the treatment interview may include almost any topic in the combined experiences of the client and the worker. The appropriateness of the topic itself depends on how it will be utilized to forward the treatment goals. Since, however, the worker must take into account the fact that any information will have a multiplicity of meanings for the client, special caution is advisable in the utilization of personal information. In at least some instances, the meaningfulness of the treatment experience may depend upon the client's ability to feel, in some concrete manner, the fundamental genuineness and humanness of the worker/client relationship.

Wendy was a young woman in her 20s who, though reasonably intelligent and a college graduate, was severely impaired emotionally. She had been hospitalized for a period of a year following a nearly successful suicide attempt involving multiple gunshot wounds. The only child of elderly parents, both of whom were born in another country, Wendy had no extended family. Although she hungered for connections with other young adults, her severe lack of social skills generally left her an outsider, even in groups designed for very isolated individuals. Wendy's social dilemma was made more complex by her awareness that her parents stilled carried on with each other an old argument as to whether or not they should have had a child in the first place. Thus, as Wendy expressed it, while others were fighting for their social rights, she was still somehow having to fight for her birthright. This was, of course, something she felt quite literally—that is, she wondered about her right to exist at all.

When entering therapy immediately after discharge from the hospital, Wendy indicated that her goal was to become an "actuarial." Wendy did have an intellectual knowledge that an actuarial was someone who calculated probable life expectancies for insurance companies and that such a position would require extensive mathematical knowledge and ability. Wendy had neither education in this field nor any interest in such training. Instead the appeal of such a position was that it would provide her with an insight into how long she could expect her parents to live and whether or not she herself could expect to survive without them. Although at the time of her suicide attempt she had so despaired of her chances of survival that she had wished to precede her parents in death, she had determined during her hospital treatment that she did wish to find some way of continuing to live.

During Wendy's treatment her dogged determination to find some insurance of survival carried her through numerous failures to find meaningful relationships in social groups. Finally she began to experience some degree of acceptance in a women's organization whose membership came almost exclusively from the same ethnic background as her parents. This group was easier for Wendy to handle than others as it did not involve any pressures toward sexual intimacy and the most common activity of the group was cooking at socials. As long as she could help in the cooking, Wendy could be with people while having to engage in very little direct communication with them. As this group became increasingly important and helpful to her, Wendy began to question the worker's ethnic identity. Having discovered that the worker's forebears were from a country neighboring that of her parents' birth, Wendy wondered if the worker had any family recipes and suggested she would like to engage in a sharing of these recipes.

For Wendy the sharing of recipes in treatment became an important way to establish and maintain a literally life-giving relationship with another human being; a means of assuring herself, both literally and psychologically, that she would know how to feed herself after losing her parents; a means of symbolically reversing a relationship with her mother in which she had felt starved; a rehearsal of how to talk with other women in the group; and a means of deepening her sense of a socially connected self through a comprehension of some of the customs and meanings of her own ethnic background. The worker's willingness to share parts of her own identity was critical to the success of the treatment.

The beginning clinician has a personal identity within the operational self, but does not have a professional identity. The initial part of training as a clinician involves the differentiation of that professional identity within the operational self. It is normally quite difficult for beginning clinical practitioners to feel confident in utilizing parts of the personal self in treatment. Indeed, since in the early stages of learning treatment much energy must go into the empathic tracking of the client's self system and there is not yet great confidence in knowing how to time appropriate treatment interventions while avoiding countertransference problems, it is usually advisable for inexperienced workers to avoid too much sharing of personal material. As a professional identity becomes a more enduring, stable, and differentiated part of the operational self of the clinician, the selection of parts of the personal self for utilization in the therapeutic encounter becomes easier. The achievement of skill in the utilization of the parts of the actual self in the interest of the client's well-being is one of the hallmarks of the mature and creative clinician.

The parts of the self that are shared with the client must be genuine parts of the individual clinician. The desired treatment effectiveness will not come from a superficial imitation of some admired mentor or famous therapist unless the worker also has those qualities. The sharing of a "false self" clinician in a therapeutic relationship at best can result in the production of a "false self" in the client. Therefore, while there may be generalizable methodologies that can be identified and taught, there are no simple memorizable or prescription-type rules for technical application in all situations. Each client and each situation is unique and must be treated as such.

In relation to all topics of discussion in treatment, there minimally must be a freedom, and frequently a necessity, to return to the topic to check out what the shared information came to mean for the client. The clinician cannot assume that he or she knows what anything means to the client unless this has been directly elicited. Furthermore the existence of multiple levels of symbolic meaning, as well as of the ubiquity of ambivalence in all meaningful relationships, will always make the treatment relationship a complex entity to comprehend. It is inevitable that even in the most skilled and successful of treatment endeavors, some countertransference, understood as a genuinely negative event, will occur. The experienced practitioner will come to expect this and be willing to accept responsibility for such errors by acknowledging them and working toward improved future performance. After all a client cannot be expected to accept responsibility for the results of his or her actions in an environment that permits the worker to evade similar responsibility. It should be repeated again, however, that treatment is concerned with issues of ownership of behavior, not with reward and punishment.

Concordance: The Therapeutic Culture

Meaning is invariably determined to a significant extent by context. This is true of any concrete external thing, of the written word, and of human behavior. For example, an individual stands in front of a group and delivers a monologue. If the context is that of a classroom, the person well might be revered for wisdom as well as paid for that which is considered work. If the context is a street corner, the person might be considered mentally ill and taken to a hospital. If there is current disorder in the social system in which the street corner is located, the person might be considered an undesirable agitator and taken to jail. In all three instances, the words and actions of the individual might be identical, but the interpretations of the onlookers regarding the person's motivation would be different even though those onlookers may have had no access to how the person understood his or her own behavior.

It is, of course, fundamentally because of a common-sense comprehension that meaning cannot be understood in the absence of a consideration of context that social work has always defined its sphere of operation as the person/situation configuration. Personal identity, defined here as the individual's meaning system, cannot really be comprehended without an understanding of the context in which it was formed. The "reality" with which the individual initially is fused psychologically does not consist only of other individual human beings, but of other artifacts as well. The inanimate world— the presumed external environment—of the individual is important in regard to the manner in which the individual comprehends himself or herself and his or her functioning. In Chapter 2, for example, it was thought that Blanche had to return to the environment of her youth simply because she could not find in-depth meaning for herself in another environment. Her personal meaning system was embedded in the context or culture in which she had been raised.

Culture, civilization, or social order—whichever concept one choses to utilize—is a human invention. Although there is presumably an independently existing external world, human beings can know that world only imperfectly through an active construction of knowledge about it. No single piece of data, point of view, or knowledge system about anything in human experience can be understood to have a final and unquestionable significance of its own. There is, therefore, no guaranteed ultimate truth. Furthermore the number of classification systems within which any particular piece of data might be organized is probably infinite. But since human beings cannot function in and cannot tolerate an environment in which there is no predictability, a meaning system that is socially shared (in other words, a culture) must be invented. Those things that are generally considered "facts" are facts simply because there exists a social consensus or agreement to consider them as such. "Reality" is defined by social agreement.

There is, however, no single reality in the external world. There is a wide range of social groupings, even in a relatively monolithic society, that are based on a variety of classifications such as age, sex, family, religion, social class, occupation, geographical location, or political belief. Because of the particular perspective of the membership in each of these groups, the negotiated consensus about the nature of reality will vary from one group to another. In other words, just as there is identity complexity, there also is social complexity, with each group having some validity as to its own point of view about the nature of the world but with none of them owning an "ultimate truth." Throughout history it appears to have been that when any particular social group claimed exclusive ownership of truth, the worst conditions of injustice and oppression have occurred [see Bronowski (1973) for a more complete explication of this point].

Social diversity is unavoidable in today's world, but it also appears to be healthy and desirable. Conflicts and varying interests within and between groups cannot be prevented and are not in and of themselves evidence of pathology. The strength of any group is probably best measured by its ability to tolerate conflict without either group dissolution or the scapegoating of a particular member. Social groups are also not mutually exclusive. Thus any given individual usually holds membership in a variety of such groups at any one time, and while membership in some may last a lifetime, membership in others will shift at different points in life. The individual, therefore, will be presented with a series of competing definitions of reality and will have to make some choices as to how to organize and prioritize all of the data. Such an organization can be accomplished, of course, through repression—through a limitation of functioning. On the other hand, it also can be accomplished through the abstraction made available by the development of a highly differentiated and articulated meaning system.

In most social orders, the family group is the primary reference group from which the infant acquires initial group memberships. It is usually this group that has the right and responsibility for assisting the child in the formation of the basics of a meaning system. The family's task is twofold. It must enable to child to function in the context of the particular family unit, but it must also foster the development of the skills whereby the child will acquire the ability to reality-process in the environment beyond the family system. In some families the strain caused by actual or threatened internal chaos results in the child's exposure to limited or very rigid ways of coping with other social systems. This explains why clinicians have consistently found that even very bizarre bahavior on the part of quite disturbed individuals seems much more comprehensible when viewed in the context of the family system. The meaning system developed by the child may work within the family but may not be applicable beyond that group. In extreme cases in which this is the case, of course, the individual is usually diagnostically considered to be functioning in a schizophrenic manner.

The development of a personal meaning or self system requires an interactive relationship with another human being. But it also requires a context or a culture that will be favorable to its growth. Understood as a differentiated, articulated, and integrated comprehension of the nature of the self, the nature of the external world, and the relationship between the two, the meaning system must be able to acquire, experience, and process data about all these items to be able to practice and refine its functioning. The client, of course, already has an environment and a culture that are part of his or her normal life. Under most circumstances the client will, and indeed should, continue to function in that environment. Whereas in situations of extreme pathology in either the self system, the environment, or the interaction between the two, removing the client from the natural environment may become necessary, ordinarily this only encourages the cessation of the functioning of the transitional self, which will result in its atrophy.

Most human growth occurs outside of a therapeutic relationship. It is preferable that this should be the case. Treatment thus is indicated only when the goals of the client exceed the capacity of the natural environment to allow or encourage the desired growth. There are, of course, instances in which some interventions directly into the natural environment of the client can alter that environment so as to make it more comprehensible to the client's existing meaning system or more hospitable for client functioning. This may be particularly true in cases where client problems relate to difficulties of inter-relationships with societal organizations designed for the delivery of basic social services. Such interventions should always be considered an integral part of an overall treatment plan. When the operational and/or transitional self temporarily malfunctions or needs basic long-term help to continue functioning, environmental adjustments or supports may be critical in the retention of whatever capacity remains.

In most instances involving clinical social work treatment, however, there has been some failure in the interrelationship between the client and the natural environment that has resulted in a less than ideal climate for client growth. While removal of the client from the current natural environment may not be indicated, there may need to be an additional environment within which the growth can be more readily fostered. In instances in which the client has a deficit in the development of the meaning system that occurred in the past, the client may wish to have the current natural environment be available for his or her personal use as a thing-of-action as part of any attempted growth. In such circumstances the client may have to confront the normal social demands of mutuality in relationships, particularly in regard to responsibility and accountability for behavior. A social order should maintain expectations of positive contributions from its membership while also providing assistance when this is needed. Expecting from people performance at a level above that of which they are capable can be punitive, but a generalized lowering of expectations may also be antitherapeutic since this can serve as a message that the person is deficient in some manner.

The achievement of a solid working alliance in treatment sometimes requires considerable effort on the part of both the worker and the client. In some instances in which a major part of the client's problem has been the erection and maintenance of too much nontraversible interpsychic space, the development of the capacity for a working alliance may even be the most significant part of the therapeutic accomplishment. Even so, however, the achievement of a relationship with a client cannot be a goal in itself. This achievement must transfer in some way into accomplishment or the potential for further accomplishment in the client's life outside the treatment. Thus the reason that the achievement of a working alliance in the therapy is important is that it is presumed there will be some transferred ability to form better relationships with humans in the client's natural environment.

Client growth, however, generally requires more than simply a working alliance. It requires a context within which to exercise and practice the functioning of the self system. It requires, in fact, a culture within the treatment situation itself. Human relationships do not and cannot operate without a social environment and a social meaning system. The therapeutic relationship is no exception. The worker and the client, therefore, together utilize their relationship to create between them a culture within which to foster the client's growth. It is because of and within this cultural system that the worker and the client can communicate with each other. It is also within this culture that the client and the worker will examine and define the meaning of their relationship and of the world of reality.

In professional literature it is not uncommon for clinicians to report that, following a period of successful treatment, a client began dealing with some significant other or some piece of the external world as it "really was." This is frequently the case even when the significant other may be a long deceased person with whom the client no longer can interact and whom the worker has never seen. Surely neither can legitimately claim to know who that person "really was" in any objective sense. What can be meant by such claims? The reality is, of course, a part of the culture developed in the therapy—that is, it is how the client and the worker have agreed to define the nature of the significant other. This "reality," like many other "realities" in the world, may successfully capture at least some of the actual qualities of the significant other, but undoubtedly will neglect others. Normally, however, in reporting that the client is now dealing with the significant other as the other "really was," what the clinician is actually reporting is the client's improved ability to accept, integrate, and process complexity.

To date one of the major difficulties for social work in utilizing many of the available theories for the purpose of explaining therapeutic processes has been that these theories usually either focused on the person or on the situation. Any means of bridging and integrating concepts between these two aspects of the totality of the problem with which the social worker is confronted have been poor or nonexistent. Just as personality theory has tended to assume a constant environment in the course of the development of the individual, so many treatment theories have assumed constancy in the therapeutic environment. It is important to recognize that the clinician may utilize the professional self in a variety of ways to provide the client with the maximum possible therapeutic assistance in achieving his or her goals. However, it now may be even more important to recognize that ideally the client and the worker together create and define the therapeutic culture within which they work.

The idea of a variable and mutually created therapeutic culture would appear to be so important as to require, in clinical social work terminology, its own special name. It is therefore proposed that such a culture be referred to as the therapeutic concordance. The implication of this term is that of a harmony of voices. Total fusion of the points of view of the social worker and the client is neither possible nor desirable. Concordance also implies the element of a negotiated agreement. The idea is that a therapeutic concordance that is ideal for one client may not be at all useful for another client. The clinician utilizes the professional self in a variety of roles and functions in accordance with the assessed needs of the individual client. The clinician should also participate in the creation of a variety of concordances in concert with client need and desire. Together the client and the worker will then utilize the concordance in which they operate to practice and refine the client's meaning system, as well as to examine its relationship to the meaning systems that predominate in the social systems of the client's natural environment.

12 Implications For Technical Application

Chapter 1 raised the question, "What makes treatment work?" That question now can be answered. Treatment works through the construction of a therapeutic concordance within which the client and the clinician, in their working alliance, practice and refine reality-processing skills, which the client later can utilize in cultures external to the concordance itself. There is a degree of satisfaction in being able to answer such an important question in only one sentence. Such satisfaction, however, must remain short-lived since, like most answers, this one raises a great many more questions. In addition it should be subject to much more examination as to its relative adequacy for meeting the needs of the practicing clinical social worker. Nevertheless this answer seems to have some promise of utility for clinical social work.

The recent popularity of separation–individuation theory, for example, in some instances has led to the equation of the ultimate goal of treatment to that of autonomous individual functioning (e.g. Blanck & Blanck, 1974). While separation–individuation theory has had much to contribute to the understanding of human development, this equation has been unfortunate for social work clinicians. Equating autonomy and maturity may serve as a means of excusing traditional psychoanalytic theory's failure to deal with the connections between the individual and the environment, but has constituted a step away from the clinical social worker's quest for an increasingly more sophisticated means of comprehending that same person/situation configuration.

The utilization of developmental theory does not depend on the conceptualization of maturity as being that of autonomous functioning in which the ideal person has no need of others. It is quite possible to consider that the ultimate goal for the individual is the achievement of the greatest possible utilization of his or her own potential and of an identity complexity. Human beings are never truly autonomous of their physical and social environments. Philosophically it would appear that there is some appeal to the conception of the human as ultimately capable of self-direction rather than as essentially driven by either internal instincts or social necessity. However, a theory involving an identity complexity, with the individual capable of making choices as to the manner in which he or she wishes to interact in a complex social system, can achieve the same end.

Social workers have always known that cultural factors are important for the individual, but have had difficulty in knowing how to integrate knowledge about cultural phenomena into conceptions of treatment. Workers have frequently found themselves pulled between ignoring important cultural data because of an inability to know how to integrate and interpret the data and a rather concrete system in which it was assumed that membership in a particular cultural group meant that any individual automatically shared in the generalized meaning system of that group. The notions of identity complexity, social complexity, and concordance may help the worker achieve a more adequate way of considering these relationships. It is, after all, not healthy for any individual to deny past or present identities in the sense of membership connections with particular groups. However, the extent to which the person will share in a particular group's consensual meaning system is a matter of individual choice.

An emphasis on the fact that clinical treatment requires the construction and utilization of a concordance—of a culture specifically its own—also may help in furthering the understanding of relationships between clinical aspects of social work and social policy. The clinical failure to pay sufficient attention to the therapeutic cultures in which they worked has contributed to some failures in making a distinction between role descriptions and agreements appropriate to the treatment situation and those appropriate to external social groups. As has been noted, an agreement to forgo to a significant extent the right to mutual need consideration in a therapeutic concordance is a fundamental part of the professional nature of a clinical relationship. However, the larger society simply cannot and should not be expected to excuse some of its membership from obligations to make positive contributions or from responsibility for the consequences of behavior.

Society can and should make allowances for the fact that the capacities and roles in which individuals can make positive contributions vary considerably. The difficulty is that making judgments about individual capabilities is tricky business even for the clinician in the relatively protected atmosphere of the concordance. Individualizing performance expectations at a societal level may be an ideal but impossible task. Nevertheless efforts at promoting a recognition of the necessity for societal complexity in the general population seem possible. Furthermore the identification and further study of aspects of concordances may help clinical social workers find more constructive ways in which to utilize clinical knowledge in the broader social environment.

For the individual clinician, it may be extremely important to recognize the necessity of constructing a boundary between professional and personal cultures. Far too many social workers have become accustomed to forgoing personal needs in treatment relationships and then have failed to expect mutuality in relationships outside the treatment situation. A failure of this sort frequently leads to worker burnout. A similar failure to pay sufficient attention to the variable nature of contexts within which relationships may be used to promote human growth has also at times led clinical education into confusion over the differences between therapy and educational supervision.

The past 15 to 20 years have seen remarkable developments in the area of family therapy, and much more growth in the utilization of group treatment as a modality. In these areas, as well as in the more traditional utilization of individual treatment, a whole array of treatment methods and modalities has come to the fore. While some of these newer forms of treatment appear to be faddist movements with little to recommend them in the long run, most of the methodologies have been seriously proposed by competent clinicians and do have some positive qualities. Another few may represent creative approaches that will have serious and lasting effects on the manner in which treatment is conducted. In general, however, that there has been so much interest and invention in the field of therapy would appear to be fundamentally a healthy thing.

Although family and group treatment methodologies have indeed proliferated, and certainly have proved to be effective, they do seem to a considerable extent to have been methodologies in search of a theory. This has caused even the practitioners of some of these models to adapt essentially antiintellectual stands, in which the question of why or how such techniques work has been dismissed as irrelevant. Clients are precious human beings whose interests deserve more serious attention than that. Adherence to outmoded theory that no longer seems to match observational data from practice will not lead to good treatment, but neither will the superficial and unquestioning acceptance of apparent "facts" without an attempt to integrate these data into a more complete explanatory system.

Another of the less constructive of the newer developments in relation to the proliferation of therapeutic modalities and techniques has been a tendency for professional divisions to advocate the exclusive effectiveness of particular technologies. It appears important to acknowledge that insufficient attention has been paid to the utilization of varied cultures in treatment and to the potential of identifying some framework for the guidance of the worker and the client in selecting the cultural types that might be most useful in reaching an individual client's particular goals. The construction of a concordance that has a membership of more than two people would seem to be a perfectly reasonable use of the therapeutic process. Once the worker can be freed from the notion that somewhere there is an ideally designed but stereotypical therapeutic context, far more creativity in the utilization of each of the modalities and techniques, alone or in combination, is likely to eventuate.

It is not unreasonable to think that the conceptualization of operational and transitional selves as the structures that need to be tracked in the empathic process of treatment might prove available as a basis for comparison of client data in individual, group, marital, and family treatment. These conception do, after all, seem to have the potential for integrating, into one general framework, data that have in the past rigidly been considered to be specifically either intrapsychic or interpersonal. The notion of a validly considered third dimension in the form of the interpsychic as a part of communication and interaction seems not to have been given sufficient consideration, although this would have practical as well as theoretical potential. For example, it can be pointed out that a worker's content focus on the state of the therapeutic relationship tends to reduce interpsychic space, while focus on concrete external aspects of the environment tends to increase it. Such guidelines should be capable of much more refinement to provide an aid to workers in making decisions regarding specific interventions.

216

Implications For Technical Application

Many of the newer models, partly on the basis of a realization that older versions of treatment did not take action sufficiently into account, have been quite activity oriented. Advocates of such therapies are apt, for example, to point out that action precedes insight, not the other way around. This would seem to be a valid point. Furthermore many of the theories seem to be questioning the role of "interpretation" in treatment. Certainly, from the point of view of the theory proposed here, the notion of interpretation as a pronouncement about the nature of reality on the part of an expert clinician following a revelation similar to a confession by the client would seem to have little place in a theory of treatment. On the other hand, interpretation, if defined as a harmonious agreement about the meaning of observational data, would be central to that theory. This latter type of interpretation can take place, of course, only after an event or action has occurred. It has limited, if any, predictive power for future events or action.

The present work has not been essentially about technique. Although the theoretical structure outlined has serious implications for technical application, any adequate consideration of the various aspects of such implications would require a much more ambitious project. The book has attempted, however, to articulate a theory of a therapeutic process that might underlie a variety of current types of clinical social work. Whatever usefulness the process described here ultimately is considered to have, it is hoped that at the least the reader has been impressed with the idea that the imposition of a particular treatment technique or culture upon all clients because such reflects worker skill or agency preference is a failure to comprehend the individuality of client/situation configurations. Thus it eventually must lead to stereotypic rather than creative practice.

The identification of the potential utilization of concepts such as concordance and the transitional and operational selves may prove to be a step in the direction of a reorganization of treatment theory clinical social work that will allow for more articulation of complexity in the comprehension of that process. The simple labeling of these ideas is not enough, however. Only their application by professionals and the further sharing of perceptions within a contemplative framework will provide evidence of their relative strengths and weaknesses in enhancing comprehension of and communication about just how it is that treatment works.

Bibliography

Alexander, Franz and French, Thomas M. 1946. *Psychoanalytic therapy.* New York: Ronald Press.

Arieti, Silvano. 1976. *Creativity: the magic synthesis.* New York: Basic Books.

Basch, Michael Franz. 1976. "Psychoanalysis and communication science," *The annual of psychoanalysis.* Chicago Institute of psychoanalysis, ed., New York: International Universities Press, 385–420.

Bettelheim, Bruno. 1950. *Love is not enough.* Glencoe, IL: the Free Press.

Bibring, Edward. 1953. "The mechanisms of depression." *Affective disorders.* P. Greenacre, ed., New York: International Universities Press.

Blanck, Gertrude and Blanck, Rubin. 1974. *Ego psychology: theory and practice.* New York Columbia University Press.

_____. 1977. "The transference object and the real object." *International Journal of Psychoanalysis.* Vol. 58, 33–44.

_____. 1979. *Ego psychology II.* New York: Columbia University Press.

Blatt, Sidney J. 1974. "Levels of object representation in anaclitic and introjective depression," *Psychoanalytic study of the child.* New Haven: Yale University Press, Vol. 29, 107–157.

Blatt, Sidney J. and Wild, Cynthia M. 1976. *Schizophrenia: a developmental analysis.* New York: Academic Press.

Bowlby, John. 1969. *Attachment and loss.* New York: Basic Books.

Brazelton, Barry. 1974. *Toddlers and parents: a declaration of independence.* New York: Delacorate Press/S. Lawrence.

Breger, Louis. 1969. "An information processing model, *Clinical cognitive psychology.* New Jersey: Prentice-Hall, Inc., 182–227.

Brody, Sylvia. 1956. *Patterns of mothering.* New York: International Universities Press.

Bronowski, Jacob. 1973. "Knowledge or certainty," *The ascent of man.* Boston: Little, Brown & Co.

Brown, Roger. 1973. *A First language.* Cambridge, MA: Harvard University Press.

Bruch, Hilde. 1969. "Hunger and instinct," *Journal of nervous and mental orders.* Vol. 149, 91–144.

Burnham, Donald and Gibson, Robert. 1969. *Schizophrenia and the need/fear dilemma.* New York: International Universities Press.

Chomsky, Noam. 1968. *Language and mind.* New York: Harcourt, Brace and World.

Coddington, R. Dean and Bruch, Hilde. 1970. "Gastric perceptivity in normal, obese, and schizophrenic subjects," *Psychosomatics.* Vol. 11, 571–579.

Cohler, Bertram. 1981. "Adult developmental psychology and reconstruction in psychoanalysis", *The Course of Life.* Greenspan, Stanley and Pollock, George, eds., U.S. Dept. of Health and Human Services, Public Health Service, Vol. III: Adulthood and the Aging Process, 149–199.

Cooley, Charles H. 1956. *The two major works of Charles H. Cooley: human nature and the social order and social organization.* Glencoe, IL.: The Free Press.

Despert, J. Louise. 1949. "Dreams in children of preschool age," *Psychoanalytic study of the child.* New York: International Universities Press, Vol. III–IV, 141–180.

Donaldson, Margaret. 1978. *Children's minds.* New York: W.W. Norton and Co.

Dowling, Scott. 1982. "Mental organization in the phenomena of sleep," *Psychoanalytic study of the child.* New Haven: Yale University Press. Vol. 37, 285–302.

Durkheim, Emile. 1953. *Sociology and philosophy.* Translated by D. F. Pocock and J. G. Peristiany. Glencoe, Il: The Free Press.

Epstein, Laura. 1973. "Is autonomous practice possible?" *Social work.* Vol. 18, No. 2, 5–13.

Erikson, Erik. H. 1963. *Childhood and society, second edition.* New York: W. W. Norton.

―――――. 1964. *Insight and responsibility.* New York: W. W. Norton and Co.

Escalona, Sybil. 1968. *The roots of individuality: patterns of normal development in infancy.* Chicago: Aldine Publishing.

Fraiberg, Selma. 1977. *Insights from the blind.* New York: Basic Books.

Bibliography

Freud, Anna. 1946. *The ego and the mechanisms of defense.* New York: International Universities Press.

Freud, Sigmund. 1900. "The interpretation of dreams," *Standard Edition.* Vols. 4 and 5, London: Hogarth Press.

_____ 1914A. "On narcissism," *Standard edition.* London: Hogarth Press. Vol. 14, 69–104.

_____ 1914B. "The unconscious," *Standard edition.* London: Hogarth Press, Vol. 14, 159–216.

_____ 1923. "The ego and the id," *Standard edition.* London: Hogarth Press, Vol. 19, 19–27.

_____ 1920. "Beyond the pleasure principle," *Standard edition.* London: Hogarth Press, Vol. 18, 17–64.

_____ 1933. *New introductory lectures on psychoanalysis.* ed. James Strachey. New York: W. W. Norton, 1965.

Fromm-Reichman, Freida. 1959. "Problems of therapeutic management in a psychoanalytic hospital," *Psychoanalysis and psychotherapy.* Chicago: University of Chicago Press, 137–159.

Gaensbauer, Theodore J. 1982. "The differentiation of discrete affects," *Psychoanalytic Study of the Child.* Vol. 37, 29–66.

Germaine, Carel B. 1976. "Time: an ecological variable in social work practice," *Social casework.* Vol. 54, 323–330.

Gilligan, Carol. 1982. *In a different voice: psychological theory and woman's development.* Cambridge MA: Harvard University Press.

Gillman, Robert D. 1982. "Preoedipal and early oedipal components of the superego," *Psychoanalytic study of the child.* Vol. 37, 273–281.

Greenson, Ralph. 1960. "Empathy and its vicissitudes," *International journal of psychoanalysis.* Vol. 41, 418–424.

Hartmann, Heinz. 1958. *Ego psychology and the problem of adaptation.* New York: International Universities Press.

_____ 1964. *Essays on ego psychology.* New York: International Universities Press.

Hartmann, Heinz, Kris, Ernst, and Loewenstein, Rudolph M. 1950. "Notes on the theory of aggression," *Psychoanalytic study of the child.* Vol. 3/4, 9–36.

Hebb, D. O. 1949. *The organization of behavior.* New York: John Wiley and Sons, Inc.

Hill, Lewis. 1955. *Psychotherapeutic intervention in schizophrenia.* Chicago, IL: University of Chicago Press.

Holder, Alex. 1982. "Preoedipal contributions to the formation of the superego," *Psychoanalytic study of the child.* New Haven: Yale University Press, Vol. 37, 245–272.

Holt, Robert R. 1976. "Drive as wish: a reconsideration of the psychoanalytic theory of motivation," *Psychology versus metapsychology: psychoanalytic essays in honor of George S. Klein.* M. M. Gill and P. S. Holzman, eds., *Psychological issues.* New York: International Universities Press, Monograph 36, 159–197.

Jacobson, Edith. 1971. *Depression.* New York: International Universities Press.

———— 1964. *The self and the object world.* New York: International Universities Press.

Josselyn, Irene M. 1976. "Concepts related to child development," *Infant psychiatry.* Eveoleen N. Rexford, Louis N. Sander, and Theodore Shapiro, eds., New Haven: Yale University Press, 148–171.

Kagan, Jerome. 1984. "The emergence of self," *Annual progress in child psychiatry and child development.* Stella Chess and Alexander Thomas, eds., New York: Brunner/Mazel, Inc. 5–28.

Kagan, Jerome, Kearsley, Richard B., and Zelazo, Philip R. 1978. *Infancy: its place in human development.* Cambridge, MA: Harvard University Press.

Keller, Helen. 1903. *The story of my life.* New York: Doubleday, Page and Co.

Kernberg, Otto. 1975. *Borderline conditions and pathological narcissism.* New York: Jason Aronson.

Kestenberg, Judith and Weinstein, Joan. 1978. "Transitional objects and body-image formation," *Between reality and fantasy: transitional objects and phenomena.* Simon A. Grolnick, Leonard Barkin, and Werner Muensterberger, eds., New York: Jason Aronson, 75–95.

Klein, George S. 1976. *Psychoanalytic Theory.* New York: International Universities Press.

Kohut, Heinz. 1971. *The analysis of the self.* New York: International Universities Press.

———— 1977. *The restoration of the self.* New York: International Universities Press.

———— 1980. "Reflections," *Advances in self psychology.* Arnold Goldberg, ed., New York: International Universities Press.

Krystal, Henry. 1977. "Aspects of affect theory," *Bulletin of the Menninger clinic.* Vol. 41, No. 1, 1–16.

Lacan, Jacques. 1981. *The four fundamental concepts of psychoanalysis.* New York: W. W. Norton and Co.

Lewis, Michael and Brooks-Gunn, Jeanne. 1979. *Social cognition and the acquisition of self.* New York: Plenum, Press.

Lichtenberg, Joseph. 1978. "The testing of reality from the standpoint of the body self," *Journal of the american psychoanalytic association.* Vol. 26, No. 2, 357–385.

Lichenstein, Heinz. 1977. *The dilemma of human identity.* New York: Jason Aronson.

Loevinger, Jane. 1966. "The meaning and measurement of ego development." *American psychologist.* Vol. 21.

Loewald, Hans W. 1951. "Ego and reality." *International journal of psychoanalysis.* Vol. 32, 10–18.

———— 1960. "On the therapeutic action of psychoanalysis," *International journal of psychoanalysis.* Vol. 41.

_____ 1976. "Perspectives on memory," *Psychology versus metapsychology: psychoanalytic essays in honor of George S. Klein. Psychological Issues.* Merton M. Gill and Philip S. Holzman, eds., Vol. 9 No. 4, Monograph 36, 298–325.

_____ 1978. *Psychoanalysis and the history of the individual.* New Haven: Yale University Press.

_____ 1980a. "Ego organization and defense," *Papers on psychoanalysis.* New Haven: Yale University Press. 174–177.

_____ 1980b. "On motivation and instinct theory," *Papers on psychoanalysis.* New Haven: Yale University Press. 102–137.

_____ 1980c. "Primary process, secondary process and language," *Papers on psychoanalysis..* New Haven: Yale University Press. 178–206.

_____ 1980d. "The waning of the oedipus complex," *Papers on psychoanalysis.* New Haven: Yale University Press. 384–404.

Mahl, George F. 1982. "Father-son themes in Freud's self-analysis," *Father and child.* Stanley Cath, Alan Gurwitt and John Ross, eds., Boston: Little, Brown and Co.

Mahler, Margaret. 1969. *On human symbiosis and the vicissitudes of individuation, Vol. I. Infant Psychosis.* New York: International Universities Press.

Mahler, Margaret S., Pine, Fred, and Bergman, Anni. 1975. *The psychological birth of the human infant.* New York: Basic Books.

Maslow, Abraham Harold. 1971. *The farther reaches of human nature.* New York: Viking Press.

Mead, George H. 1934. *Mind, self, and society.* Charles Morris, ed., Chicago, IL: University of Chicago Press.

Meissner, W. W. 1981. "Internalization in psychoanalysis," *Psychological issues.* New York: International Universities Press, Monograph 50.

Modell, Arnold H. 1968. *Object love and reality.* New York: International Universities Press.

Nemiah, John C. 1965. "The development of intrapsychic conflict in Freud's writing," *International journal of psychoanalysis.* Vol. 22.

Overbeck, Ann. 1977. "Life stress antecedents to the application for help at a mental health center: a clinical study of adaptation," *Smith college studies in social work.* Vol. 47, 192–233.

Parens, Henri. 1979. *The development of aggression in early childhood.* New York: Jason Aronson.

Parsons, Talcott. 1964. "The superego and the theory of social systems," *Social structure and personality.* Glencoe, ILL: The Free Press.

Piaget, Jean. 1962. *Play, dreams, and imitation in childhood.* New York: W. W. Norton and Co.

_____ 1976. *The grasp of consciousness: action and concept in the young child.* Cambridge, MA: Harvard University Press.

Piaget, Jean and Inhelder, Barbel. 1973. *Memory and intelligence.* New York: Basic Books, Inc.

Piers, Gerhart and Singer, Milton J. B. 1971. *Shame and guilt.* New York: W. W. Norton and Co.

Pruyser, Paul W. 1979. "An essay on creativity," *Bulletin of the Menninger clinic.* Vol. 43, 243–250.

Rapport, David. 1951. *The organization and pathology of thought.* New York: Columbia University Press.

Reynolds, Bertha Capen. 1942. *Learning and teaching in social casework.* New York: Farrar and Rinehart.

Richmond, Mary E. 1917. *Social diagnosis.* New York: Russell Sage Foundation.

Robbins, Fred P. and Sadow, Leo A. 1974. "A developmental hypothesis of reality processing," *Journal of the american psychoanalytic association.* Vol. 22, 344–363.

Rose, Gilbert J. 1974. "Some misuses of analysis as a way of life," *International review of psychoanalysis.* Vol. 1. 509–515.

_____. 1980. *The power of form: a psychoanalytic approach to aesthetic form.* New York: International Universities Press.

Rosenblatt, Allan D. and Thickstun, James T. 1977. "Modern psycho-analytic concepts in a general psychology," *Psychological issues.* Vol. 11, Nos. 2 and 3, Monograph 42/43.

Ross, John Munder. 1982. "In search of fathering: a review," *Father and child.* Stanley Cath, Alan Gurwitt and John Ross, eds., Boston: Little, Brown and Co., 21–32.

Rycroft, Charles. 1956. "Symbolism and its relationship to the primary and secondary process." *International journal of psychoanalysis.* Vol. 38.

Saari, Carolyn. 1976. "Affective symbolization in the dynamics of character-disordered functioning," *Smith College studies in social work.* Vol. 46, 79–113.

Schafer, Roy. 1960. "The loving and beloved superego in Freud's structural theory," *Psychoanalytic study of the child.* Vol. 15. 163–188.

Schafer, Roy. 1968a. *Aspects of internalization.* New York: International Universities Press.

_____ 1968b. "The mechanisms of defense," *International journal of psychoanalysis.* Vol. 49. 49–62.

_____ 1970. "The psychoanalytic vision of reality." *International journal of psychoanalysis.* Vol. 51, 279–297.

_____ 1974. "Problems in Freud's psychology of women," *Journal of the american psychoanalytic association.* Vol. 2.

Schimek, Jean G. 1975. "A critical reexamination of Freud's concept of unconscious mental representation." *International review of psycho-analysis.* Vol. 2, No. 1, 171–187.

Searles, Harold F. 1959. "Oedipal love in the countertransference." *International journal of psychbanalysis.* Vol. 40, 180–190.

_____ 1960. *The non-human environment.* New York: international Universities Press.

_____ 1975. "The patient as therapist to his analyst." *Tactics and techniques in psychoanalytic therapy, Vol. II: countertransference.* Peter Giovaccini, ed., New York: Jason Aronson, 95–151.

Seton, Paul H. 1981. "Affect and issues of separation-individuation," *Smith college studies in social work.* Vol. 52, No. 1, November, 1–11.

Singer, Margaret T. 1965. "Thought disorder and family relations of schizophrenics, IV. results and implications," *Archives of general psychiatry.* Vol. 12. 201–212.

Spaulding, Elaine. 1982. "The formation of lesbian identity during the 'coming out' process," Unpublished doctoral dissertation. Smith College for Social Work, Northampton, MA.

Spitz, Rene A. 1965. *The first year of life: a psychoanalytic study of normal and development of object relations.* New York: International Universities Press.

_____ 1966. *No and yes: on the genesis of human communication.* New York: International Universities Press.

Tolpin, Marian. 1971. "On the beginnings of a cohesive self," *Psychoanalytic study of the child,* New York: Quadrangle Books, Vol. 26, 316–352.

Vygotsky, Lev S. 1962. *Thought and language.* Cambridge, MA: The M.I.T. Press.

Werner, Heinz and Kaplan, Bernard. 1963. *Symbol formation.* New York: John Wiley and Sons.

White, Robert W. 1963. "Ego and reality in psychoanalytic theory," *Psychological issues.* Vol. 3, No. 3, Monograph 2.

Whorf, Benjamin, L. 1971. *Language, thought and reality.* Cambridge, MA: The M.I.T. Press.

Winnicott, Clare. 1978. "D. W. W.: a reflection," *Between reality and fantasy: transitional objects and phenomena.* Simon A. Grolnick, Leonard Barkin and Werner Muensterberger, eds., New York: Jason Aronson, 17–33.

Winnicott, D. W. 1971. "The location of the cultural experience," *Playing and reality.* New York: Basic Books, 95–103.

_____ 1975a. "The anti-social tendency," *Through paediatrics to psychoanalysis.* New York: Basic Books, 306–315.

_____ 1975b. "Hate in the countertransference," *Through paediatrics to psychoanalysis.* New York: Basic Books.

_____ 1975c. "Transitional objects and transitional phenomena," *Through paediatrics to psychoanalysis.* New York: Basic Books. 229–242.

Wolff, Peter. 1976. "Developmental and motivational concepts in Piaget's sensorimotor theory of intelligence," *Infant psychiatry.* Eveoleen N. Rexford, Louis W. Sander and Theodore Shapiro, eds., New Haven: Yale University Press. 172–186.

Zetzel, Elizabeth R. 1970. "On the incapacity to bear depression," *The capacity for emotional growth.* New York: International Universities Press, 82–114.

Author Index

Subject Index